If You're Talking To Me,
Your Career Must Be In Trouble

Joe Queenan writes regularly for the *Washington Post*, *The Wall Street Journal*, *Rolling Stone*, *GQ*, *Time*, *Spy*, *Movieline* and the *New York Times Book Review*. He is the author of *Imperial Caddy*, a book about Dan Quayle, who is not yet a movie star.

'Joe Queenan is the funniest writer in America and he's very probably the funniest writer in the world including England . . . he's the perfect gentleman: while being unfailingly courteous to his readers and other social inferiors . . . he is unflinchingly rude to the rich and famous. He's so good that he doesn't even make me feel envious – just pleased that he's alive and published in an age when so many journalists are so mealy-mouthed and self-deceiving that they could almost be, you know, actors'
Julie Birchill, *Spectator*

'His writing on film is so trenchant that when he recently asked seventy-five of Hollywood's biggest names for interviews for his book, they all refused. Even George Hamilton. Unfazed, Queenan culled his best columns into the aptly named *If You're Talking To Me Your Career Must Be In Trouble*, one of the most devastatingly funny books ever written about the film business . . . Throughout the book, Queenan continually exposes Hollywood's tenacious grasp on reality by trying unsuccessfully to re-enact key scenes from various films, such as taking a prostitute to a business dinner where she acts sophisticated (*Pretty Woman*) or convincing a beautiful blind-folded woman to swallow disgusting objects (*9½ Weeks*). Even Jimmy Stewart's roof-

top vault in *Vertigo* is shown to be implausible. Most critics only talk about films, this man likes them, and they make his life hell'
Stephen Amidon, *Esquire*

'There aren't many journalists who are just so damn good at what they do that you should buy any magazine they appear in. This has an index that makes better reading than the real bits of most other books'
Mark Edwards, *The Face*

'Writers who make you laugh are rare, and Queenan is one of them. He claims that his gleeful, ego-spearing iconoclasm is written in "a spirit of cheerful, life-affirming malice rather than noxious, downbeat variety", but I particularly enjoyed the random, thoroughly gratuitous swipes at such inoffensive people as Diane Keaton. By his own admission, Queenan "makes his living by watching unspeakably foul, hopelessly incomprehensible movies and then issuing belated, useless warnings to the viewing public telling them not to go see movies they've already seen". This may not be the noblest of occupations, but it has produced one of the funniest books of the year'
Vogue

'Shows a man with the potential to be a frighteningly good critic . . . He sparkles when he's icon smashing'
Deborah Bosley, *Literary Review*

'The P. J. O'Rourke of the movies, a deeply irreverent chronicler of Hollywood foolishness'
Arena

'Just buy it'
Sky

If You're Talking To Me, Your Career Must Be In Trouble

MOVIES, MAYHEM, AND MALICE

Joe Queenan

PICADOR

First published 1994 by Hyperion, New York

First published in Great Britain 1994 by Picador
a division of Pan Macmillan Publishers Limited
Cavaye Place London SW10 9PG
and Basingstoke

Associated companies throughout the world

ISBN 0 330 33148 5

The essays in this book have previously appeared in *Movieline* magazine
between the years 1990–1993, except for "The Lapp of Luxury," "Miss
Congeniality," and "Oh, You Beautiful Doll," which appeared in *Rolling Stone*
magazine between 1989–1990, and "No Way Out," which appeared in the
Washington Post on February 16, 1992.

Lyrics from "Passion Is No Ordinary Word" by Graham Parker reprinted
with permission. Copyright © 1979 Geep Music Ltd.

5 7 9 8 6 4

A CIP catalogue record for this book is available from
the British Library

Printed by Cox & Wyman Ltd, Reading, Berkshire

To Alan Abelson

Quotation to Make Book Seem Really Important, Like Barbarians
at the Gate*:*

I try to act amazed, but it's an act,
The movie might be new, but it's the same soundtrack.

—Graham Parker
''Passion Is No Ordinary Word''

CONTENTS

ACKNOWLEDGMENTS

I am deeply indebted to Virginia Campbell, Ed Margulies, Laurie Halpern Smith, Jill Feldman, Anne Volokh, and my dear friends at Videophile in Tarrytown.

I am slightly less deeply indebted to Josh Mooney, Heidi Parker, Teresa Lopes, Tom Cooney, Jeff Nisbet, and David Handelman.

I am *very* deeply indebted to my editor Patricia Mulcahy and to my agents Joe and Janis Vallely.

I am mildly indebted to my wife and kids.

INTRODUCTION

IF YOU'RE TALKING TO ME,
YOUR CAREER MUST BE IN TROUBLE

In December 1992, I sent out polite, neatly typed letters to seventy-five actors and actresses requesting interviews for a book I was writing about the movies. Some of the letters were a bit hazy about the book's theme, but most of them did contain at least a passing mention of my interest in discussing the fleeting nature of fame, a subject with which many of them were quite familiar. The people I wrote to included the rich and famous (Kevin Costner, Mel Gibson, Daryl Hannah, Goldie Hawn), the previously rich and famous (Ursula Andress, Bo Derek, Isaac Hayes, Margot Kidder, Liza Minnelli, John Travolta), the previously reasonably well known and/or probably still fairly rich (George Hamilton, Judd Nelson, Eric Roberts), plus a bunch of people like Pam Grier, Helen Slater, and Vincent Spano. Only two of the seventy-five responded; Liza Minnelli's and Raul Julia's publicists wrote back to say no.

The stars' and ex-stars' lack of interest in this project did not catch me entirely by surprise. Over the previous five years, while writing for publications as varied as *Spy*, *GQ*, *The Wall Street Journal*, *The New York Times*, *Time*, *The New Republic*, *Rolling Stone* and, most especially, *Movieline*, I had developed a reputation as a bit of a hatchet man, the sort of mean-spirited turnip whose work would never be allowed to grace the covers of such ferociously accommodating publications as *Entertainment Weekly*, or such overtly supine magazines as *Premiere*. During those five years, I had developed a reputation as a writer who did not seem to have the stars' best interests at heart. This became apparent when I attempted to become the first American journalist to write an article about Susan Sarandon without mentioning her incredible breasts, an attempt that failed miserably. I also disappointed my interview subject when I devoted the lion's share of an article about Sean Young to the troubled thespianess's shocking deficiencies in algebra and trigonometry, intellectual gaps I had inadvertently stumbled upon when the svelte but unhinged actress forced me to sit in her Greenwich Village living room for an hour, paging through stacks of coffee table art books, while she struggled through her weekly algebra lesson with a local high school teacher.

More recently, I had gone two weeks without bathing, shaving, washing my hair, or changing my clothes in preparation for writing a story called "Mickey Rourke for a Day," a project in which I literally entered the renowned actor's skin for a day: degrading numerous women, smoking eighty-two Marlboros, rolling around in the gutter on the Bowery, picking fights with complete strangers, lighting cigarettes off comatose alkies' feet, and setting a new indoor and outdoor world's record for use of the word "motherfucker."

None of the subjects featured in these articles had subsequently phoned or written to thank me for the coverage, nor had any of them instructed their publicists to include my work in their press kits, or to send me flowers or chocolates. Not even the legendarily gallant Rourke.

Similar lack of enthusiasm was exhibited by Jessica Lange's

publicists at PMK, who strongly objected to an article entitled "Is This Any Way to Run a Career?" What seemed to annoy the spin doctors for this talented but perverse actress, aside from the gratuitously snide remarks about her polo-playing husband, was my likening her to Frances Farmer, the blond bombshell from the 1940s who was eventually forced to undergo a lobotomy and to appear on *This Is Your Life*. During my interview with Lange, I had mentioned, without going into too many details, the amazing parallels between her life and Farmer's, parallels that Lange categorically denied. The article arising from the interview pointed out that both Lange and Farmer were gorgeous Middle-American blondes who started out playing bimbos, rebelled against their image, made enemies in the business, gradually found it harder and harder to get decent roles, and ended up marrying pretentious playwrights. Other than that, of course, there were no similarities whatsoever. In retrospect, Lange may have been right about my going overboard with this thing—after all, Frances Farmer had never had a kid by a Russian dancer, and Jessica Lange had never been lobotomized. Though she did make two movies in one year with Robert De Niro.

Lange was not the only actress to express displeasure with my work. A phone call to the offices of *Movieline* by Barbra Streisand's press agent confirmed my suspicion that the erstwhile political radical and Neil Diamond collaborator was not thrilled by my career survey, "Sacred Cow." In this article, I had seriously questioned the cultural and economic savvy of the director and screenwriter of *Nuts*, accusing them of gross ignorance of the economics of the prostitution business. My basis for this accusation was the fact that they had cast Streisand as a $500-a-night call girl capable of "taking your body to heaven and sending your mind south." I had had personal experience with this subject, having had my body sent to heaven and my mind sent south on several occasions, and had also interviewed friends who had had their bodies sent to heaven and their minds sent south. All parties agreed that $500 was a bit steep for a call

girl answering the general physical description of Barbra Streisand, that $85-a-night was more in the general price range.
Room included.

Given this unenviable record as a journalist, I was not entirely
shocked when none of the seventy-five actors and actresses I
wrote to agreed to talk to me. For one thing, my interviews with
Lange, Sarandon, and Young had been pure flukes anyway.
Basically, I was a journalist who only dealt in troubled merchan-
dise, who only got to meet movie stars when they themselves had
a gun cocked to their heads by their studios and were literally
forced to go out and do interviews with unpleasant people. They
were forced to do interviews with people like me because they
had megaduds in the can. Fortunately for them, there *are* no
other people like me.

Thus, the Susan Sarandon I got to interview was not the
triumphant Susan Sarandon of *Thelma and Louise* or *Bull Durham*, but the Susan Sarandon who had two turkeys—*The January
Man* and *A Dry White Season*—in the can, and who needed all
the publicity she could get. The Sean Young I got to interview
was not the radiant supernova fresh from her triumph in *Blade
Runner* or *No Way Out*, not the up-and-coming femme fatale who
had the whole world at her feet, but the head case who'd been
given early dismissal from *Wall Street*, who'd been written out of
Batman, who'd been interrogated by the Los Angeles Police
Department after allegedly depositing a mutilated doll on the
doorstep of James Woods's girlfriend, and whose career was
headed straight for the bargain-rental video rack inhabited by
people like Shannon Tweed.

Similarly, the Jessica Lange I got to interview was not the
Oscar-winning alumna of *Tootsie* or the resurgent star of *Cape
Fear* but the disgruntled veteran of a string of stinkeroos (*Everybody's All-American, Crimes of the Heart, Far North*) and interesting failures (*Sweet Dreams, Country*), who now had two more
bombs/interesting failures—*Men Don't Leave, Music Box*—ready

to be released. If you were talking to me, it seemed, your career was in big trouble.

This being the case, the fact that I failed to get a single positive response from the seventy-five actors and actresses did not totally floor me. Since my rap sheet includes such offenses as "Dark Side of the Moon," an article exploring the role of Melanie Griffith's formidable butt in her astonishing rise to fame, and "The Stone Age," in which I pinpointed an obsession with head trauma as the principal theme in the work of Oliver Stone, it would have been foolhardy for any of the stars—even Susan Anton—to agree to talk with me. Even though many of the stars' best work was far behind them, it was still safe to say that they had better things to do with their time than to talk to the author of "If You Can't Say Something Nice, Say It in Broken English," an exhaustive study of the history of bad accents in motion pictures (including the first annual Horst Buchholz Nine Hours to Rama Award), or "Clerical Errors," a cine-theological essay exploring the world of bad-priest movies in an effort to determine which actor, actress, director, producer, and best boy would spend the longest time in Hell for his or her participation in motion pictures attacking the Catholic Church, the Virgin Mary, the Holy Eucharist, the Immaculate Conception, the Blessed Trinity, the Mystical Body of Christ, or any combination thereof. Even Vincent Spano had better things to do with his time than talk to me. Ditto David Carradine.

I hope that the reader will not feel cheated by all this. I hope he will not find himself halfway through this book saying, "Hey, where the hell's the goddamn interview with Casey Siemaszko?" or, "Twenty-two bucks and I don't even get to meet Valerie Perrine up close and personal?" And I hope he will not feel shortchanged by the recurring personal remarks about people like Danny Aiello and River Phoenix. Yes, in working his way through this book, the reader may be surprised and even annoyed to discover more than one reference to Emilio Estevez's height, Kathleen Turner's weight, the questionable casting of Charlotte Rampling as a really smart marine biologist in *Orca*, and Lou Diamond Phillips's existence. This is *not* the result of an editing oversight. Rather, this repetition of certain pejorative remarks stems from my personal belief that it is impossible to remind the public too often that Diane Keaton is a really awful actress, just as it is impossible to make too many nasty remarks about short, bad actors related to Martin Sheen. With this in mind, I would hope that the reader would look upon these running jokes not so much as running jokes, but as *leitmotifs*. *Leitmotif*, for the uninitiated, is one of many words that Lou Diamond Phillips probably cannot spell.

Most of the mean-spirited, journalistically irresponsible, completely unbalanced articles that appear in this collection first reared their ugly heads in *Movieline*, a West Coast magazine published by people who are not very nice. The remainder of the mean-spirited, journalistically irresponsible, completely unbalanced articles in this collection first appeared in *Rolling Stone*, while they still had mean-spirited editors working there. (They have since been purged, or have gone back to Philadelphia where they belong.) The one story in this collection that is unquestionably mean-spirited and unbalanced but is not journalistically irresponsible first appeared in the Washington *Post*, a fine newspaper in an awful city.

I would also point out that even though these stories were written in a spirit of complete and utter malice, they were written in a spirit of cheerful, life-affirming malice, not the noxious, downbeat variety. By this I mean that although on an intellectual level I despise most of the people that I write about, just as I despise most of the awful movies that they appear in, I do not despise the movie industry per se. For movies, even the very worst movies, are miracles that remind us that the world is a mysterious place where strange, utterly inexplicable phenomena keep happening. Movies are the last place on earth where science holds no sway. Science can explain a miracle like the birth of the oceans or the existence of the heavens above. Science can explain a miracle like the Empire State Building. Science can explain a miracle like Babe Ruth or Michael Jordan. But no power on earth can explain how people like Melanie Griffith and Christopher Reeve can continue to find work in Hollywood. Their careers are living proof that there are some things that take place on this planet for which we mortals will never have an explanation. Not until we pass through the Pearly Gates and meet our Maker will any of us ever know why God created Ryan O'Neal, what pivotal role Mariel Hemingway is playing in the Almighty's master plan, and to what extent Satan himself was involved in the final editing of *Beastmaster III*.

Actually, of the seventy-five people I wrote to, I really did think I had an outside chance with James Brolin.

IF YOU'RE
TALKING TO
ME, YOUR
CAREER MUST
BE IN
TROUBLE

1 BABY LOVE

It was a tragic affair when we first heard of it, and it is a tragic affair now. A pretentious middleaged intellectual sets up house with an attractive woman a few years his junior. Alas, their love eventually sours as he becomes obsessed by his wife's beautiful but cerebrally impoverished teenage daughter. One day, his wife stumbles upon a supremely damaging piece of physical evidence confirming her suspicion that her mate has fallen in love with her child. An eruption occurs. Soon, the older man is involved in a wild affair with the young girl, even though he is assailed by pointed inquiries from his concerned neighbors, and is even awakened in the middle of the night by calls from total strangers demanding to know more details about his seemingly immoral relationship with his young mistress. His reputation is destroyed, his career lies in ruins, as friend and foe alike condemn his immoral behavior. The verdict of society is clear: James Mason (Professor Humbert) had no right to take up with his wife's daughter by a previous marriage, Sue Lyon (Lolita). As boring and conventional and thoroughly bourgeois as it may have been, Mason should have done the right thing and remained true to Shelley Winters (Mrs. Hayes) till death did them part.

It is now thirty-one years since Stanley Kubrick directed his groundbreaking, highly controversial *Lolita*, yet the screen version of Vladimir Nabokov's famous novel has lost none of its power to shock, amaze and, yes, even horrify. Of course, the film's message is particularly relevant in the year 1994 because of all those shocking revelations about Woody Allen's infidelity to his longtime companion Mia Farrow, a breach of faith culminating in his apparently sordid liaison with his apparent common-law daughter Soon-Yi Previn.

It is not our intention here to judge Mr. Allen or Ms. Previn, nor to draw unflattering comparisons between the often eccentric behavior of Ms. Farrow and her somewhat more rotund screen counterpart, Shelley Winters, which may have contributed to the Messrs. Mason's and Allen's decidedly idiosyncratic behavior. But we would be most remiss as film connoisseurs and *auteur* buffs if we did not underscore the disturbing similarities between the events depicted in *Lolita* and the events that have actually transpired in the Allen-Farrow contretemps. And we would be even more remiss if we did not wonder aloud how it was possible for an individual as steeped in cinematic lore as Mr. Allen to ignore the moral warning signs that had been planted firmly in his path by a film such as *Lolita* and others of this ilk—black-and-white pictures that regularly played at the Bleecker Street Cinema, the Carnegie Hall Cinema, the Thalia, the Regency, and all the other arty Greenwich Village and Upper West Side film houses where Allen spent his formative years.

The arts—and yes, that term does include motion pictures—are the deepest repositories of a civilization's values, guideposts planted on the Highway of Life to assist the young and the untutored in finding their moral bearings (obviously, there are exceptions to this rule—Russ Meyer, David Lynch). Motion pictures such as *Lolita* are not mere diversions, mere entertainments, mere *amusements*; oh no, they serve a higher purpose.

And what is that purpose if not to guide the viewer toward the One, the True, and the Beautiful? Their purpose, their raison d'être, is not merely to help a bored filmgoer while away a few stolen hours. Their purpose is to warn the viewer to eschew the crass, the vulgar, the base. Their purpose is to warn the viewer to keep one's eyes on the prize, one's chin up, one's nose to the grindstone, one's eyes *on* the road, one's hands *upon* the wheel. Conversely, their purpose is to warn the viewer to keep his hands *off* his wife's or girlfriend's daughter, and at all costs to avoid public liaisons with obvious jailbait.

By choosing to ignore the lesson James Mason learned—at such bitter cost—in *Lolita*, Woody Allen has displayed a truly remarkable naïveté. For that lesson is simple: May/December romances are to be avoided at all costs. They are messy. They are difficult. People's hearts get broken. Unwanted babies get born. Alimony and child-support litigation can occur. And sometimes the man ends up in jail.

It is not as if *Lolita* was the first or only time that the motion picture industry had dealt with the subject of older men's fatal infatuations with younger women. Perhaps the most memorable treatment of all was *The Blue Angel*, the 1930 film that made Marlene Dietrich an international star. In that film, a doddering old professor played by Emil Jannings falls hopelessly in love with a cabaret singer wearing ruffled panties, a garter belt, and a top hat. *It can happen.* But the relationship doesn't work, nor did it ever have a chance of working. Yet *The Blue Angel* is one of those films that has been a staple on art house programs for more than half a century. Therefore, we know, without a shadow of a doubt, that Woody Allen had to have seen it at some point in his career, and may even have seen it several times. Yet for some strange reason he chose to ignore its message.

He also chose to ignore the none-too-subtle message of *Baby Doll*, the 1956 Elia Kazan film in which the downwardly mobile cotton gin operator Karl Malden has his life ruined after falling in love with a nineteen-year-old girl who still wears ruffled baby doll pajamas and sleeps in a baby's crib. *Hey, the heart has its reasons.* Although this film is the trashiest of the trashiest, even by the standards of mid-fifties, Johnny Reb *film noir*, we know that Woody Allen had to have seen it because it was directed by the cultural avatar Elia Kazan and was based on a screenplay by Tennessee Williams, and was therefore a staple on the art house circuit for decades. Yet for some strange reason he chose to ignore its message.

The list of arty films warning older men not to screw around with teenyboppers goes on and on. In 1978, the pretentious French director Louis Malle explored the subject in *Lolita Does the Big Easy*, also known as *Pretty Baby*. This film features putative human Keith Carradine as a pretentious photographer, totally obsessed with his art, who helps the downtrodden Susan Sarandon start a new career by using her in his pictures, and who then starts screwing around with her gorgeous daughter. *Pretty Baby* has been a staple on the art house circuit for years; it was released a year before Allen's *Manhattan*. Woody Allen, an incredibly pretentious guy who is totally obsessed by his art, who helped Mia Farrow start a new career by putting her in his pictures, and who then got involved with her gorgeous daughter, had to have seen it. Yet for some strange reason he chose to ignore its message.

Even before Louis Malle sank his teeth into it, the Italian director Bernardo Bertolucci had explored the subject in his 1972 film *Last Tango in Paris*. Although this film has quite a bit more stuff about rat's assholes and pig's vomit and conventional sodomy than any of the other films we have mentioned, it nonetheless contains a reasonably straightforward moral message: Don't mess with the young stuff. *Last Tango* has been a staple on the art house circuit for twenty years, so we know that Woody Allen has to have seen it. Yet for some strange reason, he chose to ignore its message.

Since the disclosures about Allen's affair with Ms. Previn have become public knowledge, there has been much discussion in the press about the striking similarities between Allen's 1979 masterpiece *Manhattan* and his own life. In that film, it will be recalled, the twice-divorced Allen character, having broken up with the neurotic Diane Keaton, ends up winning back Mariel Hemingway, the cuddly high-school girl he jilted earlier in the film. In the final close-up, Allen seems to be saying that it is possible to fool around with borderline jailbait and get away with it, the very opposite of the message conveyed in *The Blue Angel*, *Lolita*, and *Pretty Baby*, all of which are unbelievably pretentious art house films that we know that he saw. How, then, was it possible for someone like Woody Allen to have ignored the warnings he was being given in these films?

The answer is actually quite simple: He saw those pictures on a double-bill with films like *Sabrina* and *Georgy Girl*, and those flicks confused the issue. In Billy Wilder's 1954 classic, *Sabrina*, the pixieish chauffeur's daughter Audrey Hepburn is torn between falling in love with William Holden, a man twenty years too old for her, or Humphrey Bogart, a man forty years too old for her. She finally settles on Bogie, and the two live happily ever after. In *Georgy Girl*, Silvio Narizzano's 1966 classic, James Mason plays a dirty old man who falls in love with a girl thirty years younger than him, and ends up marrying her. *Sabrina* and *Georgy Girl* have both been staples on the art house circuit for years, and almost certainly appeared on the same bill as pictures such as *Lolita*, *Baby Doll*, *Pretty Baby*, and *Last Tango in Paris* many times over. Woody, who seems like an impressionable man, may have been confused by the contradictory messages he was receiving from the morally self-canceling double bills, and decided that screwing around with girls thirty years younger than him was a judgment call. This almost certainly contributed to the cradle-robbing mentality we first saw in *Manhattan*, and have now seen in Manhattan.

Another factor contributing to Woody's moral disorientation is the fact that most of the movies that have dealt with this subject in the past decade—while Ms. Previn was growing up—have been trashy, low-budget productions that Allen would never have seen, not only because they never made it onto the art house circuit, but because the art house circuit in New York no longer exists; developers tore down all the art-film houses. Here, we are talking about movies such as *Blame It on Rio, Sunset, Creator*, and the spectacularly ungodly *Butterfly*. In each of these movies, an old coot, played, variously, by Michael Caine, James Garner, Peter O'Toole, or Stacy Keach, falls in love with a girl roughly thirty years younger than him, usually with disastrous results. But Woody Allen would not have seen *Blame It on Rio*, because Demi Moore was in it; would not have seen *Creator*, because Vincent Spano was in it; would not have seen *Butterfly*, because Pia Zadora was in it; and would not have seen *Sunset*, because Bruce Willis was in it, and because, well, nobody saw it. Let's face it: The man who is arguably America's greatest living director did not get that way by wasting his free time watching Vincent Spano movies.

Thus, even though the movie industry, all through the 1980s, continued to churn out movies warning senior citizens like Woody Allen to keep their hands off tykes who were barely out of diapers, those films were no help to Woody because they were so awful that they never made it onto the art house circuit, which doesn't exist anymore anyway, so he never got to see them. He had to rely on old standbys like *Sabrina* and *Georgy Girl*, and they clouded his judgment.

As a public service to older men who are thinking about getting involved with girls thirty or more years younger than themselves, or who are giving serious thought to moving in with their common-law wives' daughters and then saying something like "The heart has its reasons" or "Let he who is without sin cast the first stone," I have compiled the *Essential May/December Video Library*, also known as *The Jailbait Baker's Dozen*. These are not the only movies that deal with this treacherous subject, nor are they necessarily the best. Rather, they are the only films the local video store had in stock the night I stopped in. For

purposes of thematic and gender consistency, I have ignored
older woman–younger man films such as *Golden Boy* and *Harold
and Maude,* and have also avoided older man–younger boy films
such as *Death in Venice* because they do not apply to people like
Woody Allen, and because they have too much depressing
Austrian music. Still, the compilation is of sufficient breadth and
scope that it would make a fine addition to any film library, even
though it might make your babysitter nervous to see them all
together, side by side, on the shelf. Here then is our list:

Baby Doll (1956). Fortyish Karl Malden, a complete asshole,
has a weird, unconsummated marriage with nineteen-year-old
Carroll Baker, who is first seen sucking her thumb in a crib,
clad in baby doll pajamas with ruffled shorts. Baker is seduced
by Eli Wallach, an immigrant cotton magnate, who chases her
around the house while clutching a riding crop, then gets all
tuckered out and has a nap in her crib. Malden, having burned
down Wallach's cotton mill, ends up getting hauled off to jail for
arson, which suits everybody just fine. The movie is memorable
for Wallach's subtle remark: "This world is built on the principle
of tit for tat," and because Malden keeps a look of wide-eyed
terror on his face for two hours, not unlike a guy who's just had
all of his American Express travelers checks stolen.

Blame It on Rio (1984). Fiftyish Michael Caine falls in love
with his best friend's nineteen-year-old daughter (Michelle Johnson), who sleeps with a teddy bear and who shares a bedroom
with Caine's own nineteen-year-old daughter, played by Demi
Moore. Yes, Caine's Lolita is named Jennifer, and, yes, she has
breasts that are not to be believed, though Caine certainly has
no trouble believing them. Best line: "I love it when your glasses
steam up." ATTENTION, PARENTS: Film contains rabies jokes
and Valerie Harper.

The Blue Angel (1930). Emil Jannings plays a crusty old
professor who falls in love with Marlene Dietrich, a talented,
pre-Nazi Madonna in slightly roomier underwear. The relationship ends in tragedy, though many would argue that if you're

going to have your life end in tragedy, there are worse fates than having your life end in tragedy involving Marlene Dietrich. Especially in that get-up.

Butterfly (1981). Stacy Keach, an unsuccessful mine-shaft security guard, makes love to Pia Zadora, even though he thinks he's her father. Meanwhile, Pia already appears to have gotten knocked up by Edward Albert, whose parents are played with zest and verve by June Lockhart and Ed McMahon. (McMahon was chosen for the role because he was the only actor stupid enough to be credible in a role as a man who would welcome Pia Zadora into his family.) As things turn out, the baby did not spring from the Albertian loins, but was actually sired by Pia's mother's lover, James Franciscus. Moreover, Pia may even be Franciscus's daughter, meaning that she has slept with one dad then with another man who *thinks* he's her dad. Keach now begins to suspect that Pia may be a tramp, and murders Franciscus before he has a chance to sleep with anyone else and further complicate the plot. Keach, an ex-jailbird in real life, is convicted of incest and sentenced to ten years in jail at a trial presided over by Orson Welles, who spends a considerable amount of time gaping at Pia's formidable knockers.

"He didn't do anything to me that I didn't want to happen," declares Pia, a statement the court has no trouble believing. This film is memorable because of the wonderful scene where Keach teaches Pia optimal mining techniques, and because it demonstrates that no matter how bad Woody Allen's problems are, they could be a whole lot worse.

Georgy Girl (1966). James Mason plays a wealthy, dirty old man who dreams of taking the plump, dowdy Lynn Redgrave as his mistress. Instead, Redgrave falls in love with the flashy mod Alan Bates, who has just knocked up Charlotte Rampling, who, in one of her first films, is ingeniously cast as a slut. Redgrave adopts the baby, is deserted by Bates, and ends up marrying her aging, wealthy benefactor. A film best remembered for its truly ghastly theme song, *Georgy Girl* is basically a fat girl's *Lolita*.

Last Tango in Paris (1972). Fiftyish Marlon Brando sodomizes twenty-year-old Maria Schneider, volunteers to prepare a dead rat for dinner, plays "Shenandoah" on the harmonica, and says a lot of things like "I'm gonna get a pig, and I'm gonna have the pig fuck you, and I want the pig to vomit in your face," then wonders why the relationship doesn't work out. European.

Lolita (1962). James Mason, a pretentious urbanite obsessed by art, marries a strange woman, falls in love with her jailbait daughter, forces her to take piano lessons and go to museums, brings her *Portrait of the Artist* while she's in the hospital, and drives her to Los Angeles, where he is supposedly working on a film about existentialism. Any similarities between Vladimir Nabokov's screenplay and Woody Allen's entire life are purely coincidental.

Pretty Baby (1978). Keith Carradine, a corpse masquerading as an actor, marries Brooke Shields, a charismatic, twelve-year-old prostitute. But not even she can breathe any life into this anorexic deadbeat.

Susan Sarandon steps out of character by showing off her breasts.

Sabrina (1954). Audrey Hepburn spends two hours dressed like a wholesome Jean Seberg, while aging juvenile playboy William Holden gets champagne flute fragments impacted in his ass. Humphrey Bogart, inexplicably cast as a Wall Street tycoon, wears a dapper homburg, mumbles a lot, and eventually sails off to Paris with the perky *gamine*. John Williams, cast as Hepburn's chauffeur dad, hams it up. From the unchallenged genius Billy Wilder.

Voyager (1991). In a real stretch, Sam Shepard plays a mopey hydroelectrical engineer who falls in love with the daughter of a woman he deserted twenty years earlier because she wanted to have a baby, while he had a good job offer in Baghdad. The girl gets bit by a poisonous snake, but doesn't die from the snakebite. Instead, she dies from the bump on her head caused by keeling over onto a rock after the snake bit her. Mom sees Sam off to the airport, but expresses no interest in resuming their admittedly offbeat relationship. Oedipal.

The final three movies in our collection all showcase the work of one of the silver screen's living legends: Mariel Hemingway. It is often said that fine wines get better as they get older. But Mariel Hemingway comes straight from the vineyards of Ernest and Julio Gallo. She was passable as the high school senior Woody Allen fell in love with in *Manhattan*, but was ludicrous as the white-trash babe Peter O'Toole falls for in *Creator* (1985), and was unspeakable as the nymphet James Garner gets involved with in *Sunset* (1988).

In fact, Mariel Hemingway's three incursions into May/December romances underscore why movies of this ilk are generally so bad. May/December—or jailbait—films by their very nature juxtapose a young actress with a much older actor. This almost invariably results in a profound dramatic imbalance, because the veteran actor can usually act the pants off the female newcomer. The result is something akin to Muhammad Ali sharing the ring with Richard Simmons, contributing to such unlikely pairings as:

James Mason/Sue Lyon
Peter O'Toole/Mariel Hemingway
Orson Welles/Pia Zadora
Marlon Brando/Maria Schneider
Michael Caine/Michelle Johnson

All things considered, it's surprising that the films aren't a lot worse.

On the other hand, they're bad enough. In the horrendous *Creator*, Mariel plays a trash-talking truck-stop babe who gets involved with the donnish physicist Peter O'Toole, who is attempting to genetically reconstruct his wife, dead for thirty years (her amino acids are out of sequence, so that's the reason for the holdup). Vincent Spano is also in this film, but let's not get into

that. Mariel is especially unconvincing in a scene where, bathed
in grease, she repairs a pick-up truck while singing "I'm a
Woman—W-O-M-A-N." In another scene, she falls asleep on
the couch, and as the camera lovingly hovers above her face, the
viewer is treated to indisputable celluloid evidence that Mariel
can *act bad in her sleep*, no mean feat.

Then there's *Sunset*, Blake Edwards's extravagant 1988 bomb,
in which Mariel plays a cross-dressing bordello operator who
falls in love with James Garner, who plays a ninety-year-old
Wyatt Earp who has come to Hollywood to work as a consultant
on a cowboy movie starring Tom Mix, played with verve, gusto,
and panache by Bruce Willis. *I*, as the saying once went, *kid you
not*.

Unbelievably retrograde as these films are, they form essential
components of the *Home Nymphet Video Collection*. Despite their
absurd plots, their horrible scripts, their eighth-rate acting, and
Vincent Spano, these films, viewed as a unit, provide an indispensable moral compass that horny, middle-aged men everywhere can use when reaching a decision about preying on women
who are old enough to be their children, grandchildren, great-
grandchildren, or nieces once removed by marriage. Had Woody
Allen looked at these films, or looked at them more carefully, he
would have been less reckless in making the decision to abandon
Ms. Farrow and take up with one of her numerous United Colors
of Benetton daughters. Woody would have learned from Mason,
would have learned from Brando, would have learned from Keach.
Oh, he might momentarily have been blinded by the moral frappé
served up in numbskull piffle such as *Sabrina* and *Funny Face*,
but had he really studied these movies, and studied them
carefully, the way he studied *The Seventh Seal* and *Grand Illusion*
and *Les Enfants du Paradis*, he would have clung to the straight
and narrow. Instead, he has strayed far from the path of righ-
teousness, and must now accept the same verdict from society
that Sue Lyon once handed down to James Mason: "You're sick.
You need help."

Only Pia would disagree.

2 MICKEY ROURKE FOR A DAY

Several months ago, I began to suffer from extreme stomach pains. The pains were of mysterious origin, but were so persistent and excruciating that I soon became convinced that I was dying of cancer. Like most people who unexpectedly find themselves in such a situation, I immediately began to regret all the dreams I would never get to fulfill in my life were I to die before my time. I would never get to see the Parthenon. I would never get to see the Philadelphia Eagles win the Super Bowl. I would never get to cuddle my grandchildren. I would never get to sweep through the Scottish heather like Paul McCartney does in "Mull of Kintyre." But my greatest regret of all was that I would never get to spend an entire day being Mickey Rourke.

Like most American males, my single most cherished fantasy has long been to spend an entire day in the shoes, in the skin, nay, in the psyche of Mickey Rourke. With his uncompromising artistic vision, Rourke embodies a particularly heroic strain of American manhood that is constantly threatened with extermination by venal corporate philistines. More than Brando, more than Elvis, more even than Jim Morrison, Mickey Rourke is the incarnation of a recalcitrant American rebelliousness that refuses to kowtow to the demands of Wall Street, Madison Avenue, or even La Cienega Boulevard. "Live free or die!" is the motto Mickey Rourke has always lived by, a motto that I—and most American males—have only lived by in our dreams.

What is most appealing about Mickey Rourke qua man is that he has obliterated the distinction between his own personality and those of the characters he plays on the screen, engendering a sort of cosmic Mickey Rourkeianism that straddles the real and the celluloid world. That's why my premature burial would have chagrined me so, because I would not only have missed out on being the Mickey Rourke who kicks people's asses in the movies, but the Mickey Rourke who kicks people's asses in real life; not only the Mickey Rourke who brutalizes women in the movies, but the Mickey Rourke who brutalizes women in real life; not only the Mickey Rourke who looks like a complete scuzzball in the movies, but the Mickey Rourke who looks like a complete scuzzball in real life.

In May one of New York's finest gastroenterologists informed me that I was not suffering from stomach cancer and was not going to die, but was merely suffering from stress, a rotten diet, and nervous exhaustion. He recommended that I eat more salad and start enjoying myself more. I took him up on it. I immediately booked a summer trip to Scotland, and by mid-July was joyously sweeping through the northern heather just a stone's throw from Loch Ness. I set up a writing assignment that would require a spring 1993 trip to Athens. I started talking to my eight-year-old daughter about the joys of teenage pregnancy. Last, but not least, I started gearing up to be Mickey Rourke for a day.

My preparations fell into three categories. First, I would have to look like Mickey Rourke. Physically, this was no problem at all. Mickey Rourke and I are both fabulously handsome Irish-Americans, so appearancewise I was a natural for the part. But my line of work—journalism—generally requires more than a passing acquaintance with normal human hygiene. Not so Mickey's. So the first thing I had to do was to grunge up for a week, religiously abstaining from bathing or washing my hair for seven days. In addition, I jogged and played basketball every day for a week to augment the pungency of *l'arome de Rourke*. I did not shave for fourteen days, cultivating a rich, grainy stubble, and I let my hair grow out for five months preceding my adventure. By the time the big day arrived, I looked like a complete thug.

Sartorially, I prepared for being Mickey Rourke by buying a jet black sports coat, jet black jeans, jet black shoes, jet black socks, a jet black shirt, a jet black belt, and jet black sunglasses. This would take care of the Mickey Rourke of *Diner*, *The Pope of Greenwich Village*, *Angel Heart*, *Year of the Dragon*, *Desperate Hours*, and *9½ Weeks*. For the Mickey Rourke of *Barfly* I would have to switch to a grubby gray sweatshirt with a beer mug on the front; for the Mickey Rourke of *A Prayer for the Dying* I would don filthy blue jeans, a faded green fatigue jacket, and a pair of brown combat boots. The Mickey Rourke of *Harley Davidson and the Marlboro Man* would require a Confederate flag bandana, an earring, and a tattoo; the Mickey Rourke of *Homeboy* would involve stripping down to boxer's trunks.

Psychologically, I prepared for being Mickey Rourke by watching all of his movies and memorizing particularly memorable snippets of dialogue. It was important for me to spend my day as Mickey Rourke by not only speaking in clipped, guttural tones the way Rourke does both in his films and in real life, but by reproducing verbatim some of his most memorable remarks. At all times, I reminded myself that I must never let more than fifteen words pass through my lips without using Mickey Rourke's favorite term—read *any* of his interviews?—"motherfucker."

The ground rules for the project were simple: I would spend an entire day, from the moment I rose until midnight, doing things Mickey Rourke had actually done in his films and in real life, and saying things Mickey Rourke had actually said in his films and in real life. I would dress like he dressed, speak like he spoke, eat like he ate, smoke like he smoked, and fuck with people like those he fucked with. Only then could I meet my Maker in peace.

5:00 Rise, smoke first Marlboro.

5:01 Smash bathroom mirror with fist (*Pope*), curse unidentified motherfuckers who want me to compromise my principles and suck their cocks.

5:04 Smoke second Marlboro.

5:05 Take thirty $10-bills out of my shoes (*Pope*).

5:06 My children wake, come to hug me. "I really like this family," I snarl, pushing them away, "but you're pushing my patience." (*Desperate Hours*).

5:08 Smoke third Marlboro.

5:15 Hit local diner, sprinkle raw sugar all over my tongue, then wash it down with glass of Coke (*Diner*).

5:21 Kick over two trash cans. (*Pope*).

5:26 Smoke fourth Marlboro, grind out butt with heel of my boot.

5:27 Work out on speed bag at gym. (*Johnny Handsome*).

5:45 Kick over two more trash cans (*Pope*).

5:49 Order French fries with gravy (*Diner*).

5:52 Smoke fifth Marlboro.

5:54 Call passing motorist "motherfucker."

5:56 Get in line for train to New York. Man tries to sneak ahead of me. "Fuck you, motherfucker," I snarl. "You fuck with me, we're gonna fucking get down. You're not gonna cut off my balls the way they cut off Michael Cimino's."

Ancient, short retiree skulks off.

5:58–6:25 Sneer and snarl a lot on train to city.

6:25 Get off train at 125th Street and run madly through streets of Harlem (*Angel Heart*).

6:28 Madly dash back to safety of train platform, away from mean streets of Harlem.

7:12 Arrive at Grand Central Station. Eighth Marlboro.

7:23 On the lookout for the kind of prostitute Mickey Rourke hires to fondle Kim Basinger in *9½ Weeks*, I visit sex shop on 42nd Street. No prostitutes, but I can't pass up the opportunity to watch *Latex Submission*. Grind out tenth Marlboro with heel of my boot.

7:48 Visit dirty-book store in Times Square. Page through *Bondage Life*, *The Tickling Scene*, and *Foot Notes*. Smoke eleventh Marlboro.

8:02 Visit porn palace on Eighth Avenue and watch *Ready, Willing and Anal*.

8:13 Pop into cheap dive on Eighth Avenue. Order four Scotches (*Barfly*). "Hey, if these motherfuckers pay me enough money, I'll talk to anybody they want me to," I tell the bartender, who doesn't seem entirely sure what I plan to do with the four Scotches. (I don't drink, but I feel that in order to be just like Mickey Rourke it's important to at least *order* the same drinks that he orders in his movies.) "Every once in a while you've gotta roll the potato." (I'm not sure what Mickey Rourke meant by this when he said it in his interview with *Smart* magazine, and I can tell by the look on the bartender's face that he has no idea what it means to roll the potato. But when a grunged-up fuck all dressed in black comes into your shithole dive at eight o'clock in the morning and says that he wants to roll the potato, hey, you let him roll the motherfucking potato.)

8:19 Grind fifteenth Marlboro into sidewalk with heel of my boot.

8:27 Visit scuzzy diner on Ninth Avenue. Order French fries with gravy. Wash it down with mouthful of raw sugar and Coke chaser.

8:38 Guy hassles me on Ninth Avenue. "Let's rock 'n' roll, motherfucker!" I exclaim (*Harley Davidson*). Seventy-year-old Chinese-American handing out fliers for local drugstore cowers in corner and meekly skulks away.

8:55 Spy a passed-out drunk lying on street outside bus depot. Put my foot across his neck, just like Mickey Rourke does in *A*

Prayer for the Dying. The drunk doesn't budge, so I figure I'll get a two-fer by lighting a match off his shoes just like Mickey does in *Angel Heart.* The drunk still doesn't budge, but unfortunately I only have book matches, which are hard to light off shoe leather. What I need are stick matches like the ones Mickey uses in the Fifties-era *Angel Heart.* I scour the neighborhood looking for chi-chi restaurants that give away stick matches, but it's too early in the morning, and, besides, it's a non-chi-chi neighborhood. I eventually decide to go back and light the match an inch away from the drunk's feet. I then smoke my twentieth Marlboro and grind it into the sidewalk with the heel of my boot.

9:23 Check into an Eighth Avenue diner and ask the waiter, "Is there any pussy on the menu? I heard the special is warm pussy salad."

"Whaaa?" says the waiter.

"I'll just have some French fries and gravy," I tell him. "Every once in a while you've gotta roll the potato."

9:35 Time to intimidate the press. Call Martin Beiser, managing editor of *GQ*, to threaten to rearrange his fucking face if he ever fucks with me again. But he hasn't come to work yet, so I leave a message saying I'll call back later.

9:45 Read a few passages from Tennessee Williams's *A Streetcar Named Desire* in the lobby of a seedy Times Square Hotel, just the way Mickey Rourke used to do when he first came to New York.

10:02 Stand in pulpit of St. Malachy's: The Actor's Chapel on West 49th Street, right off Broadway, and slip effortlessly into role of Martin Fallon, the IRA terrorist Mickey played in *A Prayer for the Dying.* "Fodder, we are fundamentally aloon . . ." I tell no one in particular, though secretly I am speaking directly to God. "Nothing lasts," I continue. "There's no purpose to any of it." A female penitent enters the church and kneels down a few feet in front of me. I descend from the pulpit. "There's nothing worth killing or dying for," I whisper to her, as I sweep past.

"And the real truth is . . . there's nothing worth living for." A certified non-babe, she looks like she's used to this kind of stuff.

10:35 Still on the lookout for the *right* kind of prostitute, I visit a porn palace ("LIVE GIRLS!!!") on 42nd Street and ask to see a live girl in a fantasy booth. The palooka at the counter tells me the live girls don't come on until eleven. For the first time, I feel really stupid and out of character. Mickey would have known what time the live girls come on.

10:40 Smoke twenty-sixth Marlboro.

10:42 Black pimp remarks, "That's a nice outfit you got on. John Wayne style—all black." A movie buff, fer sure.

10:50 Order a beer and a chaser in sleazy Eighth Avenue bar. "Even the most primitive societies have respect for the insane," I quote from Mickey's Motorcycle Boy in *Rumble Fish* to the disinterested drunk sitting next to me.

11:00 Visit porn palace where blond bombshell admits—as Mickey Rourke makes Kim Basinger confess in *9½ Weeks*—that she's been "a nosy Parker" and deserves a good spanking. She turns, lifts her skirt, and bends over, but the glass partition in the booth comes down suddenly, and I don't feel like giving her another $20 tip, so I leave.

11:15 Kick a car and briefly obstruct traffic just like Mickey Rourke does in *Homeboy*.

11:17 Call Andy Aaron, a freelance journalist, to threaten to kick his fucking head in if he ever fucks with me again. But he's not home.

11:21 Smoke thirty-first Marlboro. Throat getting kind of hoarse.

11:34 Take subway down to mean streets of Chinatown, where I run madly through the streets like Mickey Rourke does in *Year of the Dragon*.

11:37 Stop for lunch at Double Hey Rice Shop, but notice chicken hanging from windows and leave in a hurry. "I've got a thing about chickens," I tell waiter, quoting from *Angel Heart*.

11:51 Report to U.S. Court House to see if there are any wise guys in the vicinity I can hang out with or kiss on the cheeks like Mickey Rourke did during John Gotti's trial. But clerk says it's lunchtime.

11:59 Smoke thirty-third Marlboro.

12:03 Visit OTB and hang out with Little Italy and Chinatown lowlifes.

12:17 Walk through streets of Little Italy arm in arm with a reasonably handsome male friend so we look like a pair of raging queens just like Mickey Rourke and Eric Roberts in *The Pope of Greenwich Village*.

12:19 My friend buys a sausage sandwich from a vendor, just like the safecracker in *Pope*. "Hey, that stuff'll fucking kill you," I exclaim, yanking it from his lips and tossing it into the trash just like Mickey Rourke (*Pope*).

12:32 Spit on black guy's shoes just like Mickey Rourke does in *Homeboy*. Eighty-five-year-old derelict does not emerge from coma.

12:35 Sit on chopper outside Bowery eatery.

12:59 Visit Fetish Fantasy Video on Lower East Side in hope of finding a prostitute to recreate that *9½ Weeks* scene. None available, but since I'm here, what the fuck, I watch terrific movie about English schoolgirls who deserve, and receive, proper canings.

1:12 Wander past Hell's Angels clubhouse and smoke fortieth Marlboro. Briefly toy with idea of going inside and striking up conversation with spiritual kinsmen, but then recall that I am not really a badass motherfucker like Mickey Rourke but a pussy magazine writer masquerading as a badass motherfucker. Decide to leave the Angels to their own devices and go fuck around with some women instead. Hey, every once in a while you've gotta roll the potato.

1:38 Visit apartment of female friend and tear white blouse off her just like Mickey Rourke does to Kelly Lynch in *Desperate Hours*, then spray Perrier between her legs just like Mickey does to Kim Basinger in *9½ Weeks*. Next I force her to kneel in front of me with her eyes shut as she sips a mouthful of Vicks Formula 44D Cough Syrup just like Kim Basinger. I guzzle down the Perrier and finish my forty-third Marlboro, then kiss her passionately, forcing my tongue between her teeth.

"Kim Basinger once said that kissing Mickey Rourke was like kissing an ashtray," I tell my friend. "Is kissing me like kissing an ashtray?"

"No," she replies. "It's like kissing someone who's been smoking a lot of cigarettes." She pauses. "But then again, my mouth tastes like cough syrup."

2:25 Visit bombed-out bar on Lower East Side and nuzzle on up to pathetic female rummy. "People in my business, they want to own your ass, they wanna squeeze your balls, they wanna control you," I tell her, quoting from real-life Mickey Rourke's interview. "I'll go fifty-fifty, but I won't kiss nobody's ass." She asks me to buy her a drink.

2:48 Intimidate the press by stopping off at *Spy* magazine and threatening to kick editor Kurt Andersen's motherfucking face in if he ever fucks with me again. He giggles, apparently used to visits from people dressed like Mickey Rourke threatening to kick in his motherfucking face.

3:05 Buy a bag of goldfish, then set them free in the Hudson River just like Mickey Rourke did in *Rumble Fish*.

3:12 Buy a cheap, temporary tattoo depicting a skull surrounded by a snake.

3:16 Put out fiftieth Marlboro with heel of my shoe.

3:23 Stop off at cheap dive on Second Avenue and tell bartender: "A man is not a gentleman unless he knows how to mix a proper martini." (*Desperate Hours*).

3:27 Using Mickey's Snagglepuss accent from *Barfly*, I tell the lowlife sitting next to me: "Some people never go crazy; what truly horrible lives they must lead."

3:48 Pick fight with drunk at corner of 12th Street and Avenue A. "You know, if I had a nickel for every time some piece of shit pointed a gun at me," I remark, quoting Mickey as Harley

Davidson, "I'd be a rich man." The bum is not actually pointing a gun at me, but I jab him in the shoulder anyhow. "Catch you on the rebound, asshole."

4:08 Visit a cemetery while carrying a lot of money, just like Mickey does in *Johnny Handsome*.

4:23 Stop by a female friend's house and ask if she will wear a black-cat mask and black panties and fuck a complete stranger while I watch just like Mickey Rourke did with Carré Otis in *Wild Orchid*. She politely declines.

4:38 Stub out fifty-third Marlboro with the heel of my boot.

5:12 Stop by a Lower East Side church and say the brief prayer that Mickey recites in *Harley Davidson*: "Oh God, if you do exist, and you're up there watching from wherever it is you're watching from . . . stay away from me."

5:23 Stagger into cheap dive in fringes of Little Italy and tell drunken scum sitting right next to me, "Your mother's cunt stinks like carpet cleaner." (*Barfly*). He doesn't confirm or deny it.

5:37 Briefly roll around in gutter outside bar.

5:39 Remark to passerby: "Anybody can be a non-drunk; it takes a special talent to be a drunk." (*Barfly*).

5:59 Shoot some pool. (*Rumble Fish*).

6:11 Stub out fifty-ninth Marlboro with heel of my boot.

6:17 Sprinkle tongue with raw sugar, followed by Coke chaser.

6:25 Emulating Mickey, who regularly induces servile intermediaries to do the talking for him in public, I ask a friend to go into a Pakistani deli and tell the clerk: "Mr. Queenan would like you to sell him a pack of Marlboros."

6:59 Visit Times Square dive and watch cruddy porn flick. Attempt to ream my cock through bottom of popcorn container the way Mickey Rourke did in *Diner*, but have no luck. Realize that nineties-era container has solid bottom, rather than folds that were popular in *Diner* era. Also realize that hot butter could scald my ponderous manhood anyway. Stub out sixty-second Marlboro with heel of my boot.

7:12 Visit friend and complain about Spike Lee's movies

causing Los Angeles riots. "I'd like to investigate his asshole with a baseball bat," I say, citing real-life Mickey Rourke interview on another subject.

7:28 Invite female friend to hit me in the face like Daryl Hannah does to Mickey in *The Pope of Greenwich Village*. She does. The fucking bitch.

7:43 Steal a Hershey bar from Times Square bodega the way Mickey used to when he was a down-at-the heels actor struggling to make ends meet back in the seventies.

7:58 Grab a guy by the ear (*A Prayer for the Dying*).

8:15 Stub out sixty-seventh Marlboro with heel of my boot.

8:38 Blindfold female friend, then ask if she would mind having ice cubes dripped all over her lips and chin (*9½ Weeks*). She says this is no problem, but when she goes to the kitchen there is no ice in the refrigerator. I send her out to get some ice from a deli.

8:45 While she's out, I smash the refrigerator (*Pope*), shadowbox for ten minutes (*Johnny Handsome*), and call up her mother to ask what her daughter's favorite food is, just like Mickey Rourke does to Carré Otis in *Wild Orchid*. The woman's mother says she will need a day to think about it.

9:02 Friend returns with ice cubes that I refuse to pay for. I reblindfold her, then drip ice all over her lips and chin. After I finish she asks if I'm going to do anything with a riding crop. I say I don't have one. As luck would have it, *she* does. I try it out. Smooth. "Dominatrixes suffer from carpal tunnel syndrome due to repetitive use of the same muscles," my friend explains, mysteriously. "Look," I tell her, "you stay here and be Madonna, I've got to get back out on the streets and be Mickey Rourke."

9:27 Slosh down mouthful of sugar with Coke chaser, then stub out seventy-third Marlboro with the heel of my boot.

9:58 Check in to Sixth Avenue dive for a couple of Cokes and a mouthful of sugar. Strike up conversation with wino to my left. "I lost something a long time ago," I explain, quoting from Mickey Rourke's IRA terrorist in *A Prayer for the Dying*. "Everything . . . everything got very black like dried blood, and something started to stink. And every day it got worse, sometimes so bad I couldn't get out of my bed. I sat there in the darkness like a wee scared boy not being able to breathe or speak my name. I saw myself lying in the street dying, not wanting to die." Then the big wind-up: "Maybe there's something wrong with me."

The wino keeps watching the Mets game.

10:23 Dog-tired of being Mickey Rourke, I chat up a Puerto Rican prostitute on Eighth Avenue and ask if she'll fondle a blond girl's breasts just like the hooker did to Kim Basinger in *9½ Weeks*. She says she'll do it for $80, but I have to tip the blonde, too. I don't have $80, and, besides, Mickey Rourke doesn't have to tip *nobody*.

11:15 Catch the train home, referring to numerous bag people, conductors, and passengers as motherfuckers.

11:23 Shadowbox for ten minutes in train bathroom, then light up eighty-first Marlboro in area clearly marked "No Smoking."

12:00 Arrive home exactly at midnight, stub out eighty-second Marlboro with heel of my boot, pull off my jet black sunglasses, and officially stop being Mickey Rourke.

Was being Mickey Rourke for a day the emotionally transcendent experience I had long expected it to be, the unforgettable event that would enable me to go to my grave in peace? Yes. Getting to step on a bum's neck, to wear sunglasses in a pulpit, to force a woman to kneel in front of me while I force-fed her Vicks Formula 44D Cough Syrup, and to threaten the press with serious physical harm are about as uplifting experiences as I have ever had, and I also enjoyed watching *Ready, Willing and Anal*. Oh, sure, there were disappointments—I never got to see a man strangle another man on his own penis the way Mickey Rourke does in *Angel Heart* and I never got to see my girlfriend shoot herself with a pistol I lent her the way Mickey Rourke did with Carré Otis and I never got to jam a sharpened butcher knife between a person's fingers the way Mickey Rourke does in *Desperate Hours*—but on the whole I felt that I had accomplished what I had set out to accomplish. Within the parameters of Mickey Rourketude that I had delineated, I was satisfied that I had truly been Mickey Rourke for a day.

Did I learn anything from my day-long masquerade as one of the legends of the silver screen? Yes, being Mickey Rourke is a lot more physically demanding than I could possibly have imagined beforehand. Smoking eighty-two cigarettes when you've never smoked more than twenty-five in a single day in your entire life really leaves your nerves frazzled. Same deal with the seven mouthfuls of sugar followed by Coke chasers. Moreover, your ankles get tired from stubbing out eighty-two cigarettes, and your jaws get tired from repetitive use of the muscles needed to form the word "motherfucker." But all in all, I came away from my Day of the Rourke feeling as emotionally sated as I have ever felt in my life.

Still, by the time midnight arrived, I knew that it was time for me to start coming down, time to enter an emotional decompression chamber, time to start making the break from being Mickey Rourke. Otherwise I'd be tying my wife to the chandelier with a rattlesnake whip and coldcocking my little kids when they got up in the morning to go to school. I realized that it was vitally important for me to establish a clean break with the Mickey Rourke persona than I had inhabited for the past twenty-four hours. So I tearfully pulled off my Confederate flag headband. I yanked out my earring. I dragged off my black Guns N' Roses T-shirt. I took off my black boots. I stripped off my black jeans.

And then I took the first of four very long baths.

3 IT'S A MAN'S, MAN'S, MAN'S WORLD

At the very beginning of Oliver Stone's most interesting movie, *Salvador*, sleazeball photojournalist James Woods's nagging wife gets ready to pack up her bawling infant and go back to Italy, tired of waking up every morning to find eviction notices, a grimy apartment, and sleazeball photojournalist James Woods. Desperate for cash, Woods seeks an immediate assignment in El Salvador, but has the phone slammed down on him by a cold bitch of an editor. While he is on the phone, Woods is harassed by a fat bitch who wants to make a call herself, and after he gets off the phone he is arrested for speeding by a tough bitch of a cop. Bail is posted by his pal Jim Belushi, a sleazeball deejay who has just broken up with his Yuppie bitch of a wife because she wants him to stop being a sleazeball deejay and start being a sleazeball computer salesman.

The lurid Jims now decide to head south to Guatemala, but not before dropping by the local dog pound to pick up Belushi's beloved mutt. Alas, the dog has already been dispatched to the great kennel in the sky, and it is a cold-hearted bitch of a dog trainer who breaks the bad news to the boys. Thus, perhaps ten minutes into Stone's most successful movie (even though it's really just a remake of *Under Fire*, which appeared three years earlier), Jim & Jim have had miserable dealings with two nags, one bitch, and three cunts. No wonder they now find themselves on the way to merry El Salvador, where even though they'll have to deal with a moronic female journalist, an overbearingly pious nun, and a local witch doctress who ramrods a huge needle into Belushi's huge buttocks; at least, as Woods says, "[you can] get a virgin to sit on your face for seven bucks."

I think this says a lot about Oliver Stone's worldview.

Because most of Stone's movies deal so intensely with political themes—the war in Vietnam, the assassination of John F. Kennedy, the inexplicable rise of hate groups hellbent on killing performance artists like Eric Bogosian—there is a tendency to discuss his films as if they were *primarily* political films or, as some critics have dubbed them, as *propaganda*. But this ignores the underlying theme that binds *all* Oliver Stone movies together and accounts for their box-office appeal to a primarily male audience. Oliver Stone, whether he is directing, producing, or writing the screenplay for a film, basically makes buddy movies.

In buddy movies, women do not exist, or, if they do exist, they don't exist for very long. Yes, *JFK* is a profoundly disturbing film about the threat posed to this excellent, pluralistic republic by the sinister machinations of the military-industrial complex, but it's also a buddy movie about a crusading district attorney and a bunch of his pals who try to pin the rap for the president's murder on Tommy Lee Jones and his buddy Joe Pesci, and *his* buddy Ed Asner. The major female character is a nagging bitch (Sissy Spacek) who periodically surfaces to make dinner, put the kids to bed, and complain. *Salvador* is a buddy movie about a couple of fuck-knuckles who go to Central America to get wasted and have virgins squat on their faces. The major female character is a Latino madonna who periodically surfaces to chide James Woods for little things like getting her kid brother abducted, tortured, and murdered by death squads. *Wall Street* is a buddy

movie about Charlie Sheen and his sleazeball buddy Michael
Douglas who rig the stock market. The major female character is
Daryl Hannah, an entirely ornamental interior decorator, a role
she was *born* to play. *The Doors* is a buddy movie about the
adventures of Jim Morrison and his pals Robbie, Ray, and John
in Never-Never Land. The major female character is the hilari-
ously miscast Meg Ryan (*When Sally Met the Lizard King . . .*),
the wholesomest groupie since Barbra Streisand charmed the
leather pants off Kris Kristofferson in the thirty-sixth remake of
A Star Is Born. Platoon is a buddy movie about a bunch of guys
like Oliver Stone going through hell in Vietnam; there is no major
female character. *Born on the Fourth of July* is a wheelchair
buddy move about a bunch of guys like Oliver Stone going
through hell in Vietnam. The major female character is a dim-
bulb cupcake played with consummate verve by the indefatigably
bland Kyra Sedgwick. Throughout the movie, intransigent heterosexual paraplegic Tom Cruise repeatedly complains that because
of Vietnam, he'll never be able to use his penis again. Wasted
tears, Tommy-boy; in an Oliver Stone movie where the hell would
you find a woman you'd want to stick your penis into? You're
lucky if you can find a virgin to sit on your face for seven bucks.

The buddy theme goes all the way back to movies Stone merely
scripted. *Scarface* is a buddy movie about a bunch of Cuban
dirtballs who come to the United States and have a lot of
interesting adventures in the cocaine trade. The major female
character is Michelle Pfeiffer, a coke-snorting slut, though she
does get some serious competition from Mary Elizabeth Mastrantonio, a coke-snorting slut. *Talk Radio* is a buddy movie about a
couple of late-night buddies trying to make a big splash on the
national scene. The major female character is a prim cutie-pie
who favors those neat little neckties that businesswomen from the
Midwest always wear in a desperate attempt to be taken seriously
by their male colleagues. *Conan the Barbarian* is a Stone Age
buddy movie about a mighty Vikingish warrior and his somewhat
less mighty chum who lock horniness with James Earl Jones and

his two gigantic, long-haired buddies, who look like power forwards in the Ozzy Osbourne Lookalike Basketball League. The major female character is Sandahl Bergman, who has enough muscles for eight buddies. And you really can't get a more explicit buddy movie than *Midnight Express*, which is, after all, set in the ultimate buddy environment: a Turkish prison. The *only* female character in this cheerful affair is Brad Davis's girlfriend, whose one big scene involves squishing her bare breasts up against a glass partition so that her imprisoned boyfriend can lick her reflection.

I think this says a lot about Oliver Stone's worldview.

I don't want to spend too much time dwelling on the pathetic cartoons that pass for women in Oliver Stone's movies, but it's a pretty damning statement when the most fully realized female character in any film Stone has ever been associated with is the Thighmaster pinup girl played by Sandahl Bergman in *Conan the Future Republican. At least she has a job.* The rest of the Family Stone are trophy wives, girls next door, and an endless parade of coke-sniffing whores and Yuppie bimbos. If Stone were not peddling a politically fashionable anti-Americanism that never goes out of style in Hollywood, feminists would be all over him as one of the most reactionary, sexist movie makers alive.

Stone is, of course, one of our most sadistic *auteurs*, whose particular brand of mayhem involves the surgical removal of important body parts from their customary moorings. Stone's first major motion picture was *The Hand*, a 1981 film that announced the director's fascination with dismemberment by portraying a cartoonist (Michael Caine) whose severed Cockney hand starts running around murdering people. (Let your fingers do the stalking.) The next year, when writing the screenplay for *Conan the Future Kennedy In-Law*, Stone worked his way further up the human anatomy: The film begins and ends with a decapitation, but also features a scene in which what appear to be vestal virgins or vestal vixens (I can never tell the difference) drink a puke-colored bisque containing skulls and human hands—Cro-

Magnon nouvelle cuisine, if you will—and apparently enjoy it. After *Conan*, Stone scripted *Scarface*, which features a man who has his head cut in half with a chain saw, and *Year of the Dragon*, in which the villain drops a bloody head onto his plate in the middle of an otherwise refined business luncheon with the Khmer Rouge. This certainly gets everyone's attention.

Salvador, which Stone directed in 1986, features no explicit decapitations, but there are plenty of bullet holes in the forehead and numerous references to another recurring Stone theme: castration. In fact, the movie's climax occurs when James Woods is threatened with a machete poised perilously close to the crown jewels, which elicits memories of the scene in *Midnight Express* in which Randy Quaid is beaten so badly that he loses a testicle, and then is beaten so badly that he loses the other (N.B.: Even in macho Oliver Stone films, men are limited to two testicles per customer). This was certainly one way to make Quaid less randy.

Platoon is filled with numerous dismemberments and disfigurements, as is *Born on the Fourth of July*, in which Tom Cruise gets his sex organs blown to smithereens in Vietnam. Male urinary-tract problems resurface in *The Doors*, where Val Kilmer's propensity to show off his tumescent manhood results in all sorts of legal wrangling and leads to several unparalleled American tragedies: Morrison's death, the subsequent death of his wife, and the release of the song "Touch Me, Babe." Then, in *JFK*, Stone returns to the leitmotif that has served him so well in the past: exploding skulls. When *JFK* was released, a friend of mine speculated that Stone's next movie would be about Jim Jones or the Moonies or the Church of Scientology, but I disagreed. When you're dealing with a guy as obsessed with decapitation and ball-busting sluts as this guy, you've got to figure Marie Antoinette is going to turn up eventually.

All this said, it would be a mistake to dismiss Oliver Stone's movies as merely spectacularly obvious, misogynistic buddy films in which people lose important parts of their bodies. Oliver Stone's movies are spectacularly obvious, misogynistic buddy films in which people lose important parts of their bodies that already have lots of drugs in them. *Midnight Express* is a movie that deals with testicle loss in which the drug of choice is hashish. *Scarface* depicts the bifurcation of a human skull with a chain saw; the drug of choice is cocaine. *Year of the Dragon* has decapitation, bullet holes in the cheeks, and strangulation with piano wire; the drug of choice is heroin. In *Born on the Fourth of July*, a paraplegic *Platoon*, the drug of choice is tequila (yes, kids, alcohol is a drug). *Platoon* itself showcases men shot in the head and nailed to trees; the drug of choice is grass. *JFK* focuses on exploding skulls; the drug of choice is cocaine. *Conan, the Buddy of Kurt Waldheim* deals with crucifixion, decapitation, and having one's flesh ripped apart by vultures; the drug of choice is mead.

Oliver Stone certainly knows how to recycle his best material. Buoyed by the audience response to the scene in *Midnight Express* where Brad Davis bites a nice chunk of flesh off the prison snitch's face, Stone reprises the scene in *Conan*, instructing Arnold Schwarzenegger to rip a vulture's lungs out with his teeth. (Young Arnold, who had not yet learned his *craft*, is pretty awful in this film, but this scene is a whole lot more convincing than the one where he makes love to Sandahl Bergman in what amounts to a steroid version of *Wuthering Heights*.)

Buoyed by the audience response to the scene in *Year of the Dragon* where a Chinese-American undercover cop has a half-dozen bullets rip through the back of his skull and come out through his suddenly ruddy cheeks, Stone reprised the scene in *JFK*, where the audience repeatedly is treated to the sight of the president's head flying off in Jackie's general direction. Nice touch, Ollie.

Thematically, Oliver Stone conveys three messages that are repeated over and over again in his films. They are:

1. America sucks.
2. If you get too caught up in your work, it's going to ruin your family life.
3. Beware of foreigners.

The first message is so obvious that we need hardly belabor it. But what kind of an Oliver Stone article would this be without a little belaboring of the obvious? So let's do it. *Salvador* and *Born on the Fourth of July* tell us that Republicans are ruining the country with their filthy little wars. *Platoon* and *JFK* tell us that Democrats are ruining the country with *their* filthy little wars. *Wall Street* tells us that greedy businessmen are ruining the country. *Scarface* tells us that Latin American cocaine dealers are ruining the country. *Eight Million Ways to Die* also tells us that Latin American cocaine dealers are ruining the country, but throws in alcohol for good measure. *Year of the Dragon* tells us that Chinese heroin dealers are ruining the country. *Talk Radio* tells us that redneck assholes who murder people like Eric Bogosian are ruining the country. *Midnight Express* tells us that Turks are ruining the country, or at least making it hard for clean-cut American hashish smugglers to travel abroad without being hassled. I don't have any idea what *The Doors* tells us, except not to whip out your cock in Dade County. In any case, once you've blamed all of the country's woes on Republicans, Democrats, businessmen, drug dealers, drunks, foreigners, and rednecks, that only leaves three entirely blameless people: Bill Moyers and Ben & Jerry. This is ultimately what is wrong with Oliver Stone's movies: If you blame *everyone* for *everything*, it's impossible to blame *someone* for *something* or *anyone* for *anything*.

Stone's second message is a tad more subtle, but if you look at his movies from the American Heart Association's point of view, one message comes through loud and clear: Type A behavior is going to ruin your family life. Consider the following chart.

WHAT HAPPENS TO GUYS WHO GET TOO CAUGHT UP IN THEIR WORK

CHARACTER, FILM	RESULT
Mickey Rourke, *Year of the Dragon*	Wife leaves him, then gets strangled.
Val Kilmer, *The Doors*	Band breaks up, common-law wife leaves him, he dies.

Charlie Sheen, *Wall Street*	Ruins family, loses good job, goes to jail.
Arnold Schwarzenegger, *Conan*	Girlfriend dies, no kids.
Eric Bogosian, *Talk Radio*	Wife leaves him, he gets murdered, show canceled.
Brad David, *Midnight Express*	Life sentence in Turkish jail, loses girlfriend, wrecks family.
Kevin Costner, *JFK*	Wife gets really pissed off, loses case anyway.
James Woods, *Salvador*	Loses wife and kid; best friend gets killed taking dumb photo that wasn't going to win any Pulitzer Prize anyway.
Al Pacino, *Scarface*	Wife leaves him, sister tries to kill him, mom won't talk to him, ends up with 500 bullet holes in his body.
Jeff Bridges, *Eight Million Ways to Die*	Loses nice wife and cute daughter; ends up with Rosanna Arquette.
Tom Cruise, *Born on the Fourth of July*	Becomes paraplegic, loses girlfriend, wrecks family.
Tom Berenger, *Platoon*	Kills fellow officer, turns into real asshole, dies horrible death.

The Oliver Stone Health Advisory reads like this: Type A behavior is going to ruin your marriage, wreck your health, fuck up your personality, and just generally screw up everything you've worked so hard to achieve. So get your schnozzola out of that mountain of coke, shelve that hypodermic, and stop swallowing those worms with all that tequila, you big knucklehead. And keep your eyes peeled for guys with chain saws in their suitcases.

Not surprisingly, the Gospel According to Stone even dominates movies that he did not write or direct, but merely produced. *Reversal of Fortune* is a film about a woman who hits her head on the bathroom floor because she has too many drugs in her body; the principal character is a lawyer whose obsession with his work has ruined his marriage. *Blue Steel* is a movie about a young female cop whose obsession with her job ruins her life. (She's dating a guy who's trying to murder her, which is just flat-out dysfunctional behavior.) *Iron Maze*, the 1991 Bridget Fonda vehicle (as in *tricycle*) that absolutely no one but me saw (I checked), deals with an overly ambitious Japanese guy who gets so caught up in his work—dismantling a Pennsylvania steel mill and turning it into an amusement park—that he nearly gets himself killed. How? By having a gigantic steel pipe dropped on his skull. What subtlety. What imagery. What . . . nuance. Incidentally, the alternate title for the story you are reading was *Head Shots*.

We now come to the third ubiquitous element in Oliver Stone movies: Always set up a moral conflict in which the forces of good are represented by white males—even if they're a bit on the jackassish side—while the forces of evil are represented by ethnics, homosexuals, or ethnic homosexuals. In *Scarface*, the villains are Cubans. In *JFK*, the villains are Cubans and Bourbon Street gays. In *Year of the Dragon*, the bad guys are Chinese and Thais. *Platoon* and *Born on the Fourth of July* target the Vietcong, though the latter film also thoroughly vilifies Mexican whores who specialize in sleeping with paraplegics. *Salvador* and *Eight Million Ways to Die* finger Hispanics, while *Midnight Express* blames it all on those stinking Turk prison guards. Well, what did you expect from a guy who writes a movie (*Conan the Austrian*) based in some misty, prehistoric era in which the villain (James Earl Jones) just happens to be the only black person in the movie with a speaking part. Let's face it, Ollie boy, ethnics are scary.

Do I accuse Oliver Stone of deliberately targeting the ethnic groups America loves to hate as a pandering sop to xenophobic audiences? Hell, no; he's just making movies, and in the world of movies, inscrutable ethnics with facial scars who pronounce the word *shit* by saying "chit" fall under the general category of "color." Stone probably isn't even aware that he's made the same movie ten times, that he's used coke-sniffing whores and fiendish Orientals and head trauma every chance he gets. He's merely dancing with the one who brung him. Who just happens to be a gook slut.

I hope I have not created the impression that I dislike Oliver Stone films. Far from it. To give the Man of Stone his due, his movies zip along at a nifty pace, he is a master at creating a sustained mood of imminent menace, and his screenplays, except for the obligatory harangue in which he feels compelled to actually explain what his transparently obvious films are about, are quite good. He gets terrific performances from people you'd expect it from—James Woods, Kevin Costner, Willem Dafoe, Gary Oldman—but also gets terrific performances from people you wouldn't expect it from—Tom Cruise, Charlie Sheen, Michael Douglas. His movies are always obvious (*Salvador*, *Platoon*, *Wall Street*, *Talk Radio*) and frequently stupid (*JFK*, *The Doors*), but I'd take obvious antiwar movies and stupid films that spark national debates rather than *Driving Miss Daisy* or another goddamn E. M. Forster film any day of the week. *All* antiwar movies are good movies. *All* movies that demand an explanation of John Kennedy's death are worth making. Even if they are stupid. Great art and incredible stupidity frequently make comfortable bedfellows. Just look at the Rolling Stones. Or Frank Sinatra. Or Richard Burton.

On the other hand, we're not talking about a John Ford or a Jean Renoir here. We're talking about a John Cameron who's read one more book. Great filmmakers look at complicated things— love, politics, crime—and show you that the world is a complicated place where moral decisions are often difficult to make. Filmmakers like Oliver Stone look at complicated things and tell you that the world is a simple place, where all you have to do is to be like Oliver Stone. This explains Stone's obsession with JFK, because, like all conspiracy-theory devotees, Stone would rather believe that we live in a world where sinister forces pull all the strings than that we live in a world where things just happen. But the truth is: We do live in a world where things just happen. Otherwise, how do you explain Dan Quayle?

When *JFK* was released just in time to bring us all some Yuletide cheer in 1991, Stone came in for tremendous criticism from all sides. Virtually all of that criticism focused on the story line in *JFK*, taking Stone to task for hawking the least plausible of the myriad JFK assassination theories, and for deliberately twisting the facts to suit his purposes. But just about none of the criticism was directed at the film qua film.

Here, I would like to put in my two cents on the subject. Personally, I found *JFK* quite engaging, and was very impressed by the performances of Gary Oldman and Kevin Costner. But the film doesn't work for me, because at no point could I even come close to buying Stone's theory about the assassination.

Why did I have so much trouble swallowing the theory that the United States government was in on Kennedy's assassination? Basically, because of Joe Pesci's wig. Joe Pesci is a preposterous-looking guy in the best of times, but that radiant shock of tangerine-hued fabric that was supposed to pass for Pesci's hair looked like something the wardrobe department bought mail-order from the Vito's Hair Research Center on Channel 67. To my way of thinking, if the creep played by Joe Pesci had anything to do with Kennedy's assassination, the CIA and the mob and the Pentagon and the military-industrial complex and the KGB and Lyndon Baines Johnson and Fidel Castro would have chipped in to give him enough money to buy a better wig. They did not; he wore the ridiculous wig to his interrogation by Kevin Costner; and for me the whole conspiracy theory fell apart right there.

La coiffe Pesci was not the first time that a movie Oliver Stone had worked on was stopped dead in its tracks by a mutinous hairstyle. Lamentably, Stone seems to have learned about hair grooming from the same people who taught him editing: Michael Cimino and Brian De Palma. Mickey Rourke's hair in Cimino's

Year of the Dragon, dyed white to make him look like a middle-aged asshole instead of a youthful asshole, had the inadvertent effect of making Rourke look like a chemotherapy patient trying to unravel an international heroin conspiracy on an outpatient basis. In De Palma's *Scarface*, Mary Elizabeth Mastrantonio looks like she broke into the Pam Grier Memorial Museum and purloined an Afro-American fright wig. Hair also plays a major role in *Wall Street*, where Gordon Gekko's do very nearly upstages the man sporting it; in *Conan the Kennedy*, where James Earl Jones looks like a sun-tanned Dungeons & Dragons Cher impersonator; and in *The Doors*, where the actor playing Ed Sullivan appears to have enlisted the styling assistance of Herman Munster.

But if Stone is to be taken to task for Pesci's absurd coiffure in *JFK* (and don't get me started on Tommy Lee Jones's dapper locks), he must be applauded for the decision to airlift the intransigently chemotherapeutical Donald Sutherland into the movie two-thirds of the way through the proceedings. A lot of critics have objected to Stone's use of this entirely fictitious deep throat, but I think Stone's decision to use Sutherland was brilliant. Sutherland, it must be recalled, can talk faster than anyone in the history of motion pictures, meaning that in one twelve-minute set piece he can advance the plot of a movie by at least two hours. Without the intervention of Donald Sutherland, *JFK* would have been five-and-a-half hours long. We *all* owe Donald a debt of gratitude; his exemplary work in *JFK* very nearly makes up for such previous crimes against humanity as *The Wolf at the Door*, *Revolution*, and siring Kiefer.

In summing up the work of Oliver Stone, let me cite two highly autobiographical chunks of dialogue he has written for his characters over the years. The first comes from the street-smart cop played by Mickey Rourke in *Year of the Dragon*, who tells his jaded colleagues: "I give a shit, and I'm going to make you people give a shit." This is the Stone credo in a nutshell: This is a man who gives a shit and who is going to make other people give a shit, even if they don't give a shit about the things he gives

a shit about, or think that he's full of shit, or that he is a shit, or
think that the things he gives a shit about are a load of shit.

The other illuminating passage comes from the mouth of Hal
Holbrook, who plays a dignified old stockbroker in *Wall Street*
(one assumes the character is based on Stone's deceased father,
a stockbroker to whom both *Wall Street* and *Salvador* are dedi-
cated). At the very end of the movie, just as Charlie Sheen is
about to be nailed by the feds for insider trading, Holbrook wraps
his arm around the youthful sleazeball and says: "Man looks in
the abyss. There's nothing staring back at him. At that moment,
man finds his character. And that is what keeps him out of the
abyss."

Actually, man looks in the abyss and Oliver Stone is staring
back at him. And *that's* what keeps him out of the abyss.

4 DON'T TRY THIS AT HOME

In the memorable opening sequence from Alfred Hitchcock's *Vertigo*, the already fortyish James Stewart, playing a high-ranking detective in the San Francisco Police Department, leaps across an alleyway to a sharply sloping tiled rooftop approximately five feet away while pursuing a criminal. Immediately losing his grip, Stewart slips off the rooftop and only escapes plunging to his death many stories below by securing a shaky hold on a rainspout. His flatfoot companion, cognizant of Stewart's plight, abandons the rooftop chase and comes to his aid. Gingerly clutching one of those flimsy roof tiles, the cop sticks out his hand, only to lose his own grip, and falls to a horrible death, triggering Stewart's vertigo for the remainder of the film.

Ever since I saw this movie at age ten, I have been troubled by this heart-stopping opening sequence. At first I thought that my problem was the absurd physical setup of the scene: When Stewart first leaps across the void, the gap between buildings is only around five feet, but when his cop buddy plunges to his death far below, the alleyway is clearly some twenty feet wide. Equally perplexing is Stewart's dubious motivation for attempting such a dangerous acrobatic feat: Why would a middle-aged man who entertains serious hopes of being the next Police Commissioner of San Francisco risk his life attempting to collar some small-time hood?

But as I watched the movie for perhaps the tenth time recently, I realized that neither of these things was what *really* bothered me about the sequence. What *really* bothered me was the doomed cop's rescue attempt. How could a 185-pound, middle-aged man leaning down from a sharply sloping roof, clinging to a chintzy ceramic tile, possibly think that he could haul another man of the same general size and build to safety—with just one hand? Rarely in the history of cinema have viewers been subjected to such a smorgasbord of aerodynamic and hydraulic lunacy as Hitchcock serves up in *Vertigo*. Which brings me to my central thesis: that movies are an inherently stupid art form that often relies on scams, tricks, stunts, gambits, ploys, ruses, or gags that are logically or physically impossible, and often both. The obvious corollary to my thesis is that no intelligent person should fashion a lifestyle based on things he has seen in the movies. That would be dumb.

To illustrate my contention, I recently selected crucial scenes from a dozen motion pictures and went out and made an attempt to recreate them in the real world. Some of these scenes involve scams (*Paper Moon*, *What's Up, Doc?*), some involve sex (*9½ Weeks*, *When Harry Met Sally*), some involve feats requiring immense physical prowess (*Vertigo*), and some involve practical jokes (*Bananas*, *Annie Hall*). One film (*Spellbound*) required me to apply for a job, another (*Dial M for Murder*) to enlist a friend in a fiendish murder plot, a third (*Pretty Woman*) to seek out the services of a prostitute who would accompany me to a formal dinner at which I would discuss the hostile acquisition of my guest's corporation. Almost without exception, my findings confirmed my original thesis: Things that work in the movies simply do not work in real life. So if you're thinking of lending some glamour to your hopelessly dreary existence by imitating things you've seen in the movies, think again. Here's why:

Freeloading. In the 1972 Peter Bogdanovich film *What's Up, Doc?*, Barbra Streisand picks up a phone in a hotel lobby and says, "Room service, please. Hi, room service, this is Room 1717. I would like a double-thick roast beef sandwich medium rare on rye bread with mustard on the top, mayonnaise on the bottom, and a coffee hot fudge sundae with a large bottle of diet anything. You got that? Yeah, Room 1717. Oh, and room service, would you put it in the hall outside the door? I mean, don't bring it in or knock on the door because I'm just putting my little one to sleep. Thank you."

In the movie, the scam works like a charm: Room service delivers the food, and Streisand wolfs it down without ever actually checking into the hotel or even signing for the order. Seeking to establish once and for all whether this scam would work in real life, I trekked down to the Vista Hotel in the World Trade Center in lower Manhattan, picked up a house phone, and mouthed Streisand's order verbatim.

"You'll have to repeat that," the woman from room service said. Then, when I got to the part about the "large diet anything," she said, "Twelve ounces is the largest size we have; would you like me to send up two of them?" Yes, I told her, I would. But in response to my request that room service leave the food outside the door, the young woman said, "He'll knock lightly, but you have to sign for the check." She then said the food would arrive in twenty-five minutes.

I hung around the lobby for around twenty minutes, then went up to the seventeenth floor. Sure enough, a few minutes later, the bellboy appeared with my order. He knocked very lightly at Room 1717, not wishing to rouse my young'un. No answer. He knocked again. Still no answer. After a third knock, he went away. I dialed room service and asked where my sandwich was.

"We brought it up to you and he knocked lightly, but there

was no answer," the woman said. "Somebody has to sign for the check."

I paused for a few moments to consider the implications of all this. On the one hand, I was suprised that room service had even delivered the food; I felt for sure that they would have called back to confirm the order. And in a certain sense the ruse came near to working: I could have simply walked up to the bellboy and signed for the check in the hall while pretending to be the occupant of Room 1717. But he probably would have become suspicious if I had not immediately gone into my room to eat the food. Moreover, ordering food is merely a prank, whereas signing for it is theft. And while I may be a prankster, I am not a thief. In any case, the scam did not work the way it worked in *What's Up, Doc?*, which is all we are really concerned with here. Proving, beyond the shadow of a doubt, that a freeloader cannot avoid starvation by tricking room service personnel in major metropolitan hotels into leaving food unattended in the hallway. It just won't work.

Changing Careers. The entire plotline of Hitchcock's *Spellbound* hangs by a single, fragile thread: No one at Green Manors Psychiatric Institute has ever met the world-famous Dr. Anthony Edwardes, author of *The Labyrinth of the Guilt Complex*, before he accepts a job as new director of the prestigious institution. In reality, Dr. Edwardes has already been murdered by the demented Leo G. Carroll and has been replaced by the out-to-lunch Gregory Peck, recently demobilized from the army, who doesn't know anything about psychiatry or medicine, yet is called upon to participate in major surgery by his newfound colleagues. Since nobody, it seems, has ever seen the real Dr. Edwardes, nobody objects when he starts futzing around with the scalpels. The health-care ramifications of all this are too terrifying to contemplate.

Seeking to determine if it was possible to obtain a job as director of a world-class psychiatric institution where I would be able to perform brain surgery on complete strangers without any formal medical training and without ever having to appear for a face-to-face interview, I called Bellevue Hospital, New York's most celebrated loony bin, and asked about the top job.

"We're not hiring," barked a woman in human resources.

"But I'm a world-famous psychiatrist," I shot back. "I'm the author of *The Labyrinth of the Guilt Complex*."

"We're not hiring," she reiterated. "It's a matter of money. We have no money."

"Not even for a world-famous psychiatrist?"

"No. We're facing layoffs here."

Purely in the interest of bicoastal scientific balance, I next called the Betty Ford Clinic in Rancho Mirage to see about nailing down the top spot. The Betty Ford Clinic was not facing layoffs, doubtless having plenty of spare cash, and the woman from human resources was a whole lot friendlier and more helpful than her East Coast counterpart.

"This is Dr. Anthony Edwardes," I explained. "I'm the author of *The Labyrinth of the Guilt Complex*. I'd like to apply for a job as director of the clinic."

"Well, I'll send out an application today."

"Would it be necessary for me to come in for a face-to-face, in-person interview?" I inquired.

"Usually, but they would let you know," she replied.

"But I would probably have to come in for an interview, right?"

"Yes," she replied.

See?

Breaking and Entering. About halfway through *The French Connection*, Roy Scheider knocks on the door of Gene Hackman's New York City apartment. Hackman, who has been chained to his bed with his own handcuffs by a young woman he had picked up earlier in the day, tells his partner to go ahead and let himself in. So Scheider extracts a credit card from his wallet, slides it through the crack in the door, jiggles it around a bit, and enters.

Let me make this perfectly clear: This trick will not work. Oh, maybe it'll work in Trenton, or Chippewa Falls, but it will not work in New York City. New York City apartment owners have big thick Medeco locks—usually two of them—plus chains, grates, alarms, and tables stuck up against the doorknobs in their grimy, depressing, microscopic apartments. I tried Scheider's ploy on four different friends' apartment doors, with Mastercard, Visa, American Express, and even my Citicorp ATM card. No dice. The trick will not work now, but, more to the point, it would not have worked twenty years ago when *The French Connection* was being filmed. It's just another example of the incredibly idiotic stuff that passes for realism in movies.

Sleight of Hand. In another absolutely peachy Peter Bogdanovich movie, *Paper Moon*, small-time con man Ryan O'Neal hands a cashier a $5 bill to pay for 15 cents worth of hair ribbon for his daughter Tatum, then distracts her with small talk to camouflage his convoluted con game. After she hands him the correct $4.85 change (while resting the fiver on top of the till), he tells her he'll give her the four ones plus another single for the five; then, distracted by his chatter, she is tricked into giving him a $10 bill for the five ones plus the fiver from the top of the cash register. All told, he comes out $4.85 ahead on the deal.

I was less successful. I went to three different Woolworth's in three different parts of New York City on three different days, and could never get this scam to work. Everytime I gave a cashier a fiver, she immediately put it in the till. Whether I talked about the heat, the humidity, the economy, or life in these here United States, they just put the money in the till. No matter how I tried to cajole them, beguile them, distract them, they all just put the money into the cash register. This stuff probably only worked back in the Depression era of *Paper Moon* because cashiers were a whole lot dumber than they are today.

Grifting. I took in *The Grifters* hoping to cadge some angles to raise the scratch to put my brats through the College of Knowledge. Forget it, Freddy. Numero uno, if you're going to bilk bookies out of big bucks, you should have enough nuggets in your noodle to put the moolah in eighteen-month CDs or variable-rate annuities or government-insured money market funds, instead of stashing the swag in the trunk of your T-Bird the way A-1 bimbo Anjelica Huston does.

(For purposes of stylistic decorum, the rest of this section will be written in non-grifter English.) As for John Cusack's folded $20-bill trick, well, just can that idea. I hit three bars and two diners in Manhattan, flashing a twenty when ordering a drink, then replaced it with a folded ten, hoping I would get change for a twenty, just like Cusack did the first time he tried it in the film. *No way, José.* For staters, bartenders and waitresses don't hop to attention just because you flash a twenty, and for another thing modern cash registers have separate compartments for ones, fives, tens, and twenties, so when the cashier puts the money away, he or she tends to put it in the right place. Nobody gave me change for a twenty. Nobody said, "Hey, didn't you just flash a twenty?" Nobody said, "Hey, what the fuck are you trying to pull here, asshole?" On the positive side, nobody did what they did to Cusack, either—no one rammed a billyclub into my guts, causing near-fatal hemorrhaging. Which is good, because the magazine that commissioned this story doesn't pay for gastro-intestinal surgery resulting from freelance assignments.

Ordering Takeout. In *Bananas*, Woody Allen walks into a nonde-script diner in the middle of an unidentified South American jungle and orders coffee. Then he says, "I also want something to go. Do you have any grilled cheese sandwiches?"

"Yes sir," the counterman replies.

"Well, let me have a thousand, and three hundred tuna fish and two hundred bacon, lettuce, and tomato sandwiches."

Without blinking an eyelash, the man at the counter asks Allen if he wants the cheese on rye. "Four hundred and ninety on rye," replies Allen, "and let me have a hundred and ten on whole wheat and three hundred on white bread, and one on a roll." He also orders 700 regular coffees, 500 cokes, and 1,000 7-Ups. Finally, he asks for 900 side orders of cole slaw.

The budget for the story you are reading was not large enough to pay for a trip to a South American jungle, so I went to the next-best place: the Lower East Side of New York. At a grungy diner on Avenue A, I ordered coffee, then nonchalantly said, "Do you have grilled cheese sandwiches?"

"We don't *have* grilled cheese sandwiches," the young man behind the counter replied. "We *make* them."

"Fine, I'd like a thousand," I said. "And two hundred tuna fish, and . . ."

"We don't do catering," the waiter said. "We deliver lunch, but we don't do catering."

"Well, I need a thousand grilled cheese sandwiches and five hundred Cokes and a bunch of other stuff . . ."

"Well, you need a caterer then. Caterers do that. You have to look in the Yellow Pages."

Getting a Prostitute to Accompany You to a Business Dinner at Which She Will Have to Pretend to Be Somebody Sophisticated Named Vivian, Just Like Julia Roberts in Pretty Woman. Of all the experiments I attempted for this article, this was the one that I felt I had the best chance of succeeding at. That's because prostitutes are famous for doing *anything* you ask. In fact, one of my fantasies has always been to go to Times Square on April 14, approach a hooker who says she "will do anything" and say, "Do my taxes."

I should start off by saying that none of the women I saw on Eighth Avenue bore even a remote physical resemblance to Julia Roberts. Or, for that matter, to Eric Roberts. If anyone had made a movie about any of these tragic individuals, it would have been called *Pretty Ugly Woman*. Moreover, it wasn't always easy to establish whether the woman I was talking to was actually a woman. Or a human. In any event, I finally singled out a twentyish hooker sporting Julia Robertsish black boots and said, "I'm having dinner with a CEO whose company I'm taking over. How much to come with me to dinner?"

"Thirty dollars in your car," she replied.

"No, I want you to come with me to a business function and pretend to be a sophisticated woman named Vivian."

"Thirty dollars in your car. Fifty if you pay for the room. Come on, sugar, you want a date?"

Well, actually, no.

Eliciting Sexual Advice from Elderly Strangers. In *Annie Hall,* Woody Allen walks up to a total stranger—an elderly gent—and says, "I have to ask you a question; don't go any further; with your wife, in bed, does she need any kind of artificial stimulation, like marijuana?"

"We use a large, vibrating egg," the man replies.

It took me a while to work up the nerve to ask anybody this extremely personal question, but I finally buttonholed a harmless-looking old geezer getting off a bus on Eighth Avenue. "I have to ask you a question; don't go any further; with your wife, in bed, does she need any kind of artificial stimulation, like marijuana?"

"I'm not from New York," he said, making every effort to get away as quickly as possible. Then, over his shoulder he volunteered, "Ask the bus driver; he might know."

Inducing Women to Swallow Numerous Unappetizing Objects. In the unfailingly charming *9½ Weeks,* future pugilist Mickey Rourke persuades Kim Basinger to sit on the floor with her eyes shut while he force-feeds her olives, cherries, strawberries, pasta, jello, and jalapeño peppers, washing it all down with champagne, Perrier, and milk, before finishing up by dripping honey onto her tongue and all over her legs. My wife being a Catholic, I knew she wouldn't go for any of this kinky, produce-oriented stuff, so I called a good friend who is well known for her spirit of adventure.

"Are you asking if I would let *you* do it, or if I would let *anyone* do it?" she inquired.

"Anyone."

"Yeah."

"You would?"

"Yeah."

"Even the jalapeño peppers?"

"Yeah, why not?"

"Well, did you see *9½ Weeks?*"

"Yeah."

"Well, don't you remember that it really hurt Kim Basinger's tongue a lot?"

"Well, it depends where you bite into the pepper. If you just eat the skin of the pepper and not the seeds, it doesn't burn."

"No, I think it burns no matter where you bite into them. But never mind, let me ask you another question," I said, recalling another of the film's fun-couple scenes. "If a man threatened to hit you with a belt, would you agree to crawl across the floor like a doggie and pick up ten- and twenty-dollar bills he'd strewn on the ground?"

"No."

"Why not?"

"I just wouldn't."

"Because it's too humiliating?"

"No."

"Well, why would you let someone feed you jalapeño peppers that are going to set your mouth on fire but not agree to crawl across the floor to pick up money?"

"Because one involves food, and I like food, but the other involves money, and I don't like money."

Why ask why?

My other female friends were flat-out opposed to any of the salacious Mickey Rourkeisms I suggested. None of them were interested in being blindfolded and fondled by a prostitute, spreading their legs for Daddy while lying on a king-sized bed in an upscale department store, or looking on submissively as I tried out riding crops in an equestrian-goods shop. Still, I was astonished and a bit unnerved to find that at least one woman of my acquaintance was willing to let a man stuff a whole cornucopia of fruits and vegetables into her mouth as she knelt on the ground with her eyes closed. But New York *is* that kind of town.

The list of things that work in movies that will not work in real life goes on and on. For example, if you stand up to corrupt union officials the way Marlon Brando does at the end of *On the Waterfront*, your body will never be found. You cannot drive a car around San Francisco the way Steve McQueen does in *Bullitt* or the way Dan Aykroyd does in *The Blues Brothers* without killing pedestrians or wrecking your car or *both*. If you hit people with a pistol butt on the back of the head "to make it look good" the way they do in the old Westerns, they in fact will *die*. As for the famous scene in *When Harry Met Sally* where Meg Ryan fakes an orgasm in a Manhattan diner as Billy Crystal looks on, that would never work in real life because I can spot fake orgasms a mile away. Every woman who's ever been with me has gone directly to Jupiter, so I would *know*. Frankly, the humorous thrust of Meg Ryan's performance was always completely lost on me.

And then there is *Vertigo*. Seeking to recreate Jimmy Stewart's death-defying leap from one fifteen-story ledge to another, I jumped from my front porch to my neighbor's, a yawning chasm of, oh, about eight feet. I managed to sprawl safely onto his porch, but not without scraping my knee. However, when I proceeded to the next part of the experiment—having a friend the same size as me lean down and attempt to hoist me up onto his porch—the attempt failed miserably. And this was on a level surface, where my friend got to use both hands, and did not have to worry about plummeting hundreds of feet to a messy death. Proving that the entire opening sequence from *Vertigo* is just incredibly stupid, and that anyone who would risk his own life trying to save another person by attempting to hoist him to safety while gripping a chintzy tile high atop a sharply sloping San Francisco roof probably deserves to die.

In all of my experiments did I find any clever trick, gambit, ploy, scam, ruse, or stunt that actually did work in real life? Yes, but only if you count the jalapeño peppers. Other than that, no. But I did find one incredibly cunning ruse that actually *failed* in a movie and—get this!—*also failed in real life*. A few weeks ago, after a ferocious argument with an editor whose name will go unmentioned, I began to toy with the idea of murdering him. After much idle rumination, I finally settled on the ingenious plot hatched by Ray Milland in *Dial M for Murder*.

As the reader will doubtless recall, Milland's scheme involves a set of latchkeys, one in his wife's handbag, one concealed beneath the stairway carpet outside the apartment door. The killer hired by Milland is supposed to let himself in with the latchkey, then hide behind the curtains in the living room, and then, when Grace Kelly comes to answer Milland's call from his club, sneak up from behind and strangle her. He is then supposed to put the key back in its place beneath the carpet and get the hell out of there.

Unfortunately, Grace Kelly kills the would-be murderer, who had already put the key back in its place after opening the door, so when Ray Milland comes home, he takes the key out of the killer's pocket and puts it in Kelly's handbag, never realizing that it is actually the killer's own latchkey, and not the latchkey to the Milland-Kelly apartment door. This creates problems for Ray later in the film, when he switches keys around and his latchkey ends up in a raincoat picked up by the indefatigable Scotland Yard detective played by John Williams, whose own latchkey ends up in Milland's possession. Milland then tries to use the key in Kelly's handbag, which doesn't work on his door, since it's the killer's key. This chain of events forces Milland to open the door with the latchkey left under the hall stairs by the killer, who was supposed to keep the key until after he had disposed of Grace Kelly, but who messed up the whole plan and thus deserved to be impaled on a pair of very sharp scissors. As a result, Milland is caught out and, presumably, fries for it.

I invited a friend over to the house one afternoon and we ran through this key thing several times. I didn't tell him that I was thinking of killing anybody; I told him the little stunt was something I'd planned for a surprise party for my wife. Well, to make a long story short, we screwed up miserably. As complicated as Milland's scheme is in the film, it's even more complicated in real life, and neither I nor my friend could ever get the hang of it. This being the case, I would suggest to readers who are contemplating the murder of employers or business associates or even spouses that they stick with blowtorches or axes or AK-47s, and try to make the murder look like the work of an intruder. The movies are really no help at all in handling practical, everyday affairs. They're just incredibly stupid, and you're far better off running your life normally, like me.

5 CLERICAL ERRORS

For centuries, Catholic theologians have vainly striven to solve two seemingly unfathomable mysteries: How is it possible to reconcile the existence of a merciful, loving God with the existence of people like Mickey Rourke? And if God is truly all-knowing and all-powerful, an omnipotent force Who can make the oceans swell and the mountains tremble, why doesn't He do something about Daphne Zuniga? More to the point, why does He tolerate *anyone* who makes such blasphemous movies as *Last Rites*, *Exorcist II: The Heretic*, *A Prayer for the Dying*, and *Monsignor*—all of which deal contemptuously with the religion His well-beloved Son shed His most precious blood to establish? This is, after all, *His* universe. It's not like He *has* to put up with this stuff.

The complete answer to these questions is too convoluted to go into here, so let's just put it this way: God doesn't enjoy movies like *Last Rites* and *The Pope Must Diet* any more than the rest of us. But since the fall of man, or so Catholics believe, God has endowed all of His human creations with free will and has allowed them to determine their own destinies. For some, this means acting in, directing, scripting, being a gaffer for the second technical unit, or paying to see movies about Catholic priests. People such as this can live rich, productive, morally upstanding lives, trying to make the best of the tools God has given them, and either participate in or shell out their hard-earned money to see movies like *Going My Way* and *The Bells of Saint Mary's*. Or they can become the tools of Satan and waste their lives in charnel houses, fleshpots, brothels, and business school, producing, directing, or going to see movies like *Last Rites* and *Exorcist III*. God has made the choice very clear: You can spend your time watching wholesome, upbeat, life-affirming films and at the end of your days I will sit you at My right hand, just a few seats from John Hughes and Ronnie Howard. Or you can spend your life watching libidinous, perverse films, and at the end of your days I will cast you into the very deepest pit of Hell. (The very deepest pit of Hell, of course, is the first left past Renny Harlin's house.)

The most important thing to remember in dealing with films featuring Catholic priests is that there *are* limits to God's power, even if He is, technically, omnipotent. Not even an omnipotent creature who has ruled all of creation since the beginning of time can teach Christopher Reeve how to act. Not even the most powerful being in the universe can breathe any pep into Jason Miller. And once an implacable force of nature like Richard Burton or Robert De Niro or Sean Penn has made up his mind that he is going to wreck a film, no power in the cosmos can stand in his way.

The purpose of this article is to determine precisely which film about priests is most offensive in the eyes of God—which film has won for its producer, directors, stars, best boy, publicist, postproduction sound editor, etc., the longest and most terrifying sojourn in the Inferno. I do this, not out of some personal sense of outrage at salacious, Catholic-bashing slime such as *Monsignor* and *Last Rites* that turns my ex-seminarian's stomach, but in direct response to voluminous inquiries from *Movieline* readers demanding to know why the magazine doesn't run more stories dealing with the Sixth and Ninth Commandments, and, of course, the Seven Deadly Sins.

But first, some history. Movies about priests first came to prominence during the 1930s and 1940s, when such sturdy offerings as *Angels with Dirty Faces* and *Fighting Father Dunne* were box-office favorites. These films had three common characteristics: They all starred Pat O'Brien as a crusading priest, they all celebrated the triumph of good over evil, and not for a single moment did anyone even faintly resembling Daphne Zuniga or Genevieve Bujold offer to roll in the hay with anyone wearing a Roman collar.

These movies were succeeded by charming Bing Crosby vehicles such as *Going My Way* and *The Bells of St. Mary's (Going My Way II)*, in which the low-key crooner tried to hold his own against the radiant Ingrid Bergman, the most beautiful movie star of them all, who upon her death was immediately assumed into Heaven, Roberto Rossellini or no Roberto Rossellini. These movies bore little or no relation to what professionals call "reality," but then again, neither does Heaven.

At the same time, Gregory Peck was starring in slightly weightier films such as *The Keys of the Kingdom*, and pious chaplains were turning up in war movies all over the place. These films were made by people who did not think religion was impossibly stupid or who, if they did, kept their opinions to themselves. This is even true of Alfred Hitchcock's 1953 film *I Confess*, which deals with a somewhat thick priest (Montgomery Clift) who cannot divulge the identity of a murderer to the police because the murderer has confessed the crime in the confessional—even though this means that the priest himself may be framed for the crime. Hitchcock may have felt that this seal-of-confession business was hopeless rigamarole, but this does not come across in the film. What does come across is that Hitchcock can really use a camera and that even in black and white, Karl Malden has the biggest nose in Quebec.

Things started to change during the 1960s, as movies about

priests became grittier and less deferential. *The Hoodlum Priest* (1961) dealt with the efforts of street-smart cleric Don Murray to save the soul of teenaged hood Keir Dullea, *literally* a bad actor playing a bad actor. *The Cardinal* (1963), an interminable Otto Premingeriatricism, featured an actor who had once played a TV character named Texas John Slaughter playing a priest who falls in love with a hot little number played by Romy Schneider.

The year 1964 witnessed the making of the greatest priest film ever—*Becket*—which concerns the spiritual apotheosis of a lecher and rake, played by Richard Burton, after he is named Archbishop of Canterbury by his lecherous, rakish chum, the King of England, played by Peter O'Toole (obviously, it wouldn't have been too hard for Burton and O'Toole to switch roles). Seven years later, Ken Russell released his refreshingly depraved *The Devils*, a Hieronymus Bosch painting come to life, featuring full-service knave Oliver Reed as a priest and veteran space creature Vanessa Redgrave as a nun. This type of casting is right up there with Charlotte Rampling as a marine biologist in *Orca*, Sigourney Weaver as an expert on Middle Eastern history in *Half Moon Street*, and Diane Keaton as anyone in anything.

Since *Becket* and *The Devils*, we have fallen on hard times. In fact, with the exception of the intelligent, moving *True Confessions*, the cheerfully revolting *The Exorcist*, and such well-meaning but overwrought offerings as *Mass Appeal* and *Romero*, it's been straight downhill. We have had knuckleheadisms such as *The Rosary Murders* and *The Shoes of the Fisherman*, sadistic trash such as *Last Rites*, *A Prayer for the Dying*, and the *Exorcist* sequels, and idiotic comedies such as *We're No Angels* and *The Pope Must Diet*. What we have had is a steady diet of bad-priest movies.

There are three basic types of bad-priest movies: the priest-as-impostor picture, the seal-of-confession picture, and the Mafia-priest picture. (There is often a good deal of overlap, too: *Last Rites* is both a seal-of-confession and a Mafia-priest picture.) The priest-as-impostor picture features a bum, hired killer, or complete whip-off who disguises himself as a cleric and suddenly finds himself suffused with inexhaustible supplies of piety and goodness—just like Sinead O'Connor. The genre originated with *The Left Hand of God*, the 1955 film starring Humphrey Bogart, which is set in the mysterious East; evolved further in *Guns for San Sebastian*, the 1968 Anthony Quinn film set in the Wild West; and culminated in *We're No Angels*, the 1990 Robert De Niro–Sean Penn film set in Buffalo or Canada or points north— which is itself a remake of, yes, an old Bogart film.

The Mafia-priest picture deals with the attempts by sinister forces whose names end in a vowel to take control of the already debauched Catholic Church. The first—and most ghastly—film of this sort is *Monsignor*, a 1982 abomination so ferociously anti-Catholic one suspects that Satan himself had something to do with it. But no, it was not Satan; it was Frank Yablans. *Monsignor* stars the abysmal Christopher Reeve, features a score by the useless John Williams, and has a supporting cast headed by all-purpose ham Fernando Rey. The movie deals with the villainy of Reeve, the Vatican business manager, who plays ball with the Mafia and nearly brings the Church crashing down around him— not that Frank Yablans would care. In this sense, *Monsignor* is a little bit like *Last Rites*, which deals with a priest whose dad is a mafia don. And it's also just a teensy-weensy bit like *Godfather III*, which deals with a Vatican banker who does business with the Mafia. And, yes, it does bear ever so slight a resemblance to *The Pope Must Diet*, which deals with a shady Cardinal who is in league with the Mafia.

An unsophisticated viewer—say, Michael Medved—might have a hard time telling some of these movies apart. Each of these movies makes Italians seem vicious and Catholic clergy-men seem beastly. Each of these movies has a central character played by an actor or actress who cannot act: Christopher Reeve, Tom Berenger, Sofia Coppola, Robbie Coltrane. Each of these movies involves a Mafia hitman. How then to tell them apart? The handiest way is by remembering which illicit sexual act the major characters engage in during the movie. *Last Rites* is the one where the priest sleeps with his sister, a hit woman, as well as with a Mexican whore. *The Pope Must Diet* is the one where the priest sleeps with the mother of a dead British rock star. *Monsignor* is the one where the priest sleeps with a French nun. And *Godfather III* is the one where the priest doesn't sleep with anyone. *Godfather III* is the one where the Mafia hit man sleeps with his first cousin, who should have been Winona Ryder, but ended up being the director's daughter, a certifiable non-fox.

I hope all of this has been helpful.

Just as Mob-priest pictures seem to overlap at certain points, seal-of-confession pictures all seem to run together. Ever since Montgomery Clift clammed up about the killer's identity in *I Confess*, Hollywood has been going back to this particular well again and again and again. In *The Rosary Murders*, inexplicably set in Detroit, a serial killer confesses his crimes to Donald Sutherland, who is bound by the seal of confession not to reveal his identity to the police. In *Last Rites*, Tom Berenger's half-sister confesses that she murdered her husband, but Berenger is bound by the seal of confession not to reveal her identity to the cops. (Berenger, of course, has other reasons for keeping a lid on it; he was banging Sis when she was just fifteen.) In *True Confessions*, all-around lowlife Charles Durning tells Robert De Niro that he was banging a murdered, mutilated playgirl, but De Niro cannot report this to his flatfoot brother because of the seal of confession. (De Niro, of course, has other reasons for keeping a lid on it; he also is an acquaintance of the murdered, mutilated girl.) In *Exorcist III*, Satan himself confesses his sins to a priest, who cannot reveal his identity to the police because of the seal of confession, and also because Satan rips his head off. In *Monsignor*, scumbag mobster Jason Miller confesses his sins to scumbag priest Christopher Reeve, who cannot divulge his crimes because of the seal of confession. (Reeve, of course, has other reasons for not divulging his crimes to the cops, because the penitent scumbag happens to be his partner in crime.) Finally, in *A Prayer for the Dying*, a lowlife, gun-toting, child-murdering, IRA psychopath played by Mickey Rourke (the role was a real stretch for Mickey) confesses to a murder in Father Bob Hoskins's confessional *after Hoskins has seen him commit the crime.*

Here we get into one of the more troubling areas of *le bad-priest cinema.* Anytime a bunch of people living in Hollywood, New York, or London whose last names do not end in "i" or begin with "O' " decide to get together and make a film about the Catholic Church, they run the tiny risk of misinterpreting esoteric points of Catholic theology, and frequently end up with movies that are even stupider than they had intended them to be. For example, in *The Rosary Murders*, Donald Sutherland is told by his pastor that Catholic dogma forbids baptizing children born out of wedlock. This is not true: Ask fifty million Chinese babies baptized against their will in the 1940s. The same is true of *A Prayer for the Dying.* Once a priest has witnessed a murder, he is under no obligation to suppress the identity of the criminal, even if the criminal subsequently confesses his guilt to the priest. This is particularly true if the criminal looks like Mickey Rourke. The lesson to be learned? When making a movie dealing with subtle nuances of Catholic theology, hire a screenwriter named Patrick O'Shaughnessy, not one named Elmore Leonard.

Priest movies are loaded with repeat offenders. Jason Miller appears in three priest movies (*The Exorcist, Exorcist III, Monsignor*), as does Robert De Niro (*We're No Angels, True Confessions, The Mission*) and Charles Durning (*Mass Appeal, True Confessions, The Rosary Murders*), who bounces back and forth between being a fat, low-energy Brian Dennehy and a thin, low-energy John Goodman. Richard Burton also appears in three (*The Robe, Becket, Exorcist II*), while Anthony Quinn actually appears in four: *The Shoes of the Fisherman, Guns for San Sebastian, Behold a Pale Horse,* and *The Agony and the Ecstasy.*

These are not the only repeat offenders. Bill Conti rewrote
Samuel Barber's music for *Mass Appeal* before rewriting the
Chieftains' music for *A Prayer for the Dying.* Jogging clerics
figure prominently in *The Exorcist, Mass Appeal,* and *The Rosary
Murders.* And even though Daphne Zuniga has appeared in only
one bad-priest film to date, she is still young enough and awful
enough to have at least three more cracks at it. The one bright
spot in all this: Zeljko Ivanek is probably not going to reprise his
role as a brash, bisexual seminarian in *Mass Appeal II.*

Watching movies about priests drives home a number of
important truths about life on this planet, truths that are all too
easy to forget as we blindly pursue our daily tasks. Here are a
handful of these truths: Christopher Reeve really *is* the worst
actor who ever lived. When he puts his mind to it, Donald
Sutherland really can come off as a charter member of Bob and
Ray's Slow . . . Talkers . . . of . . . America . . . Club. When
Robert De Niro is good (*True Confessions*) he is very, very good,
but when Robert De Niro is bad (*We're No Angels*), he is worse
than Sean Penn. (What can you say about a movie in which Sean
Penn and Robert De Niro are outacted by Hoyt Axton? Well, for
starters you can say, "Boy, that movie really sucked.")

And then there is The Strange Case of Linda Blair. When
Blair starred in *The Exorcist* twenty years ago, she received
almost universal acclaim for her portrayal of a sweet twelve-year-
old girl whose body is suddenly taken over by Satan. But with
the passage of time, it has now become apparent that Linda Blair
was *always* possessed by Satan, and that the kudos she received
should have been for being a twelve-year-old demon talented
enough to deceive an audience into thinking she was ever a sweet
twelve-year-old girl.

Much the same thought occurred to me after watching *The
Poseidon Adventure,* one of those brain-dead, big-budget, all-star
extravaganzas that could only have been made in the 1970s, the
era of disco and Legionnaires' disease and the Bay City Rollers
and Jimmy Carter. Although Gene Hackman plays a minister

rather than a priest in this film, he is such a complete asshole that he could easily be mistaken for many Catholic priests, or, for that matter, for Charles Durning, so we will include him here. *The Poseidon Adventure* chronicles the daring efforts of nine characters played by Hackman, Ernest Borgnine, Stella Stevens, Shelley Winters, Carol Lynley, Roddy McDowall, Red Buttons, Pamela Sue Martin, and Jack Albertson to escape from an ocean liner that has turned completely upside down. Watching the movie, I could not help thinking how much more fun going to the movies would have been in the ensuing decade if Gene Hackman, Ernest Borgnine, Stella Stevens, Shelley Winters, Carol Lynley, Roddy McDowall, Red Buttons, Pamela Sue Martin, and Jack Albertson had actually been on a real-life capsized ocean liner and had drowned. Still, *The Poseidon Adventure* is worth seeing for four reasons:

1. Carol Lynley wears hot pants the entire movie.
2. Pamela Sue Martin wears hot pants the entire movie.
3. Stella Stevens wears panties, high heels, and a man's shirt the entire movie.
4. Shelley Winters keeps all her clothes on for the entire movie.

In addition to Gene Hackman's insane tirades against God, the last one conducted while suspended above a fiery cauldron—not a good place to be fucking with the Lord of All Creation, Whom you will be seeing in about twenty seconds on the other side of reality—the movie is memorable because it confirms that Pamela Sue Martin has the most enormous forehead in the history of show business; because it dispels any lingering doubts anyone might have that Ernest Borgnine is the second-worst actor of all time; and because it allows the moviegoing public to see Shelley Winters act underwater (she's better down there; she can't talk). After her dip, Winters succumbs to a stroke and tells Hackman: "Enough is enough." I think Shelley knew the score.

In preparing this essay I watched twenty-one different films with priests as the major protagonists. While doing so, I mentally ranked the films in order of artistic excellence and faithfulness to Catholic dogma. I rated the films on a scale of 0 to 100, deducting points if a film omitted ominous Gregorian chants (5 points), belfries (3 points), statues of the Blessed Virgin Mary with eyes that appear to move (3 points), tunnels/catacombs (5 points), prostitutes with hearts of gold (7 points), Latin mumbo-jumbo (8 points), nuns making eyes at priests (4 points), the kyrie eleison (3 points), or Charles Durning (15 points). Based on these criteria, I provide the following rankings:

CLERICAL RANK	BEST MOVIE	WORST MOVIE
Priest	*I Confess*	*Last Rites*
Fake priest	*The Left Hand of God*	*We're No Angels*
Monsignor	*True Confessions*	*Monsignor*
Bishop	*The Bishop's Wife*	*The Bishop's Wife**
Archbishop	*Becket*	*Romero*
Cardinal	*Godfather III*	*The Cardinal*
Pope	*Shoes of the Fisherman*	*The Pope Must Diet*
Monk	*The Name of the Rose*	*Stealing Heaven*
Exorcist	*The Exorcist*	*Exorcist II, III***

*This is the only movie about a bishop that I could find.
**A tie. Only a Jesuit could tell which of these monstrosities is the worst. And whatever my other failings, I am no Jesuit.

Some of these movies contain memorable scenes that will remain rooted in my consciousness for decades to come. For example, I really enjoyed the scene in *Monsignor* where Genevieve Bujold says to Christopher Reeve: "Do you think God was planning to waste a miracle on us?" *But, Genevieve, he already had. He got both of you jobs in the movies.*

Another line I cannot get out of my head is: "You might ask Sister Margaret Mary of the Holy Martyrs." This is a throwaway line someone says to Donald Sutherland in *The Rosary Murders*, yet for some reason within its terse syntactical borders it seems to capture everything that one needs to know about the nunnish subculture. "You might ask Sister Margaret Mary of the Holy Martyrs." *And if she's not available, try Sister Immaculata Redemptoris of the Holy Innocent Bystanders.*

I also took solace from Sean Penn's sermon in *We're No Angels*, where he says: "Be nice to strangers, 'cause sometimes you're a stranger, too." Add to that the hooker's remark to Father Tom Berenger in *Last Rites*: "I didn't know that priests hung out with assholes." Who did you think they hung out with, honey? Daphne Zuniga?

While watching these stupefying, immoral, cretinous priest films, one question that kept going through my head was: Who will burn in Hell the longest for making one of these things? Artistically speaking, it was hard to choose between the moronic *We're No Angels*, the depraved *Last Rites*, the sacrilegious *Monsignor*, and the boisterously shitheaded *A Prayer for the Dying*. Yet, at the last moment, my Catholic upbringing told me to eliminate *We're No Angels*, which, despite its truly awesome stupidity, was only a misfiring comedy, and also to rule out *A Prayer for the Dying*, whose central character was not the good priest badly played by Bob Hoskins but the merry psychopath convincingly played by Mickey Rourke.

This narrowed things down to *Last Rites* and *Monsignor*. Speaking in purely cinematic terms, it was impossible to choose between these celluloid abortions. *Last Rites* featured a terrible actor playing a mob priest; *Monsignor* featured a terrible actor playing a mob priest. *Last Rites* featured a terrible actress playing a psychotic hooker; *Monsignor* featured a terrible actress playing a neurotic, slutty nun. In *Last Rites*, Tom Berenger's best friend is a Mafia hood; in *Monsignor*, Christopher Reeve's best friend is a Mafia hood. Deciding which of these two flicks is the worst is like being a judge at the Twenty-fifth Annual Putrescent Fruit of the Year Awards and having to choose between a decaying apricot and a festering nectarine.

Ultimately, it came down to a question of good and evil. Since the artistic distinctions between these films were so negligible, the only way to decide which was the most morally repugnant film was to tote up the number of sins committed in each one. It was a pretty impressive list:

MORTAL SINS IN *LAST RITES*	MORTAL SINS IN *MONSIGNOR*
Priest sleeps with a whore hit woman who is not his sister	Priest sleeps with a nun
Priest sleeps with a whore hit woman who is his sister	Priest sells cigarettes to the Mafia
Priest leads Mafia to his whore girlfriend so they can ice her	Priest leads the Mafia to his best friend, so they can ice him
Priest leaves Catholic Church to become *capo di tutti i capi* in his dad's company	Priest stays in church so he can keep investing money with Mafia

VENIAL SINS IN *LAST RITES*	VENIAL SINS IN *MONSIGNOR*
Repeated profanity, fantasizing about sleeping with one's sister, mild fibbing	Not much profanity, but a lot of fibbing

On balance, I guess you would have to say that *Last Rites* is the more immoral movie of the two—this sleeping with your hit-person sister does not look good at all—and that everyone associated with it will burn in Hell for all eternity. But we mustn't overlook intangibles. *Last Rites* is so bad that it immediately went to video, so the number of impressionable youths who have seen it is quite limited. But because Frank Yablans was the producer of *Monsignor*, it was actually released theatrically, and actually filled up movie screens everywhere, poisoning the minds of children all over the country, if not the world. In terms of evil inflicted on humanity, it has probably had a far greater and far more pernicious effect than *Last Rites*.

Then we have to factor in the Christopher Reeve thing. When I say that Christopher Reeve is the worst actor who ever lived, I am not speaking off the top of my head; I have seen *all* of Lou Diamond Phillips's movies and am no stranger to the *oeuvres* of Steve Guttenberg and John Ritter. Yet this guy is head and shoulders below these guys. Indeed, Christopher Reeve's continued ability to find work would seem to prove, beyond the shadow of a doubt, that the universe has no purpose and that life has no meaning. If God truly loved us, He still might not do something about Daphne Zuniga, but He would definitely do something about Christopher Reeve. Still, in God's defense, it is not His fault. Every human being possesses his own free will, and if we choose to exercise our free will by going to see movies like *Monsignor* and *Exorcist II*, then we all deserve to burn in Hell.

See you in Hell, Mr. Yablans.

6 NO WAY OUT

Two Thursdays ago, my wife and I decided to put the kids to bed early and rent a videotape of an engaging, recently released movie. As soon as the little angels had drifted off to slumberland, I nipped out and picked up *Q&A*, the fine 1991 Sidney Lumet feature in which Timothy Hutton plays a crusading young Manhattan lawyer who discovers that the cops and his own superior, the district attorney, are on the take. One of the main themes of the movie was the threat posed to the entire community when the police start tampering with evidence in highly sensitive drug cases.

We enjoyed the movie immensely, but couldn't help noticing how much it resembled *True Believer*, the fine James Woods–Robert Downey vehicle of a couple years back that we'd rented three weeks earlier. *True Believer* deals with a crusading young Manhattan lawyer and his boss, a crusading middle-aged Manhattan lawyer, who discover that the cops and the district attorney are on the take. An important theme of the movie is the threat posed to the entire community when the police start tampering with evidence in highly sensitive drug cases.

Actually, *True Believer* wasn't entirely unlike *Presumed Innocent*, the fine 1990 film in which Harrison Ford plays a crusading young Chicago lawyer who discovers that his superior, the district attorney, is corrupt; that his adversary, the new district attorney, has tampered with evidence; and that the judge presiding over his case is on the take. We enjoyed that movie thoroughly, even though it did bear a wee, wee resemblance to *Witness*, the fine Peter Weir film of a few years back in which Harrison Ford plays a crusading young Philadelphia police detective who discovers that the cops are on the take. Of course, in a certain sense, *Witness* is a direct descendant of *Serpico*, the fine 1973 movie that deals with a crusading young Manhattan police officer (Al Pacino) who discovers that the cops are on the take. The movie, one of whose principal themes is the threat posed to the entire community when the police start tampering with evidence in drug cases, was directed by Sidney Lumet, who eighteen years later would direct *Q&A*, the fine film my wife and I rented the other night.

Last Thursday, my wife and I were again in the rental mood, so I nipped out and picked up *F/X2*, the fine 1991 film that deals with a crusading special-effects man based in Manhattan who discovers that the cops are on the take. The movie, starring Bryan Brown and Brian Dennehy, had us glued to the edges of our seats, not unlike the original *F/X*, in which Bryan Brown also played a crusading special-effects man who discovers that the cops are on the take. Thursday night was double-feature night, though, so after we'd finished watching *F/X2*, we sat back and enjoyed *True Colors*, the fine 1991 film in which James Spader plays a crusading young Washington lawyer who discovers that his best friend, a congressman, is on the take.

Much as we enjoyed that film, by the following Thursday we were a bit tired of movies about lawyers, cops, and special-effects men who find out that the authorities are on the take, so we rented *Backdraft*, a film in which a crusading young fireman discovers that the authorities are on the take. The movie, starring

Robert De Niro, was the work of Ron Howard, the fine young director whose work is so good that some people have started mentioning him in the same breath as Francis Ford Coppola. Coppola became famous by making *The Godfather*, which deals with a crusading young Manhattanite, played by Al Pacino, who discovers that the cops are on the take. Coppola also directed *Godfather II*, starring Robert De Niro, which deals with politicians who are on the take, and the fine 1991 film *Godfather III*, which deals with religious authorities who are on the take.

The other night, my wife suggested that we get a babysitter and go out and *see* a movie, instead of renting one like pathetic, middle-American couch potatoes. My suggestion was *Rush*, the fine new film in which Jason Patric plays a crusading young cop who discovers that the authorities are on the take. But my wife had other ideas. She's a big Kevin Costner fan, having enjoyed his work in *Silverado*, in which he plays a crusading young cowpoke who discovers that the sheriff (played by Brian Dennehy) is on the take; in *No Way Out*, in which he plays a crusading young naval officer who discovers that the authorities are on the take; and most recently in *Robin Hood*, the fine 1991 film in which Costner plays a crusading young Crusader who returns home to find that the sheriff (of Nottingham) is on the take. So she suggested *JFK*.

We really enjoyed *JFK*, for a number of reasons. For one, it stirred the embers in the hearth of our memories, taking us back to an earlier, simpler time before we as a people were plunged into the madness of Vietnam, Watts, and Watergate. Two, it made us hearken back to a time when we, as a people, felt that there was nothing we could not accomplish if we simply rolled up our sleeves and got cracking on a problem. But the main reason we enjoyed it is that it dealt with a crusading young lawyer who discovers that all the cops and politicans are totally and utterly corrupt, and that everybody in a position of authority is probably on the take. Quite frankly, I can't see that particular kind of movie often enough, and apparently, neither can anyone else.

7 IN THE REALM OF THE SENSELESS

> "You'd rather have nothing than settle for less."
> —Warren Beatty to Dustin Hoffman
> in *Ishtar*.

If you're like most people, you don't have time to sit at home watching idiotic, utterly incomprehensible movies like *Hudson Hawk*, *Nothing But Trouble*, *Don't Tell Her It's Me*, and *Ishtar*. If you're like most people, you have a career, a family, a future, a *life* that precludes your even thinking about wasting your time trying to figure out what *Angel Heart* or *The Two Jakes* are about. If you're like most people, the idea of paying good money to rent intergalactically stupid movies like *V. I. Warshawski* or *The Little Drummer Girl* and then sit at home trying to decipher their brain-dead plots is unthinkable. If you're like most people, you have better things to do with your time than to watch *The January Man*, *The Comfort of Strangers*, or *Joe Versus the Volcano*, and you have much, much better things to do with your time than to sit at home for an entire eight-hour day attempting to make sense out of the nearly four-hour-long *Once Upon a Time in America* and the nearly four-hour-long *Heaven's Gate*.

I, on the other hand, do not.

As readers familiar with my work know, I make my living by watching unspeakably foul, hopelessly incomprehensible movies, and then issuing belated, useless warnings to the viewing public, telling them not to go see movies they have already gone to see. Unlike most of *Movieline*'s unbelievably sophisticated, cutting-edge, *now* kind of readers, I really don't have anything better to do with my time than to sit at home wasting a whole day watching *Once Upon a Time in America* and *Heaven's Gate*. This doesn't mean that I do not have a life. It just means that I don't have much of one.

But in this particular case, there is a method to my madness. This time out, I did not spend nearly two weeks watching twenty-five uncompromisingly incomprehensible movies just for the fun of it, just so I could then write a story talking about how moronic they were. No, I'd like the reader to think of this story as a sort of extended legal brief, an *amicus curiae* filing, if you will, that may one day be used in a massive class-action suit brought by the moviegoing public against the makers of the twenty-five films in question. What I have prepared here is not so much an abusive, one-sided, monolithically vituperative broadside against the film industry, but rather a massive legal writ proving that the studios in question are guilty of false advertising, just as much as if they had advertised a love story starring Robert De Niro and Meryl Streep that actually starred Jan-Michael Vincent and Kay Lenz. (Not that the movie starring Robert De Niro and Meryl Streep would have been any better.)

Why false advertising? Because in each of the films that I watched, a screenplay credit appeared in a prominent place at the end of the horror show, stating that someone had actually been hired to write a script. Yet, as anyone who has seen *Hudson Hawk* or *The January Man* will testify under oath in court, this is an out-and-out lie. No scriptwriter ever got anywhere near *Hudson Hawk* or *The January Man*. The suggestion that anyone actually wrote a screenplay for these monstrosities is one of the grossest fabrications in the history of motion pictures.

The films in question cover the entire spectrum of cinematic imbecility. Some are new (*Hudson Hawk*, *The Two Jakes*), some are old (*The Night Porter*, *Heaven's Gate*); all are stupid. In some cases (*King David, Ishtar*) the movies briefly flirt with sanity before going off the rails, but in most cases (*The Two Jakes, Once Upon a Time in America*) it is clear from the very first scene that the scriptwriter is absent without leave and will remain that way for the entire film. In these instances, it quickly becomes obvious that by the time the studio finished paying Robert De Niro or Jack Nicholson for their "work," there was not enough money left to pay someone to write a script. In still other cases (*The Night Porter*), the story is so vile and putrescent that one suspects the screenwriter had been lured into some nefarious, sadomasochistic Teutonic ritual and murdered halfway through the film. Not that anyone would notice.

Yet, in approaching a subject such as this, it is important to distinguish between films that are utterly incomprehensible and films that are merely stupid. A good example is the recent, direct-to-video release *Backtrack*, which stars Jodie Foster as a cutting-edge political artist who happens to witness a mob murder committed by Joe Pesci, whose boss is Vincent Price. When Pesci and his associate John Turturro, an underachieving hit man, fail to polish off Foster, who, in a departure from traditional, cutting-edge political artist attire, spends most of the film in a half-slip, Price hires *professional* hit man and jazz buff Dennis Hopper to do the job. Instead, Hopper falls madly in love with Foster, abducts her, kills off all the mobsters pursuing them, and then escapes to Seattle or New Zealand or somewhere or other, where, presumably, the two will live happily ever after.

This is an unbelievably stupid plot, but within the parameters of addlepatedness clearly delineated at the outset of the film, *it works on its own terms*. Yes, *Backtrack* is a hair-raisingly imbecilic movie, but it is not a movie whose plot is hard to follow. In this sense, it is very much like David Lynch's work: insane but logical, not unlike the universe most of us—though not Dennis Hopper—are currently inhabiting. Moreover, since the viewer knows at the outset that the film has been directed by Dennis Hopper or David Lynch, or for that matter by Michelangelo

Antonioni or Jean-Luc Godard, he has no right to complain that it makes no sense. Devotees of films that make sense do not suddenly burst into the local twelve-plex at 7:30 P.M. on Friday night, waving $20-bills, and shouting, "We're members of the American Logical Society; you got any tickets left for that Dennis Hopper flick?"

Here, then, is a brief viewer's guide to movies that make no fucking sense whatsoever.

Angel Heart. Mickey Rourke plays a down-at-the-heels Gotham gumshoe hired by a shadowy, pony-tailed sleazeball (Robert De Niro) to track down an obscure '40s singer named Johnny Favorite who was last seen in a Poughkeepsie mental hospital. The trail leads him—inevitably—to New Orleans, where he gets involved with a shadowy psychic named Madame Krusemark, played by Charlotte Rampling, and a shadowy voodoo chile named Epiphany Proudfoot, played by Lisa Bonet. Rampling winds up with her heart ripped out, Bonet winds up with a pistol jammed up her privates, and a minor character names Toots Suite suffocates on his own penis. The movie seems to have something to do with evil.

The Mount Everest of moronosity in this Himalaya of horseshit occurs when De Niro and Rourke have this exchange:

DE NIRO: Well, you know what they say about slugs.
ROURKE: No, what do they say about slugs?
DE NIRO: They always leave slime in their tracks.

Mr. De Niro, I do not think this is the kind of information you need to tell Mickey Rourke.

Don't Tell Her It's Me. Steve Guttenberg plays a bald, fat loser who has just had chemotherapy because he almost died of Hodgkin's disease. His sister, a bimbo romance novelist played by Shelley Long (who apparently took the role because she was afraid she was starting to get typecast as the Rodeo Drive Vanessa Redgrave), tries to get him a date with a reporter whose name I didn't catch. The reporter gives him the cold shoulder because he's fat and bald and just had chemotherapy. Guttenberg jogs and grows his hair Andre Agassi–style and resurfaces as a New Zealanderific biker named Lobo. The reporter falls in love with him and they live happily ever after. If you're a reader dying of Hodgkin's disease you really ought to check out this movie pronto. You can probably get Medicare to cover the rental.

Hudson Hawk. Leonardo da Vinci, the smartest guy who ever lived, builds a machine that can make gold out of lead. Four hundred years later, cat burglars Bruce Willis and Danny Aiello show up. They go to an exotic locale where they sing a lot of songs by Frank Sinatra and look for da Vinci's machine. The movie begins and ends with Willis (the Hudson Hawk) asking for a cup of cappuccino. This synopsis actually makes the movie seem more coherent than it really is.

Ishtar. Dustin Hoffman plays a no-talent songwriter whose nickname is Hawk. Warren Beatty is his no-talent sidekick. After many adventures, they wind up in an exotic locale singing songs by Frank Sinatra. (Editor's note: A lot of really bad, totally incomprehensible movies seem to feature characters named "Hawk" with airhead sidekicks who go to exotic locales and sing songs by Frank Sinatra.)

The January Man. Kevin Kline plays a crack fireman who used to be a crack policeman before he got thrown off the force by his brother, who claimed he was on the take. Kline is still in love with Susan Sarandon, who is married to his brother, Harvey Keitel, whose boss, Rod Steiger, tells him to put Kline back on the force because his kid, Mary Elizabeth Mastrantonio, almost got murdered by a serial killer who only strikes on days that are prime numbers. Mastrantonio falls in love with Kline, whose office at police headquarters is taken over by a British artist played by Alan Rickman, who needs the afternoon light, and eats lots of Dunkin' Donuts.

Pissed off about these deviations from conventional office procedure, police chief Danny Aiello berates Kline with the words: "You dilettante fuck!" using a polysyllabic Gallicism one would not normally expect to hear in New York City police headquarters or in any room containing Danny Aiello. Keitel tells Kline that he's going to have a hard time finding the murderer, whose crimes also have something to do with calendars and musical notation, because "You don't get away pulling eleven separate murders unless you got a brain like a Swiss watch." The movie begins and ends with Kline begging someone, anyone, for a cup of espresso. (Editor's note: A lot of really bad, totally incomprehensible movies not only feature Danny Aiello, but also have a major character who keeps asking for an exotic beverage containing too much caffeine.)

Joe Versus the Volcano. Tom Hanks thinks he's dying, so he goes to a desert isle in the South Pacific and gets involved with aboriginals ruled by Abe Vigoda, who want him and Meg Ryan to jump into a volcano. (The movie is a thinly veiled allegory for the plight of clients of the William Morris Agency.) "You only get one or two scripts a year that really interest you," movie stars are fond of saying. This was one of them? What was the other? *Turner & Hooch*?

Worth noting is the fact that although this movie—"directed," if that's the word for it, by the alleged screenwriter—makes no sense whatsoever, one thing, at least, is abundantly clear: why Ryan, who is cast in not one, not two, but *three* roles, has never been asked to play more than one person at a time again.

King David. This is one of those movies that you can't really understand unless you've already read the Old Testament, preferably just before you turned on the VCR. *King David* seems to have something to do with God and Jews, but you can't tell any of the characters apart because everyone looks like they're from Jethro Tull. You never really find out why Saul (Edward Woodward), who really likes David (Richard Gere) a lot, tries to kill him on his wedding night; or why David, who really likes Saul a lot, goes to live with his enemies, the Philistines, just as they are getting ready to kill Saul; or why the Philistines, after wiping out Saul and his army, don't just torch Jerusalem; or why David, who really likes his son Absalom, doesn't tell his right-hand man not to run him through with a sword while he's hanging from a tree. But then again, his right-hand man probably couldn't tell it was Absalom, beloved son of David, because Absalom looks like some guy from Jethro Tull, and even back in biblical times, people went out of their way to kill guys who looked like they were from Jethro Tull.

There is one brief shining moment of lucidity in this otherwise dark hole of blather. This occurs when David, still really bummed out about Saul's death, dances into Jerusalem in his underpants. The dance, which Val Kilmer reprised in a leather-pants version in *The Doors*, is so embarrassing, and so out of character with everything else that takes place in the movie, that in a weird sort of way it starts to make sense. Looking at the expressions on the faces of David's fellow Israelites, you can sort of see them thinking: "Anyone who's a big enough asshole to do a dance like that at a funeral probably deserves to be king."

The Mission. This movie seems to have something to do with Good and Evil, but you can't understand it unless you've already read the New Testament, preferably right before you turned on the VCR. Jeremy Irons plays a devout but thimble-brained missionary in eighteenth-century Brazil, while Robert De Niro plays a conquistador/slaver who sounds like he's from Brooklyn: Ponce de Flatbush. De Niro becomes so remorseful about a murder he commits that he decides to sheathe his sword and become a servant of God. But then he changes his mind and starts killing everything that moves. *Rule of thumb:* If God Himself could not make sense out of this film, why should you? (Editor's note: A lot of really bad, totally incomprehensible movies star Robert De Niro.)

The Night Porter. More than a decade after World War II ends, Charlotte Rampling, a relatively chipper concentration camp survivor, meets her old Nazi tormentor Dirk Bogarde, who can't get a good job because of this embarrassing entry on his resume:

LAST JOB: Gestapo butcher
REASON FOR LEAVING LAST JOB: Third Reich collapsed

Not surprisingly, Dirk is now working as the night clerk in a Viennese hotel. The two wackos pick up right where they left off years earlier, scattering tiny pieces of glass all over the bathroom floor so they can cut each other's feet to ribbons and then licking the blood off each other's fingers and whatnot. The film, which features flashbacks of Rampling dolled up in an SS uniform, was made in Italy, the country where fascism was born; this makes sense, since only Europeans would be gross enough to make a movie that is more tasteless than the war that inspired it. (Editor's note: A lot of really bad, totally incomprehensible movies where the story is told in flashbacks star Charlotte Rampling.)

Nothing But Trouble. Finally, Dan Aykroyd gets to direct Dan Aykroyd. The film also stars Demi Moore, Chevy Chase, and John Candy, who plays not one but two parts.

Fill in the blanks, guys.

Once Upon a Time in America. This film seems to have something to do with the Mafia. Robert De Niro plays a mobster named Noodles, while James Woods plays a mobster who is not named Noodles, but who might as well be. Danny Aiello plays a cop who is also not named Noodles. Through a series of remarkably uninformative flashbacks, we learn that Robert De Niro helped get Woods killed thirty years earlier and has since been living in Buffalo as a kind of penance. But then it turns out that Woods is not dead after all, but has become a successful politician with wire-rimmed eyeglasses who wants De Niro to kill him for old times' sake. De Niro turns him down, saying he hasn't used a gun in thirty years, so Woods apparently kills himself by jumping into the back of a garbage truck. Woods's apparently jumping into the back of a garbage truck is apparently a Sergio Leone symbol meaning: "Crime apparently does not pay." (Editor's note: A lot of really bad, totally incomprehensible films with many uninformative flashbacks star Robert De Niro and Danny Aiello.)

Orca. Richard Harris, a downwardly mobile fisherman, kills Mrs. Orca, Orca the Killer Whale's wife, who is pregnant with Orca's child, who presumably would have been named Caitlin or Jordan or Shannon or Brittany. In revenge, Orca bites off Keenan Wynn's head and Bo Derek's leg, which motivates Harris to hie himself hither to the Canadian mainland. For reasons that are not entirely clear, Harris is unable to just get on a bus and go to Montreal or Edmonton or Moosejaw or something, where there are no killer whales, but instead has to leave town by sea. *Big mistake.* As horrified marine biologist/sex kitten Charlotte Rampling looks on, Orca kills Harris and seems to have a pretty good time doing it. (Editor's note: A lot of really bad, incomprehensible movies star Charlotte Rampling.)

Other People's Money. Danny DeVito plays a lovable corporate raider who has eaten one too many Dunkin' Donuts. He wants to take over a money-losing New England firm headed by Gregory Peck, but is stymied by Peck's illegitimate daughter, a lawyer played by Penelope Ann Miller, who uses the wily lure of sex to delay the takeover. At the very last minute, the Japanese show up, buy the company, and everyone lives happily ever after. Huh? Just for the record, if she is still alive, Penelope Ann Miller is the worst actress alive. And if she is dead, good. (Editor's note: A lot of really bad, totally incomprehensible movies feature characters who eat way too many Dunkin' Donuts.)

V. I. Warshawski. Kathleen Turner plays a fat private investigator who falls in love with a washed-up hockey star who gets murdered, leaving her in charge of his wiseass kid who wears her baseball cap backwards. The principal suspects are Boomer's two brothers, one a bland corporate type, the other a creepy sculptor who does meaningful work with metal, and who just happens to be married to the dead hockey star's ex-wife. Both brothers are keenly interested in a seemingly worthless fishing shack Boomer has bequeathed to his kid. After the Japanese suddenly turn up for no reason at all and agree to buy the fishing shack, just about everybody dies, but those who don't live happily ever after. (Editor's note: A lot of really bad, totally incomprehensible movies feature Japanese investors who inexplicably turn up at the very end of the story so everyone can live happily ever after.)

Wild Orchid. Carré Otis plays a prim, bespectacled, schoolmarmish coed living with her mom on a midwestern farm. One day she gets tired of the grind and decides to move to New York and start a job in Brazil *the next day* as an attorney specializing in international takeover law who speaks five languages, including Portuguese. Mickey Rourke plays an orphan who made a fortune in Philadelphia real estate, yet is incapable of love. His Portuguese isn't very good, either. Rourke arranges for Otis to wear a lot of masks and black string bikinis and get screwed by the lawyer representing the creep she's negotiating against in a complicated deal involving Jacqueline Bisset and some Japanese businessmen who show up near the end, enabling everyone to live happily ever after. *Wild Orchid* actually contains the line: "I stayed in the third grade for a long time; the teachers thought I was retarded."

Guess who says it?

(Editor's note: A lot of really bad, totally incomprehensible movies star Mickey Rourke and feature Asian investors who inexplicably turn up at the very end of the story so everyone can live happily ever after.)

The reader, of course, appreciates that this is only a partial list of the truly grotesque, hopelessly muddled, utterly inchoate movies that are out there waiting to be rented, perhaps this very evening. Space considerations preclude going into too much detail about *Dune*, which seems to have something to do with Outer Space; *Godfather III*, which seems to have something to do with the Mafia; and *The Comfort of Strangers*, a slightly better-lit *Night Porter* set in Venice instead of Vienna, which seems to have something to do with sex. Space considerations also preclude going into too much detail about *Winter Kills*, a baffling film about a political assassination; *Betrayal*, a baffling film about a political assassination; *The Package*, a baffling film about a political assassination; and *The Conversation*, a baffling film about a political assassination. *The Conversation* rates a mention because it falls into the same category as *8½* and *Blowup*: truly amazing films whose impact is not diminished one iota by the fact that you really can't understand what any of them are about. *The Conversation* is certainly worth having a conversation about. It's just that we're not going to have it.

We're not going to have it because there is room in this article for only one film that involves a tape recording that the main character keeps playing over and over again, hoping to unravel an enigma wrapped inside a mystery, and that film is *The Two Jakes*.

The Two Jakes. Directed with verve and panache by Jack Nicholson, and apparently edited during one of those long evenings after he'd spent the whole afternoon guzzling beer at a Lakers-Celtics game, *The Two Jakes* resembles *King David* in the sense that you can't begin to understand it unless you've already done your homework. To understand *King David* you need to have read the Bible, an incomprehensible book. To understand *The Two Jakes*, you need to have seen *Chinatown*, an incomprehensible movie, and you need to have seen it twenty seconds before you turn on the VCR. Otherwise, you're not going to be able to answer questions like: "What the hell is Chuck Newty doing here?" Instead, you're going to find yourself asking: "Who *is* Chuck Newty, and why *shouldn't* he be here?" *Rule of thumb:* If the principal characters in a movie can't figure out what's going on, why the hell should you?

At this point, I should indicate that none of the films I have described up until now have truly earned a niche in the pantheon of completely incomprehensible movies. For a movie to be considered one of the all-time scriptless wonders; to have a plot that Sherlock Holmes, Albert Einstein and, yea, verily, Jehovah

Himself could not figure out; to have a story line that can rival *Last Year at Marienbad*, *Last Tango in Paris*, *Last Exit to Brooklyn*, and all the other films that begin with "Last," it must first pass through the massive portal known as Heaven's Gate. I know of only three films that fit that bill. Here they are:

Tough Guys Don't Dance. Norman Mailer, in his staggeringly rotten directorial debut, casts Ryan O'Neal as a down-at-the-heels writer who once did three years in the slammer, and is now suspected of murdering an ex-porn star he screwed in front of her gay Limey husband in a fit of rage after his wife walked out on him. *Clear?* All of this is told in flashback to his fat, bald dad, who just had chemotherapy. Ryan gets a call from police chief Wings Hauser, who tells him to move his marijuana stash; when he does, he finds two decapitated heads in garbage bags in the hole in the ground where his stash—and movies like this—are usually found. Needless to say, Isabella Rossellini has a small role in the film, playing a mysterious asshole. The film has one redeeming moment, which occurs in the scene where Ryan tells a hood who has just killed his pet: "Your knife is in my dog." (Editor's note: Like many really bad, totally incomprehensible movies, *Tough Guys Don't Dance* features confusing flashbacks and fat, bald guys who have just had chemotherapy.)

The Little Drummer Girl. Diane Keaton plays an actress who is wooed by the Palestinian Liberation Organization, but then instead becomes a secret agent for the Israeli secret police. *Oh well, a girl's allowed to change her mind, isn't she?* Keaton helps get a famous terrorist from the PLO assassinated, but is so traumatized by the experience that by the end of the film she is no longer capable of acting. In other words, Diane Keaton, who cannot act, plays an actress who *can* act at the beginning of the film, but who *can't* act at the end.

Keaton is more convincing at the end.

Heaven's Gate. God put Michael Cimino on this earth to remind us how bad Oliver Stone would be if he didn't do *any* editing. But unlike all the other works in this survey, Cimino's bloodcurdlingly wretched film (in which Mickey Rourke has a small, but not small enough, role) is not completely and utterly incomprehensible on a frame-by-frame basis. Essentially an ethnic remake of *Shane*, where the cattlemen now murder eastern European beet farmers instead of guys like Van Heflin who just want to be left alone so they can grow 65,000 acres of barley, *Heaven's Gate* sort of has a plot that you can follow—if you can just manage to stay awake.

But you can't. I tried using an alarm clock and a paging service that would call me every fifteen minutes or so. I also had a friend sit down beside me and jostle me every so often, and I even tried getting my wife to take notes during the parts of the movie where I dozed off (twenty minutes of footage of eastern European fiddle players cavorting on roller skates around a dance floor in Casper, Wyoming, is about my limit); but it did no good. None of us could stay awake for more than eight minutes at a time. And I guess that really says a lot about me and my lifestyle and my values system. Maybe I *don't* have anything better to do with my time than to sit in front of a TV screen watching *Heaven's Gate* for 219 minutes. But I do have better things to do with my time than to stay awake.

8 LOLLOPALOOZA

B y and large, the film universe is an absolutely perfect one, where good people are rewarded and bad ones are chastised, where gifted actors and actresses ultimately receive the acclaim they deserve, while fakes, poseurs, bimbos, and callow youths end up getting exactly what they deserve: inconsequential billing in very tiny letters far below the names "Lou Diamond Phillips" and "Kay Lenz" in the credits of a Cannon-Globus Production.

Yet, there *are* exceptions to this rule. There are certain actors who never receive the kudos they merit, certain directors whose fine efforts are overlooked until it is too late, certain actresses whose phenomenal talents are obscured and ultimately overlooked because these gifts are overshadowed by their more obvious physical charms.

And so it is with Gina Lollobrigida. According to a dizzyingly encyclopedic—albeit unauthorized—biography by a Brazilian-born professor of foreign languages at Kyoto University who once worked as a clown before turning to academe, Lollobrigida—one of the biggest stars of the 1950s—was not just an unbelievably gorgeous postwar Tuscan tootsie with astonishing knockers. She was also an accomplished thespianess whose superb work in films as varied as *Fast and Sexy*, *She Got What She Asked For*, *Go Naked in the World*, *Me, Me, Me . . . and the Others*, and *Flesh Will Surrender* has too quickly been forgotten by a notoriously fickle public.

"Remember, I am an actress, not just a body!" La Lollo once declared to no one in particular, and Luis Canales, author of *Imperial Gina* (Branden Publishing, $19.95, 268 pages), has taken her at her word. Canales is an interesting case. Very possibly the only member of the Kyoto University faculty who is a Mormon, a native Portuguese speaker, and a major Gina Lollobrigida buff, Canales probably knows more about the actress than anyone alive. Not that you can translate those kinds of credentials into hard currency; *Imperial Gina* died a quiet death when it was published by a small house in Boston two years ago, and the only reason we're resurrecting it here is because it's been a slow month. Lollobrigida herself once warned Canales that if he went ahead with his lifelong obsession and wrote a book about her she'd sue his samba ass off.

She needn't have worried. *Imperial Gina* is so servilely idolatrous in its attitude toward the star of *Where the Hot Wind Blows* and *Love I Haven't . . . But . . . But . . .* that you might think it was written by her press agent. The way Canales has things stacked up, Lollobrigida's stunning physique has sadly blinded even the finest critics to the delicate talents used to such effect in *The Bride Can't Wait*, *Bride for a Night*, *Death Has Laid an Egg*, and, of course, *Fanfan the Tulip*. Were it not for her legendary bosom and winsome smile, Canales seems to argue, this "volcanic peasant girl" would be thought of as the equal of Hepburn, Magnani, Garbo, Dietrich, Bergman, and, yes, perhaps even Hawn.

"You can rate an actress's popularity by the names of her co-stars," reasoned UPI hack Vernon Scott in the early 1960s, and Canales agrees with this verdict. "Scott may be just as biased as I," he writes, "but Gina certainly starred with her share of top leading men. In the early Sixties, she had starred opposite Stephen Boyd, France's Jean-Paul Belmondo and Rock Hudson, not to mention her long list of celebrated screen stars in the Fifties." (Editor's note: Stephen Boyd played the coveted role of Jemuga in *Genghis Khan*.)

Canales concedes that Phyllis Diller's costar in *The Private Army of Sergeant O'Farrell* never appeared in a film directed by such neorealistic top dogs as Fellini, Antonioni, and Visconti, and is less well thought of as an actress than Sophia Loren, yet another volcanic peasant girl from the hills of Naples or Lombardy or Tuscany or points south. He also concedes that the star of *Flesh and the Woman* is a highly litigious sort, having sued everyone in sight—agents, producers, directors, magazines, publicists—over the past half-century. And yet, he argues, in reality Lollobrigida has "a gold heart in a tigress's body."

She also has plenty of locks on the doors to her villa. No, imperial Gina never assented to an interview with a man who says he has been obsessed with her career since he first saw one of her movies in 1957, and who is still upset that an Italian critic once used a coarse term meaning "cow udder" when discussing her breasts in a 1954 article. No, she did not assent to an interview with a man who can tell you what her measurements were ten weeks after she gave birth to her first child; a man who owns photos of the bed in which she was born; a man whose second-favorite hobby is collecting anything having to do with Yukio Mishima, the neofascist, leather-freak novelist who disemboweled himself a decade ago after an abortive attempt to topple the Japanese government; a man who writes sentences like this:

It was in the uplands of the Apennines in central Italy that the tale of the Sabine women took place approximately in the year 290 A.D.* The subjects of Romulus, founder of Rome, kidnapped the

*Canales has A.D. and B.C. mixed up, but never mind.

wives and daughters of the Sabines and when the defeated husbands were about the attack the enemy, the brave women, holding their offspring in their arms, intervened between the conquerors and the defeated.

Uh-oh.

Perhaps the most appealing feature of *Imperial Gina* is the author's own black-and-white snapshot of the green gate that bars the entrance to Lollobrigida's villa on the Appia Antica in Rome, the thoroughfare where once strode the Caesars, and now stride the Canaleses, trying to get past the gate. The gate appears to be securely locked, as well it should be. Canales ends his book with the words: "This unauthorized biography of the actress remains unfinished. There are gaps to be filled and much may be added to the life of La Bersagliera—the living legend. My search for the actress will continue. And after this book reaches the Appia Antica, if the Roman deities are on my side, I may yet have the good fortune of going beyond the green gate without the German shepherds chasing me."

I don't think so.

9 THE KING AND HIS COURT

There are certain records in the fields of entertainment, sports, finance, and mass murder that are probably never going to be broken. Wilt Chamberlain's 100 points in a single basketball game, Nolan Ryan's seven no-hitters, Josef Stalin's making thirty million Russians disappear without anyone noticing, and Steve Ross's 1990 salary all fall into this category, as do sales of Michael Jackson's *Thriller*, Joe DiMaggio's fifty-six-game hitting streak, and Fritz Mondale's amazing feat of capturing just one state out of fifty in the 1984 presidential election. True, a Pete Rose, Michael Jordan, or Michael Dukakis may from time to time come within striking distance of the accomplishments of Joltin' Joe, Flailin' Fritz, or The Big Dipper, and an enthusiastic whippersnapper like Pol Pot may occasionally give Uncle Joe a run for his money. But when the dust has cleared, the records of the immortals are still pretty much intact. And so it is with Elvis Presley.

Between 1956 and 1969, Elvis Presley, *in his spare time from being the biggest rock 'n' roll star of all time*, managed to make thirty-one of the worst movies in motion picture history, not counting two pretty dreary concert films. Even if we go easy on the guy and give passing grades to *King Creole* (Elvis as a pharmacist's son), *Flaming Star* (Elvis as a half-breed), and *Jailhouse Rock* (Elvis as a guitar-pickin' convict), we are still face to face with an *oeuvre* that is staggering in its awfulness: Elvis as a race-car driver, Elvis as a water-skiing instructor, Elvis as a sheik, Elvis in a double role as an army officer and his redneck cousin, Elvis as a sensitive doctor working in a free clinic in the ghetto. A betting man would have to say that Elvis's record for cinematic woefulness is unassailable, but what is even more astonishing about this score-and-a-half of egregious Elvisisms is that virtually all of the King's movies made lots and lots of money. Bearing in mind how big these bad films were, it is probably safe to say that no one alive today will live to see another great rock star capable of making this many unredeemably horrible, money-making films in his lifetime, nor will his chilrden, nor will his grandchildren, nor will their great-grandchildren. Nor will *their* grandchildren or great-grandchildren.

This will not, however, keep people from trying. Even as the rest of us sit around, waiting for that fourth Boston album or wondering what ever happened to Anson Williams, there are several rock stars on this very planet who are still young enough, rich enough, and conceited enough to mount at least a modest threat to Elvis's record, chillingly unaccomplished thespians who have killed before and who will kill again unless the public musters its resources to stop them. If it is true, as the English essayist Edmund Burke once said, that evil prevails when enough good men do nothing, then it can be said with equal certainty that evil occurs in motion pictures when enough so-so people pay enough good money to see enough bad movies. Actually, this happens all the time.

My goals here are modest: First, to explain why rock stars almost without exception make such terrible movie stars, and second, as a kind of *pro bono publico* service to unsuspecting Americans, to identify the living rock stars who pose the most serious threat to the King's extraordinary record of generating cinematic solid waste. Proceeding directly to the question of why rock stars so regularly bomb out as actors, one may advance two explanations: the charitable one and the uncharitable one. The charitable one is that rock stars generally are only offered roles that stink to high heaven, and are the victims of cynical manipulation by money-grubbing oligopolists who seek to cash in on the stars' fleeting popularity (Frankie Avalon in *The Alamo*, Vanilla Ice in *The Secret of the Ooze*).

A charitable corollary to this charitable explanation is that rock stars are often preyed upon by unscrupulous directors (like, say, Ken Russell) who feel that they can get the naive rock star (like, say, Roger Daltry) to make an even bigger fool of himself in public than an established movie star (like, say, Ryan O'Neal) would ever agree to.

The uncharitable explanation, of course, is that rock stars suck. Rock stars, unlike movie stars, are usually not especially pleasant to look at, so they can't get away with being terrible actors for as long as Lou Diamond Phillips or Don Johnson have. Moreover, they rely on broad, vulgar, exaggerated gestures designed to transfix the very last, drug-crazed teenager in the very last row of the very darkest multipurpose civic center, gestures that work well in Yankee Stadium and the Grand Canyon but which look ridiculous in close-up. This is the reason Morgan Freeman, and not Axl Rose, got the chauffeur's part in *Driving Miss Daisy*. Honest.

But don't take my word for it; let's go to the videotape. In recent years, we the people have been treated to the very short, bug-eyed Roger Daltry (of Ken Russell's refreshingly insane *Tommy* and *Lisztomania*); the anorexic, simian Mick Jagger (of *Performance*, *Ned Kelly* and *Freejack*); the emaciated, bug-eyed Robbie Robertson (of *Carny*); the slightly less anorexic, somewhat more bug-eyed, totally simian David Johansen (of *Let It Ride* and *Freejack*); and the phantasmagorically unattractive

Ringo Starr (star of films too repellent and too numerous to be cited this early in an otherwise wholesome article).

All of these rockers are either famous (Daltry, Starr, Jagger) or influential (Johansen was the lead singer in the godfathers-of-punk band The New York Dolls, and Robertson wrote most of The Band's golden greats and big hits), and all of them are complete duds as actors. Ringo, who cannot play the drums, also cannot act—but in *Caveman*, *Sextette*, *200 Motels*, *The Magic Christian*, and many other forlorn projects, John, Paul, and George weren't there to bail him out. Roger Daltry has nice hair, nice teeth, and that's it. (Actually, *Tommy* seems to have been a deliberate cautionary tale on the part of Ken Russell, a gauntlet thrown down to hs audience. "Think the sixties were fun?" Russell seems to be asking. "Watch this movie and refresh your memory, asshole!" After all, how could a decade have been that much fun if the Who were in it?) David Johansen does not have nice teeth or hair and he cannot act. Neither does Robbie Robertson. People who think that Mick Jagger was acting in *Performance* just because he toned down his spastic campiness a notch or two are the kinds of people who think Geraldo Rivera is intelligent because he now wears a tie. If Mick Jagger was so good in *Performance*, why was his next starring role as an Australian cowboy? And why was his next job after that a mysterious role in Werner Herzog's narcissistic, fatality-inducing, ecosystematically discombobulating *Fitzcarraldo* that he ended up getting cut out of anyway? Does anyone seriously believe that gifted actors end up spending two years in the Amazon jungle with Werner Herzog? Klaus Kinski excepted? And if Mick was so good in *Performance*, why did he have to wait twenty-two years to be in his next major film? What kind of actor waits twenty-two years to be in a movie with Emilio Estevez? Ramon Estevez?

The list of great rock stars who make bad actors is not long, but it is impressive: John Lennon as an infantryman in *How I Won the War*, Michael Jackson as a plump Scarecrow in *The Wiz*,

Keith Moon as a talentless drummer in *That'll Be the Day* and its sequel *Stardust*, and as a campy fashion designer in *Sextette*. And then there are the three-time losers, such as Bob Dylan, who has already logged in with three hair-raising performances during his career. Dylan, who is not at all good-looking, first reared his ugly head as the laconic sagebrush nihilist Alibi in Sam Peckinpah's depressingly unbuckarooish *Pat Garrett and Billy the Kid*, then directed himself in the unforgivable *Renaldo and Clara*, a kind of bloated, over-the-top, outré *Heaven's Gate*, and was last seen in *Hearts of Fire*, playing a rock star who has retreated to self-imposed exile as a chicken farmer in western Pennsylvania. It is a chilling commentary on our times that the greatest songwriter of his generation should end up making movies with people named Fiona.

All of Dylan's movies have a disturbing editorial history. *Pat Garrett* was first released in a studio-mandated, savagely truncated version in 1973, but under pressure from French film historians and other sadomasochists, the director's cut was reassembled in 1988, and the movie was rereleased in its original thirty-seven-week form. *Renaldo and Clara* first appeared in a 232-minute form in 1978, but, under pressure from French Dylan fans and the Consumer Product Safety Commission, it was later trimmed to a marginally less sociopathic 122-minute version. *Hearts of Fire* was never released in theaters anywhere, has never been trimmed to a shorter form, and is only available in the kinds of video stores that carry *all* of Dyan Cannon's movies. So far, no word from the French.

In one sense, Dylan's acting career bears a tragic resemblance to the King's. Apparently, for a short period in their lives, each of these men entertained dreams of being taken seriously as actors. Dylan and Presley were encouraged in these wild hopes by the legendary availability of powerful hallucinogenic drugs throughout the 1960s, and by the kinds of addlepated movie critics who say things like, "If it hadn't-a-been for that son-of-a-bitch Colonel Parker, Elvis could have been one hell of actor!"

and, "If Dylan had only been able to get his hands on a good script, he could have developed into a lion of the silver screen." Gosh, just think what we missed: Elvis as Henry V and Dylan as Henry Hill in *Goodfellas*. Or Elvis as Mozart in *Amadeus* and Dylan, instead of George C. Scott, in *Patton*.

One of the oddities about pop stars who try their hands at films is that the very worst rock stars often make the very best movie stars. Cher has always been a pathetic excuse for a rocker, an Ethel Merman in fishnet tights, who has attempted to compensate for her borderline vocal skills with sheer brass and bluster. The result? Twenty years of songs that sound like Journey outtakes, plus "Cherokee Woman," the national anthem of all those Designer Victims who had to suffer the slings and arrows of outrageous fortune and racial prejudice while growing up in Malibu.

Despite this, Cher has developed into a very fine actress who has turned in exemplary work in everything from *The Witches of Eastwick* to *Suspect* to *Silkwood*, and who has also performed creditably in several lackluster, generally overpraised films whose titles begin with *M*: (*Mermaids*, *Mask*, and *Moonstruck*). In fact, it is by no means inconceivable that Cher could one day make *more* movies than Elvis Presley. But that would still leave the King's record intact, because anyone can make thirty-one good movies that make money, but the King got away with making thirty-one bad movies that made money. Elvis got away with making thirty-one *atrocious* movies that made money. Thus, Cher's entry in the *Guinness Book of World Records* would still read:

Most Good Movies by a Really Bad Rock Star 400
while Elvis's entry would read:

Most Bad Movies by a Really Great Rock Star 31
Elvis still wins in a walk.

First Runner-up in the Dean Martin Memorial Sweepstakes for So-So Singers Who Make Decent Actors is Diana Ross, whose looks, not her voice, won her the lead vocalist spot in the

Supremes. An average singer fortunate enough to work with Motown's great songwriters, Ross was good in *Lady Sings the Blues*, okay in *Mahogany*, and no worse than anybody else in the nightmarish *The Wiz*, the most indefatigably cheerless musical ever made. But the hands-down winner of the Golden Deaneroonie is Bette Midler, who started out singing Barry Manilow's arrangements in New York's gay bathhouses, and who probably got her acting career off the ground after patrons of those very same bathhouses raised enough money for her to switch genres. (Bathhouses are bad enough without live renditions of songs like "Hello in There.")

Like Cher, the Divine Miss M has labored long and hard to divert attention away from her wafer-thin cabaret voice by developing a screamin'-heebie-jeebie stage show, which worked well until her screen debut in *The Rose*, the Janis Joplin gagathon that demonstrated that, while Midler couldn't really sing, she could actually act. End of *that* career.

On the other hand, being a bogus or second-tier rock star who can't sing like Elvis Presley or Little Richard will not *automatically* guarantee success in the movies. Paul Simon's hair-in-the-electric-socket sidekick was never entirely convincing as a rock star back in the parsley, sage, rosemary, and thyme era (yes, children, it happened in this very society). But Art Garfunkel has been pretty much of a Johnny One-Note as an actor, getting cast as a schmuck in *Carnal Knowledge*, as a schmuck in *Catch-22*, and as a schmuck in *Bad Timing: A Sensual Obsession*, while Simon himself, too short to rock and roll but too young to die, made his acting debut as a schmuck in *Annie Hall*, and inadvertently came off as a complete schmuck in his own production, *One-Trick Pony*. Proving that the words of the prophets really are written on the subway walls, and the words are: *Fuck you, schmuck.*

Speaking of schmucks, how about a few words vis-à-vis the Stingmeister? The Stingster, whose colossal self-importance has been captured for all eternity (well, for the next twenty-five minutes) by both Annie Leibovitz and by the Sting guy himself (in *Hold Back the Night*); he actually filmed the birth of his own son, presumably so that all those people in the Third World who don't have any children of their own could get a charge out of it. Sting is a truly appalling human being, but he's a very good rock 'n' roller and by no means the world's worst actor—so long as he's not cast as the leading man. Stiff as a board, mannered, and overrehearsed in *The Bride*, in which he was quite appropriately cast as Dr. Frankenstein, Sting was outacted not only by a dwarf (David Rappaport) but by a standup comic (Akexei Sayle) with a Yorkshire accent so thick that not even people from Yorkshire can understand it. Indeed, Lord of the Stings was so unstintingly wooden in this film that audiences the world over found themselves rooting for the star's destruction, bellowing in unison, "Sting, where is thy death?"

Still, when Stingus Supremus is cast properly—in a smaller role where he plays a sinister or vacuous figure—he is quite competent, turning in decent supporting performances in *Julia and Julia*, *Plenty*, *Dune*, and *Quadrophenia*. People who saw the Stingmensch on Broadway when he appeared in Brecht's *The Threepenny Opera* last year assure me that he cannot actually act, not in the sense of being able to behave in a psychologically coherent fashion for more than ninety seconds at a time. But, when coached properly, His Most Excellent Sting is more than equal to the minuscule demands of movie acting, trading a few lines with Meryl Streep or Kathleen Turner without being completely burned to a crisp. It ain't good, as Emmylou Harris once said in a non-Stingian context, but it ain't bad.

Some of the best acting jobs by rock stars have been served up by people who are not so univesally well known that their fame overshadows their performances. Gary and Martin Kemp are the leaders of the British art-rock band Spandau Ballet, a perfectly adequate, second-rank English rock group whose albums have not yet made *les frères* Kemp household names. Unburdened by the demands of Jaggerian, Rogerdaltryian, or Stingeroonian notoriety, the brothers were thoroughly convincing as atavistic murders in *The Krays*, once again validating the theory that English rock stars just naturally make convincing psychopaths. Along similar lines, Roland Gift of the fleetingly popular Fine Young Cannibals did a very nice job as an obsessed lover in *Scandal* and was also quite effective as a mysterious street person in *Sammy and Rosie Get Laid*. But, again, Gift is not so famous that his celebrity would overshadow his own performance, or that of any of his costars in a film. Well, maybe Bridget Fonda.

Another rocker worthy of mention is Joan Jett, who starred in Paul Schrader's exhilaratingly crappy 1987 film *Light of Day*. In this bizarre little affair, Michael J. Fox, too short to rock and roll but too young to die, is cast as the lead guitarist in an unsuccessful Cleveland bar band called The Barbusters. Jett plays his sister, the lead singer in the band, who eventually defects to join a heavy metal band called The Hunzz, but ends up back in Cleveland. Thus, in Fox we have a very successful movie star who would probably like to be a mildly successful rock star playing a very unsuccessful rock star in a movie costarring a moderately successful rock star (Jett) who would probably like to be a reasonably successful movie star but who is playing a very unsuccessful rock star. Fox is very unconvincing as a rock star, which would explain why he, after a less-than-triumphant tour of Erie, Pennsylvania, ends up back in Cleveland. But Jett, a good, real-life, second-tier rock star *is* very convincing as a rock star because she is one, so her ending up back in Cleveland makes no sense whatsoever. For what it's worth, Joan Jett can act better than Michael J. Fox, but, then again, she can probably do a lot of things better than Michael J. Fox. Or Paul Schrader.

The only top-shelf rock star in history who has consistently done memorable work on the screen is David Bowie. Debonair, good-looking, talented, and blessed with a brain roughly twice the size of everyone who ever played in the Eagles combined, Bowie has managed to avoid the dismal roles that come quite naturally to the Adam Ants and Ringo Starrs. Perfectly cast as an anorexic extraterrestrial in Nicholas Roeg's *The Man Who Fell to Earth*; he was superb as a wicked goblin in *Labyrinth*; icily mystifying as a British Army officer in *Merry Christmas, Mr. Lawrence*; cadaverously effective as an aging vampire in *The Hunger*; amusing as a con-artist bartender in *The Linguini Incident*; and the only good thing in the pestilential 1986 musical *Absolute Beginners*. With the exception of *The Man Who Fell to Earth*, all of these films are victimized by serious artistic problems—*Labyrinth* has too many Muppets; *The Hunger* has too few scenes with Susan Sarandon and Catherine Deneuve in bed together; *The Linguini Incident* has Rosanna Arquette; *Absolute Beginners* has no script; and *Merry Christmas, Mr. Lawrence* has an overbearing soundtrack, a weird plot line, and somehow manages to create the impression that Tom Conti has been airlifted out of *Reuben, Reuben* and into *The Bridge on the River Kwai* while Bowie has once again fallen to earth and been unfortunate enough to land in a part of it occupied by the Japanese army.

Still, with the single exception of the absolutely atrocious *Absolute Beginners*, all of Bowie's films are worth watching, if only because of his unrehearsed strangeness. Bowie is the only rock star to have ever brought anything to the movies that the movies didn't already have. He is also the most enduring of the seventies great glamorous weirdos. There will always be a place in my heart for the Zigster.

There will always be a place in my heart for David Byrne, as well, but it isn't really fair to call whatever the Talking Heads lead singer is doing in *True Stories* "acting." And despite the coy charm and outstanding soundtrack of this condescendingly affectionate little film about a small Texas town, director Byrne must be taken to task for giving John Goodman one of his first starring roles, thus opening the floodgates to an era in which the tubby thespian has imposed the same brutal rule of law on the American film industry that Gerard Depardieu has long exerted in France: *No movie gets made in this country unless I'm in it.*

Before moving on to the final frontier of this essay, it would be unprofessional to overlook some of the better, if quickly forgotten, acting performances by rock stars in recent years, as well as some of the worst. Tina Turner was just swell in *Mad Max Beyond Thunderdome* and *Tommy*, enlivening the proceedings with her own special brand of postnuclear oompah, and Levon Helm, the dour, low-key drummer from The Band, was splendid as Sissy Spacek's dour pappy in *Coal Miner's Daughter*. Alice Cooper was useless as a piano-playing gigolo in Mae West's unbearable 1983 swan song, *Sextette*, but certainly no worse than Arlo Guthrie in *Alice's Restaurant*, the interminable Arthur Penn movie based on Guthrie's interminable song of roughly the same name. Phil Collins was passable as a good-natured Cockney train robber in the otherwise brainless *Buster*, mustering a kind of Grade-B Bob Hoskins bluff-and-bluster, which is about what one would expect from a man who started his rock career as a drummer in the world's fourth-most-pretentious rock band (try as they might, Genesis could never wrestle the top spots away from Pink Floyd, Yes, and The Moody Blues), and who now makes his money singing bland, recycled Motown tunes. Debbie Harry, the Madonna prototype who enjoyed about three years of fame as the lead singer from the late-seventies band Blondie was passable as Sonny Bono's wife in *Hairspray*, but was useless in *Roadies*, *Videodrome*, *Tales from the Dark Side* and *Forever, Lulu*, and actually made New Jersey seem even more depressing than it really is when she played a psychopathic accountant's mousy wife in *Union City*. Last but not least,* John Doe of the very good L.A. punk band X was very bad in *Great Balls of Fire*. The film did not get an X-rating, but he should have.

Tom Waits and Lyle Lovett we are not going to mention here, even though Lovett was amusing in The Player, *and Waits has been passable in numerous films, because Waits is basically a cabaret artist and thus belongs in an essay speculating who might appear in as many bad movies as Lizi Minnelli, and Lovett is basically a country-and-western singer and thus belongs in an essay speculating who might appear in as many bad movies as Roy Rogers.*

This brings us to what Monty Python might call the fulcrum of my gist, to a discussion of the two living rock stars who are the only serious pretenders to Elvis Presley's crown of cinematic crumminess. Still young enough to make dozens of deliriously stupid movies, Madonna is not to be taken lightly. Though she started out okay, delivering an engaging performance as a feisty punk in *Desperately Seeking Susan*, and was adequate as a tart in *A League of Their Own* and as a tart in *Dick Tracy*, Madonna has also been charged with such cinematic moving violations as *Shanghai Surprise*, *Who's That Girl?* (a.k.a., *What's That Smell?*), *Bloodhounds of Broadway*, *Shadows and Fog*, and the massively hyped dud *Truth or Dare*. In *Shanghai Surprise*, Madonna clearly demonstrated that she cannot act; in *Bloodhounds of Broadway*, she clearly demonstrated that she cannot sing or dance (she is actually outclassed on both scores by Jennifer Grey), while in *Who's That Girl*, she clearly demonstrated not only that she's too chubby and ordinary-looking to replace Marilyn Monroe as the national heartthrob, but that *she's not cute*. (Casting Madonna as a girl who's supposed to be pixielike is like casting Heinrich Himmler as the Tooth Fairy.)

With five genuinely awful, money-losing movies under her belt (*Shanghai Surprise*, *Who's That Girl?*, *Shadows and Fog*, *Bloodhounds of Broadway*, *Truth or Dare*), plus her three successes, Madonna cannot be dismissed as a pretender to the King's crown. Young, rich, ruthlessly megalomaniacal and hysterically vulgar, Madonna could, given time, live to make dozens of movies as bad as *Harum Scarum*, *Kissin' Cousins*, and *Girls! Girls! Girls!* The possibilities are endless: Madonna as a pharmacist's daughter, Madonna as a half-breed on the warpath, Madonna as a racecar driver, Madonna as a crusading doctor in a free clinic in the ghetto. Leaves you, well, breathless.

Still, if the staggering cinematic records set by Elvis Presley are ever to be erased, the new name in the record book will probably not be Madonna, but her fellow midwesterner, Prince. Madonna, it must be remembered, has already wasted three golden opportunities by making a good film (*Desperately Seeking Susan*) and two passable ones (*Dick Tracy*, *A League of Their Own*). Prince, veteran of three dramatic roles, has never made a movie that is not completely and utterly idiotic, and he never will. Launching his career with the sexist, juvenile, moronic *Purple Rain* in 1984, Prince has since made the sexist, moronic, juvenile *Under the Cherry Moon*, and *Graffiti Bridge*, which is really little more than a sexist, moronic, juvenile sequel to *Purple Rain*. Too short to rock and roll but too young to die, Prince makes movies so artfully unintelligent that they make Elvis's work look like John Gielgud's.

Moreover, there are a number of haunting parallels between the lives of the King and the Prince. Both men suffered from early musical burnout, producing their best work when they were very young. Both men wear tight pants. Both men have weird facial hair. And both men are identified with second-echelon cities that begin with the letter *M*.

Ooo-ee-oh.

Though Prince may not hang around long enough to make as many bad movies as Elvis, on a frame-for-frame, reel-for-reel basis, he is already in Elvis's league, having acted in and directed three of the most uncompromisingly stupid movies of all time, movies that even the King would have to be impressed by. Like Elvis, Prince makes 'em big, and like Elvis, Prince makes 'em stupid. Now the only question is: Can Prince make 'em big and stupid in bunches?

Personally, I think the kid's got a shot.

10 SACRED COW

In Barbra Streisand's very first movie—a perky Broadway play successfully translated to the silver screen in 1968—the filmmakers immediately address the subject of the actress's unconventional physical appearance, most particularly her obtrusive nose.

"So she looks a bit off balance; she possesses golden talents—or is that a pill too bitter to digest?" inquires her mother, and, by extension, the people bankrolling this project, who were justifiably concerned about the public's digestive capacities. "You've got to face facts," Mother counsels Streisand, playing the youthful, ungainly Fanny Brice. "You don't look like other girls." Streisand, in one of the final moments of modesty in her career, agrees, conceding, "I'm a bagel on a plateful of onion rolls." The movie was the appropriately titled *Funny Girl*.

In Barbra Streisand's next-to-last movie, a gloomy Broadway play unsuccessfully translated to the silver screen in 1987, the filmmakers *do not* directly address the subject of Streisand's physical appearance, instead allowing the actress to share the screen with the only living thespian whose schnozzle can give hers serious competition: Karl Malden. This time out, the audience is asked to believe that Streisand—same eyes, same nose, same general facial contours, with twenty extra years on the odometer—is a $500-a-night call girl capable of "taking your body to heaven and sending your mind south," and of "spoiling you so bad you'll hate every other woman you touch." The film was the appropriately titled *Nuts*, which Streisand, director Martin Ritt, and everyone else associated with this dotty project quite clearly was.

It had taken Barbra Streisand a quarter-century of remorseless self-infatuation to get to the point where she would make the ridiculous *Nuts*, but that she finally arrived at her destination should come as a surprise to no one. For as long as anyone can remember, Barbra Streisand had been defying gravity, beguiling audiences into suspending belief for anywhere between 90 and 146 minutes, and accepting the premise that this intoxicatingly plain-looking, self-absorbed Tartar could pass herself off as:

1. A passionately committed communist organizer on an American college campus during the 1940s;
2. A teenaged Polish Jewess masquerading as a yeshiva boy in pre–World War I eastern Europe;
3. An incredibly talented, helpful psychiatrist;
4. God's gift to Robert Redford, Ryan O'Neal, Yves Montand, Omar Sharif, Kris Kristofferson, Nick Nolte and, by extension, all living males.

Millions of her fans have been willing to ignore the overwhelming physical evidence and swallow the Streisand schtick whole, while the rest of us look on in utter disbelief, wondering, "How the hell does she do it?"

Well, assuming that she isn't doing it with pure luck, or with an ineffable charm that has heretofore gone undetected, she must be doing it with brawn and determination and chutzpah, and with an indisputable, but invariably misdirected and abused talent. Clearly, Barbra Streisand is a talented, some might even

argue *great*, singer who has recorded a handful of fine albums; a
competent director; and an accomplished actress who has starred
in a handful of halfway decent films. She has won every acting
and singing award worth mentioning, some of them more than
once, and has been a legitimate superstar since John F. Kennedy
was in office. Save for Goldie Hawn and Jane Fonda, she is the
only actress to work continual box office magic in the past two
decades, to bring in the kinds of dollars that Meryl Streep and
Glenn Close and Jessica Lange and a host of other more gorgeous,
more gifted, more gregarious actresses can only dream of. She
is, and always has been, a force to be reckoned with.

So what? Neil Diamond is a force to be reckoned with. So are
Kenny Rogers and Barry Manilow and Dolly Parton and a host of
other MOR acts who probably seemed jaded and tired all the way
back in the maternity ward. It isn't as if America doesn't have a
tradition of rewarding its hokey old show biz troupers. It's just
that America doesn't reward *all* of them, and it doesn't reward all
of them equally. In fact, it's kind of fickle. It picks an Andy
Williams over a Vic Damone, a Dean Martin over an Al Martino,
a Hulk Hogan over a Rowdy Roddy Piper, a Merv Griffin over a
Mike Douglas. It decides that it will accept Madonna for canon-
ization, but will banish Debbie Harry to cultural Purgatory;
needs Dick Van Dyke, but doesn't need Jerry Van Dyke; wants
the Judds but doesn't want Judd Nelson. It says "Yes" to an
infantile band like the New Kids on the Block, "No" to a juvenile
band like the Bay City Rollers; "Golly, gee!" to a comeback by
Brenda Carlisle and the Four Go-Go's, "Hell, no!" to a comeback
by Frankie Valli and the Four Seasons. Fortunes have been won
and lost trying to figure out which particular load of horseshit
America will buy next.

America, in short, has a virtually limitless appetite for
schmaltz, and in the kingdom of the schmaltzeroonies, no one
has enjoyed as long a reign as Barbra Streisand. For here is a
performer who, until quite recently, has never lost sight of her
real audience: anyone who wasn't at, wanted to be at, or claimed

to be at Woodstock. And when she does make a mistake with a film project that goes awry, she quickly buries the incriminating evidence with a demographically satisfactory album. Thus, when the excessively ethnic *Hello, Dollushki!* (*Yentl*) and the claustrophobic *Nuts* failed to score big with her audiences, Streisand came right back with her overwrought collection of Broadway anthems, just as she had earlier erased the memory of disasters like *Up the Sandbox* with her uplifting TV specials and LPs. On the great Highway of Life, this is one gal who never wanders too far away from the median strip.

Unlike the Streeps and Sarandons and Langes and Hoffmans and De Niros, who seem almost embarrassed at being movie stars (though they don't mind the pay), Streisand is Miss Torch Song from start to finish, a direct descendant of such Show Biz Personalities and All-Purpose Artistes as Judy Garland, Edith Piaf, and Ethel Merman, and the spiritual mother of the most relentless self-promoter of them all: the incomparable voter-registration campaigner and fetishist Madonna. (Garland actually passed the ceremonial torch to Streisand in a memorable 1963 TV special, holding out hope that Madonna will one day gather up Streisand's fallen mantle in a big-budget, prime-time TV special, with special guests Ray Charles, Gladys Knight & the Pips and George Burns.) Like Garland and Madonna, as well as Frank Sinatra—another performer whose career hers resembles—Streisand has always been able to profit from the double-whammy effect of being both a singer and an actress.

Basically, this is a judicious form of portfolio diversification, enabling a performer to keep a flagging acting career alive by recording a successful album, and vice versa. Unlike Garland and Sinatra, however, Streisand has never been able to achieve predeath beatification, that gloriously transcendent moment when even your worst critics are willing to forget that you're basically an unacceptable human being and instead concentrate on your fabulous gifts as a performer. That's why we have The Two Franks—the one who menaces reporters and acts like a pig, and

the one who sings "I Have Dreamed"—and the two Garlands—
the one who hits the sauce, gets wasted on chemicals, and self-
destructs in public, and the one who sings "Somewhere Over the
Rainbow" and meets Louie in St. Louis. Streisand has never,
and will never, achieve that status where critics instinctively
separate the artist from the art. She'll always be Streisand; you
know, the one who fell in love with her hairdresser.

Streisand is probably the only artist of the twentieth century
who can simultaneously be compared to both Bob Dylan and
Sammy Davis Jr. Like Sammy, she started out as a gifted,
respected performer who helped breathe life into a stagnant
idiom (yes, Sammy was once considered a great jazz singer), and
like him she has ended up a show-business cliché. Like Sammy,
she started out as a critic's favorite, and like him she ended up
being thought of as a crass megalomaniac. Like Sammy, she has
led a spectacularly vulgar public life filled with trashy love affairs
and clumsy dabblings in politics and religions, and like him she
has spent a good part of her adult life trying to figure out why
she keeps getting left off the annual list of the World's Classiest
People.

The comparisons with Dylan, while less obvious, are no less
powerful. Bear in mind that at one point in the early sixties, in
the dark night before the British invasion, Dylan and Streisand
were the brightest young stars in the musical firmament, holding
out hope for those doomed to life in a universe dominated by
Leslie Gore, Frankie Avalon, Neil Sedaka, Paul Anka, and other
names too horrid to be printed in this, a family publication. Both
Streisand and Dylan worked for Columbia Records; both were, in
fact, despised by a large percentage of the powers-that-be at that
label. They were despised for what they stood for, and what they
stood for was anything that Steve Lawrence and Edie Gormé
didn't stand for. But unlike Dylan, who managed to stay on the
cutting edge of popular culture from his debut album in 1961 all
the way up until his motorcycle accident in 1967, and who has
launched at least two successful comebacks (*Nashville Skyline* in

1969 and *Blood on the Tracks* in 1974), Barbra Streisand remained on the cutting edge of this civilization for only about two hours and twenty-seven minutes in her entire career.

Having perfected her deceptively overwrought style when she was singing "People" and other numbers of that ilk, Streisand has remained locked inside a safe, traditional groove ever since, only occasionally sallying forth to briefly masquerade as something she is not (her hypocritical attempt to pass herself off as a rocker on *Stoney End* and *Emotion*) or to make a fool of herself (her disco duet with Donna Summers, her absurd *Classical Barbra*). As an actress, she made her debut by appearing in a pair of full-dress, big-budget musicals at a time the idiom had all three feet in the grave (*Funny Girl* came out the year Bobby Kennedy was assassinated, the year of the Chicago riots, the year of the Tet Offensive). As a singer, Streisand has also remained stubbornly middle-of-the-road, churning out Johnny Mathis covers when it was fashionable to cover Johnny Mathis, and then, when it was fashionable to record recycled TV jingles, she recorded recycled TV jingles with Neil Diamond ("You Don't Bring Me Flowers"). The fact that some critics treated her *Broadway Album* as a daring artistic departure shows just how daring the rest of her career has been. (It also shows that a lot of critics are stupid.) People who record Jerome Kern numbers in 1987 are not making daring artistic moves. Lou Reed makes daring artistic moves. Woody Allen makes daring artistic moves. Barbra Streisand makes the sequel to *Funny Girl* and the eight hundredth remake of *A Star Is Born*. Think of her as a thinner Elvis.

For most of her career, Streisand has had an adversarial relationship with the serious press in this country. Some of this is her own fault; if you treat journalists like you're better than they are, they will go to great lengths to remind you that you're not. Especially if you're cross-eyed and have a huge proboscis. It is odd that Streisand has not learned her lesson; surely she must have noticed that there are zillions of actors and actresses and athletes and musicians who have a glorious relationship with the press: Bob Hope, Joe Montana, Katharine Hepburn, Julius Erving, Alec Guinness, to name but a few. Of course, it helps that people like Alec Guinness don't go around marrying their hairdressers.

That Streisand cannot win the respect of serious critics must be a source of great consternation to her, because fundamentally this is a woman driven by two powerful drives: She would like to be a gorgeous sex object, and she would like to be taken seriously. Neither of these is possible—though the latter was once, before *A Star Is Born* and *The Main Event* and *All Night Long* and *Nuts* put an end to all that. The first drive was a hard sell from the word go: When you want to be a sex goddess, but Mother Nature never processed the requisition slip, you end up making an ass of yourself, as Streisand did in the vulgar aerobic sequences from *The Main Event*. When you want to end up being respected, you don't waste fifteen years of your life trying to make monstrosities like *Yentl*, a bloated, cross-dressed version of *Fiddler on the Roof*, butchering what started out as a charming short story by the great writer Isaac Bashevis Singer. (Singer hated the movie so much that he wrote an article in *The New York Times* saying how much he hated it. And Singer was a really nice man. Proving that in Streisand's case, it's the song, not the Singer, that's at fault.)

Why does Streisand do all this heavy lifting? Probably because she has figured out that history is not in the hands of the people who make it, but in the hands of the people who write about the people who make it. And, unfortunately for Streisand, movie critics of any repute by and large have very little tolerance for her trashy Vegas sensibility. Streisand may rake in megabucks off abortions such as *A Star Is Born* and *The Main Event*, but surely she realizes that when the history of the 1970s and 1980s is written, it will be Jane Fonda and Meryl Streep and Jessica Lange and maybe even Susan Sarandon who will be remembered as the interesting actresses, while Streisand—if she is remembered at all—will be celebrated as the cinematic equivalent of Fleetwood Mac: a mildly appealing MOR act who made a lot of money and then went home.

The tragedy of all this is that it could have been different. Kmart talents such as Sylvester Stallone and Julio Iglesias appeal to the same general, culturally petrified audiences as Streisand, but even if they had tried being something other than they are, they would have failed. Kenny Rogers didn't become Kenny Rogers because the Mick Jagger role was already filled; he became Kenny Rogers because he's a two-bit lounge lizard who's lucky he's not lounging with an even worse class of lizards. Streisand, on the other hand, started out with talent, panache, and even a certain bohemian charm, then worked her way down to the two-day rental bin. The Streisand of *Funny Girl*, *On a Clear Day*, *The Owl and the Pussycat*, *What's Up, Doc?* and even *For Pete's Sake*, the Streisand who had not yet succumbed to her own self-delusions, could have been a terrific comedienne, could have made a whole string of intelligent, entertaining, commercially viable comedies that would have won her the grudging esteem of the Woody Allen crowd, the revival house crowd, the postcollegiate artsy crowd. And, yes, even the critics. Well, maybe.

But, as Shaun Considine makes clear in his encylopedic and highly entertaining *Barbra Streisand: The Woman, the Myth, the Music* (which isn't nearly as pretentious as the title would suggest), Streisand didn't even like *What's Up, Doc?* She thought it was small. She thought it was beneath her. In fact, it was one of the last great screwball comedies made in this country. Released just a couple of years before the film industry would single-handedly be nuked by the cheeseball, adolescent comedy of Murray Chase Aykroyd Belushi Candy Moranis Ramis & Waterhouse, *What's Up, Doc?* is still a hilarious motion picture. "It really holds up," as those of us born less recently than Sting say. Directed by the young and still gifted Peter Bogdanovich, and featuring the young and still gifted Madeline Kahn (her debut role, in fact), the young and still gifted Ryan O'Neal, and assorted other young and still gifted actors and actresses (Randy Quaid, Michael Murphy), the movie had a clever plot, snappy dialogue, a sprightly, civilized soundtrack, a terrific car chase, and a sympathetic, winning Barbra Streisand, who had somehow been cajoled into acting, and not turning into a one-woman wrecking crew. But Streisand never made another movie like that. She wanted to do *important* work. Important work like . . . *A Star Is Born*.

A Star Is Born is the most explicitly autobiographical of Streisand's films, her ham-fisted attempt to abolish the 1960s, an era she was *in*, but manifestly not *of*. (I personally do not know anyone in my age group—the Age of Aquarius—who would admit to liking Barbra Streisand. On the other hand, I always thought that detesting people like Barbra Streisand was what the sixties were all about.) The ludicrous premise of this, her most commercially successful film, is that a good-looking, talented, yet self-destructive rock singer not unlike Jim Morrison would have fallen head over heels in love with an insipid cabaret singer not unlike Melissa Manchester. In the history of idiotic movies— and indeed in the history of idiotic movies entitled *A Star Is Born*—there are very few scenes more shamefacedly self-adulatory than the moment when Streisand, attending a benefit concert for American Indians, captivates a roomful of hard rock fans with her schlocky ballads. Such an occurrence does not square with my recollection of what was known in both the late 1960s and middle 1970s as Reality. If Barbra Streisand had appeared at, say, the concert for Bangladesh, and tried to upstage George Harrison or Bob Dylan, the fans might very well have used the money raised for the starving children of Bangladesh to buy up the world's remaining food supplies and starve her instead. In a stadium filled with real-live, hard-core, rock 'n' roll fans, Barbra Streisand would have had a hard time upstaging Badfinger, much less Ringo Starr. Unless, of course, Streisand had already sent everyone's body to heaven and mind south.

Since this article *is* being written by a man, a legitimate argument can be made that the author has a genetic indisposition toward Streisand the Emasculator. Indeed, Streisand's most enduring contribution to our civilization could be as a feminist role model: the ugly duckling who makes it big by chewing up and spitting out men. In this sense, she has much in common with Margaret Thatcher, Golda Meir, and Indira Gandhi, certified ballbusters all who didn't get where they got by being kewpie dolls. Conversely, *they* would have probably chosen better roles than *The Main Event* and *A Star Is Born*.

Continuing this thought, let us recall that, while blazing her way across the silver screen, Streisand has had the help of an extraordinarily docile group of male and male*ish* costars who apparently did not mind getting bent, torn, folded, and mutilated by their leading lady. Her list of victims include such professional pretty boys as Omar Sharif and Ryan O'Neal; a pair of post-Watergate sensitive guys (Kris Kristofferson, Robert Redford); and even a few would-be *menschen* (Richard Dreyfuss, George Segal, Mandy Patinkin, Nick Nolte) who simply didn't have the firepower to compete with what is less a living, breathing human being than a force of nature. Walter Matthau, who apparently loathed working with Streisand (he stopped loathing her after he realized he never had to work with her again), fares best against her (in *Hello, Dolly!*), with Yves Montand (*On a Clear Day . . .*) a close second. Of course, Montand, who got his start by keeping Edith Piaf—a short, French Judy Garland—amused, knows that in the war of the sexes, you sometimes have to play for a tie. Streisand makes mincemeat out of the rest of the gang, particularly Kristofferson, who caps off his desecration of Jim Morrison's memory by climbing into his sportscar, putting the pedal to the metal, replacing one of his dreary tapes with one of hers, and then committing suicide. Faced with a choice between suicide and having to listen to "Evergreen" again, I think he made the right decision.

Moreover, in depressing news for plain-looking women trying

to make it big in Hollywood, Streisand's success does not seem to have spawned a subsequent generation of Streisands. Unlike Dustin Hoffman, whose success opened the door for a lot of other short guys who don't look like Charlton Heston or Leslie Howard, Streisand has not institutionalized her success. While the ranks of male movie stars abound with actors sporting unconventional looks (Jack Nicholson, Keith Carradine, Robert De Niro, Al Pacino, Robin Williams, Bruce Willis, Richard Dreyfuss), the female stars of the 1970s and the 1980s are still pretty much the same as female stars of the 1930s, 1940s, and 1950s: babes. Plus, of course, Meryl Streep.

When all is said and done, Streisand's is one of the truly weird careers in the history of show business. At a time when Dustin Hoffman was making *The Graduate*, and everybody else was making love, not war, or some combination thereof, Streisand was making 146-minute musicals (just try sitting through one of them today). At a time when punks were trying to rescue rock 'n' roll from CSN&Y, the Hollies, James Taylor, the Eagles, assorted people named Stewart, and, yes, Yes, Streisand was making a movie about the doomed love affair between an alkie rock singer cranking out retooled Quicksilver Messenger Service outtakes and what is, for all intents and purposes, Carly Simon. Or worse. (For a monumental hoot, catch the lighter sequence at the end of *A Star Is Born*, as well as the scene where Kristofferson tells Streisand that hearing her sing was like "hooking a marlin." Which, in many ways, it was.)

But herein lies much of her appeal. Streisand embodies everything that is tacky and cheap and hopelessly corny and unsophisticated about Middle America. *A Star Is Born* is the 1960s the way the *Hello, Dolly!* crowd imagined it. *The Way We Were* is the McCarthy era the way the *Funny Girl* crowd imagined it (bear in mind that as a lefty organizer, the folks Streisand was handing out leaflets for included Josef Stalin). *Yentl* is eastern Europe, circa 1904, the way western Hollywood, circa 1983, imagined it: more songs, fewer pogroms (the educationally defi-

cient Barbra, according to Shaun Considine, was not aware that
the Nazis had destroyed the Warsaw ghetto, making it all but
impossible to shoot "Papa, Can You Hear Me?" there). All of
these films are an insult to anyone who ever grew up in any of
these places, or lived through any of these eras. Or died in any
of them. Obviously, all of them made money.

Ugh, she should have stuck to comedies, where she had the
knack. She could have been hilarious. Instead, in seeking to
carve out a larger place for herself, she made herself into a figure
of mirth. By the time she made *Nuts*, with the scenes of her
flashing her money-maker at Richard Dreyfuss, autographing
cheesecake photos, and slugging her attorney, Streisand had
completely lost touch with reality. Her mind had gone south.

I have two favorite moments in Barbra Streisand movies. The
first is the scene in *The Way We Were* where Streisand tries to talk
Robert Redford out of selling his novel to a Hollywood studio
because he's "too good" to work in the movie business. *Barbra
Streisand trying to talk Robert Redford out of going to Hollywood
because it would compromise his artistic integrity?*

I'm confused.

But my all-time favorite moment in the Streisand *oeuvre* occurs
at the conclusion of *Hello, Dolly!* Just before one of those painful,
fade-out reprises of the namby-pamby production numbers staged
earlier in the film, the newly married Streisand and Matthau
disappear into a stately home perched on a hill overlooking the
Hudson River. At first glance the house looks elegant and
charming, but when you take a second look (with the aid of a
VCR rewind unit filmgoers didn't have twenty years ago), you
notice that something is wrong. The house sort of resembles a
church, but it also sort of resembles a schoolhouse, with a
strange little belfry and a bunch of those ornamental pillars that
dominate the facade but don't actually support anything. The
house, which is supposed to be a stately home where the couple
will live happily ever after, is in fact an architectural smorgasbord, not unlike those monstrosities that people who made their

fortune in the folding-chair rental business *design themselves*, so
they can post a sign outside reading "Built Expressly for Cindy
and Kevin Tierney by Giorgio Tomasso & Sons." The house, in
short, seems daunting, impressive, and classy on the surface,
but on further inspection it reveals itself to be one huge load of
crap. Barbra was right at home.*

**Since this essay appeared in 1991, Streisand has produced, directed, starred
in, and, presumably, designed George Carlin's wardrobe in* Prince of Tides. *In
this Freud-by-numbers melodrama, Streisand plays a fabulously successful
Manhattan psychiatrist, married to a fabulously successful concert violinist,
who falls in love with a dysfunctional South Carolinian ne'er-do-well hunk.
Skillfully weaving an adroit psychic macramé of Adlerian, Jungian, and
Streisandian therapeutic techniques, Dr. Lowenstein helps her repressed white
trash patient recover from a childhood experience involving a large man who
happened to be standing directly behind him. Once again, Streisand had sent
a man's mind south. Only this time she had sent it Deep South.*

The long-suffering victim is played by Nick Nolte.

11 THE LAPP OF LUXURY

Three years ago, Renny Harlin was just another obscure Finnish director scuffling to make ends meet in Hollywood. With two low-budget films to his credit—*Born American*, a sort of *Midnight Express Goes to Helsinki*, and *Prison*, an institutional *Friday the 13th, Part VI*—and not much money to show for it, Harlin could easily have done what his partner Marcus Selin did: pack up his dreams of stardom and go home.

"But my feeling was, I'd rather die penniless here than go back," Harlin says today. Well, Renny Harlin is not going to die penniless. Impressed by his work on *Nightmare on Elm Street IV*, a $5 million film that made $50 million, Hollywood has come clambering to his door, paying him a reported $500,000 to direct Andrew Dice Clay's anxiously awaited starring debut *Ford Fairlane*, $750,000 to crank out *Die Hard II*, $1.5 million to do *Aliens III*, and $3 million to direct *Gale Force*, a *Key Largo*–type drama that has not yet been cast. The Renny Harlinization of director's salaries has not gone unnoticed; as Casey Silver, head of production at Universal, remarked in *The New York Times*: "In an environment in which Carolco pays Renny Harlin $3 million, what is Steven Spielberg worth?"

Good question, but Harlin is too busy to answer it. When visited in Los Angeles during the breakneck shooting of *Die Hard II*, Harlin was also still editing *Ford Fairlane* while scripting *Gale Force*. A handsome, likable thirty-year-old chap, Harlin sports a beard and shoulder-length hair that suggest the lingering grooming influence of Steppenwolf or one of the other sixties bands that he so admires. Patrolling the set of *Die Hard II*, the man who is not only the most famous Finnish director, but also quite probably its tallest (6'3"), seems perfectly at home in the big leagues. However, it should be noted that Harlin made what little of a reputation he has by churning out low-budget adventure movies that he managed to get done on time. When interviewed for this story, Harlin was experiencing the first cost overruns of his infant career, as Mother Nature cavalierly refused to supply the snowstorm the director so desperately needed to finish certain important scenes in the film.

The crew had already made an unsuccessful expedition to Moses Lake, Washington, and would soon depart for an equally unsuccessful junket to the wilds of northern Michigan. Meanwhile, Bruce Willis was wandering off to start work on another picture. These are the kinds of problems that Harlin never had when he was still making films like *Prison* for Irwin Yablans (*Halloween*, *Roller Boogie*); when you're working for Irwin Yablans, you don't have to worry about too many of the stars drifting off to their other major cinematic commitments. Certainly not Viggo Mortensen.

Right now, Harlin is so busy that he literally can not keep track of his own *oeuvre*. For example, when discussing *Nightmare on Elm Street IV*, he fondly recalls having written a scene in which the unappetizing Freddy Krueger munches on a slice of pizza decorated with the tiny anchovylike heads of his victims and remarks, "Ah! soul food!" But Harlin says that he was told by his producers to leave out the wisecrack, because "soul food" is a sixties allusion, and "the kids won't get that." Well, as it turns out, the soul-food comment *is* in the movie, and happens to be one of the funniest items in the whole film.

"Does he say that?" exclaims Harlin in disbelief. His face is illuminated by a huge, sheepish smile. Gee, Renny, welcome to your own life.

Poised on the edge of stardom, the Wotan the Conqueror looka-like is directing a scene for *Die Hard II* that takes place in a church somewhere in rural Virginia. In the film, a bunch of paramilitary crackpots is determined to extricate a Manuel Noriega clone from the clutches of the U.S. government, and has taken control of what is obviously Dulles Airport in Washington. (Dulles had originally supplied security guards' patches and other materials to the filmmakers, but when airport officials discovered what the film was about they withdrew their assistance and insisted that Dulles not be identified.)

In the scene being shot today, the assistant villain (played by Bill Sadler) is getting ready to give the order that will seemingly doom the airplane on which Willis's wife (played by Bonnie Bedelia) is traveling. Sadler is supposed to say something like, "Losing the whole first unit wasn't part of the plan," but after a couple of takes approaches Harlin and says, "I'd really like to say, 'Losing the whole first unit wasn't part of the *fucking* plan.'" Harlin doesn't think that's such a good idea.

"No," says the director, smiling at the actor with the sort of paternal forbearance directors have shown toward insecure thespians since the industry's beginnings. "He's in control. He doesn't *need* to curse."

Which is pretty much what you can say about Harlin himself: Until he has his first major disaster, because of cost overruns or box office boredom, he's in control. Which raises the question: What *is* the biggest difference between making low-budget schlockoids for people like Irwin Yablans and $40 million mega-blockbusters for people like Joel Silver?

"The most people I ever had in *Prison* was eighty extras," says Harlin. "Now, if I want a helicopter, I get a helicopter. If I want a thousand people, I get a thousand people. And now the special effects are safe. They don't blow up in your face anymore."

Is the most famous Finnish director on the planet surprised by how fast his star has risen? Does he ever wonder what other, more celebrated directors with more impressive track records must make of all this?

"I have no idea how they feel about it," says Harlin. "I hear some people have been saying, 'How does this accordion adjust? Where is the end of this accordion Renny has?' "

Yes, one can readily imagine people in Beverly Hills using precisely those words.

Renny Harlin was born Renny Lauri Mauritz Harjola in 1959 in Helsinki, Finland, where as a child he would sometimes accompany his father, a doctor, to his job at the local prison. These grim formative experiences would stand him in good stead years later when he made his first three movies, two of which deal with prisons and one of which deals with a nightmare, part IV.

As a youth, Harlin was greatly influenced by American movies, enrolling in film school at age nineteen. He immediately began sending scripts to the Finnish Film Foundation, which immediately began sending them back, branding them overly commercial. "Somehow the feeling seemed to be that movies are not supposed to make money," explains Harlin.

He drifted into the TV commercial business at age twenty-one, winning Finland's coveted Best Industrial Short Film of the Year Award. He also did a comedy about Finnish insurance companies—can't-miss material—before teaming up with Marcus Selin, who had made money in the video distribution business, to set up a production company. They raised enough cash to shoot twenty minutes of a very bad film called *Arctic Heat*. With this in hand, the two flew off to Hollywood.

Harlin likes people to believe that he made it to the top all by himself, but others deny this, mentioning banished friends, jettisoned sweethearts, and betrayed business associates on both sides of the Atlantic. "I pulled names of producers out of the Yellow Pages," is how Harlin describes his beginnings. "I sold my production company, my house, and took loans. I got rid of everything." Eventually, a Hollywood outfit called Cinema Group agreed to put up $1.1 million for the film.

Arctic Heat, soon rechristened *Born American*, was supposed to star Chuck Norris, but when Harlin and Selin couldn't get enough financing, they instead recruited Norris's son, Mike, who had been sent to Finland by his pop to lay the groundwork for his legendary footwork. The film is a gloomy, horribly acted, lamebrained affair about three American asshole buddies who wander cross the Finn-Soviet border to check out the scene behind the Iron Curtain, and end up blowing up a bunch of trucks and houses and killing a priest, some soldiers, and a load of peasants—not a cool thing to do in a workers' republic, where peasants have a certain cachet.

"We were drunk; we just wanted to see what it was like," explains one of the boys. "Maybe we could just say we're sorry and it was just a big mistake," says another. (Notes Harlin, who learned English in high school, "I write dialogue, but I go through it with the actors to make sure it's right.")

Finally captured by the Soviet police, the three imps are tortured and imprisoned in a dismal jail, from which only Son of Chuck will reemerge. Along the way there are rats, attempted drownings in toilet bowls, suffocation, insanity, and lots of judo kicks by Norris, who has the improbable name of Savoy Brown, a second-tier rock band of the late 1960s. (This is one of Harlin's little jokes.) The movie also features several alarmingly plump, prune-faced actresses.

"Even in Finland you have to pay a lot of money to get girls to show their tits," notes one Renny Harlin buff. "He only had a million, so this is what he got."

Bad as it is, *Born American* does have some nice touches, such as the opening scene, where an animal's death is juxtaposed with the rape of a young girl; and a few artsy shots of babbling brooks and snow-blanketed hills. Still, Harlin's best work is with explosives.

Harlin's eyes light up when the rare artistic elements in his first film are mentioned, but basically he is not very happy with the way the picture turned out. After Cinema Group got interested, he says, "it changed pretty heavily. They believed that this was a great sort of Cold War story. In our story, it was more about what happened to the boys' friendship in prison."

Indeed, Harlin has no sympathy for the boys whatsoever. "My feeling is that they were assholes," he comments. "They were behaving like jerks, and they got what they deserve." All in all, he says, he "was not terribly happy with the way the movie ended up being. All the beautiful stuff got cut out."

Did it ever. In Finland, *Born American* was condemned as a needlessly inflammatory anti-Soviet film, and was banned. According to Harlin, the last time the Finns banned a movie was 1939, another bad year for eastern European cinema. "It was the biggest film ever made in Finland and they banned it," he fumes. "Finally we went to the Supreme Court and proved that it was against the law to ban it because of politics.

"We just put it in Russia because we couldn't afford to go anywhere else," explains the director. "But it could have been Mexico. We were almost embarrassed by the Cold War element.

"Why would Russia take it seriously?" he asks, noting that the film is so cheap that at the very end, when some strange, written epilogue appears on the screen, it actually contains a typographical error.

"There was a spelling mistake, and they were too cheap to change it," Harlin observes with a grin. "They figured: Our audience is illiterate; who cares?"

Harlin says that he and his partner had to put up their own salaries ($10,000) to pay for the film's lab costs, which means that although the film did okay in foreign markets, and eventually made some money for the producers and distributors, he and Selin took a huge bath and had to spend the next year or so living off their credit cards. He still thinks the film could have done better; relaxing on the set of *Die Hard II*, a $40 million project, Harlin argues that détente and perestroika had more to do with the failure of the film than its inherent cinematic shortcomings. "It came out too late," he says, wistfully. "It came out the summer of the Goodwill Games." These were the bargain-basement pseudo-Olympics that Ted Turner took a huge bath on back in 1986. Though Captain Outrageous has never officially acknowledged it, there are some grounds for believing that Harlin's debut as a director may have had something to do with the failure of the Games.

After *Born American*, Harlin tried to get the William Morris Agency interested in his career, but they still had other clients. Fortunately, Irwin Yablans, producer of the original *Halloween*, was so impressed with his work that he hired him to direct *Prison*.

"I gues it's fair to say that I discovered him, because *Prison* was his first real movie," says Yablans. "He's my favorite protégé at the moment; John Carpenter was the first. I know him better than anyone in L.A. I paid his rent; he really was living out of his car; he had a furnished room in some sleazy part of town."

Was Yablans *that* impressed by *Born American*?

"*Born American* was not a complete motion picture," replies Yablans. "But what I look for is the best part of the movie. I don't look for a complete movie; I just look for good parts of them. There was an artsy, creative element in *Born American* in the church scenes, the underground chess scene. I liked that sense of the bizarre, his sense of imagination." (Here Yablans is referring to a subterranean chess game featuring insane prisoners as human chess pieces.)

The bizarre is certainly on full display in *Prison*, a gruesome but well made quickie that stars Lane Smith as a whacked-out warden in a haunted Wyoming penitentiary. What is most appealing about this snappily edited flick is Harlin's trademark—revolting but effective special effects. These include a cell that turns into an oven, melting sneakers, deep-fried facial tissue, disintegrating eyeglasses, blood dripping from light fixtures, microwaved skulls, and, of course, an extraordinarily uncharismatic prison guard who has his face snuggly wrapped inside a serpentine coil of barbed wire that seems to have a life of its own. Yablans is asked if Harlin does not deserve credit for making a film with such spiffy production values on such a tiny budget: around $1.7 million. Actually, he doesn't.

"Those movies are produced as much as they are directed," he notes. "I got the prison for nothing, and we got the townspeople as extras for nothing after the state of Wyoming reneged on its promise to provide extras." Yablans also says that the barbed wire scene was his idea, as were most of the other effects. "For two million bucks, it was a brilliant underground movie."

(Pretty far underground, though; no video store I knew of carried it, so I had to borrow a copy from Harlin himself when I visited L.A.)

Though he is grudging with his praise of Renny the Director, Yablans is very fond of Renny the Guy.

"He's a very well-balanced guy, except that he wants to get every broad in town," says Yablans. "He has a voracious appetite for Hollywood. I think he's the illegitimate son of Joel Silver."

Harlin got his first real agent around the time that *Prison* was released, but despite the $50,000 he made on the film both he and his partner were busted. Selin finally packed it in, but Harlin says he was "too stubborn to give up. I was living in an attic, I would save money to go to the movies every other week. I could not even buy a newspaper. But I wouldn't go back, as long as I had a place to stay."

There are several theories about how Harlin got his big break in *Nightmare on Elm St. IV.* Yablans says he went to bat for his protégé, his former personal manager (Venetia Stevenson) says that she did the leg work, and Harlin, characteristically, is kind of vague. Whatever the answer, *Nightmare on Elm Street IV* made Renny Harlin *the* Renny Harlin we know today, or will know tomorrow. Budgeted at $5.3 million, the fourth entry in this diverting series about a town that goes through one hell of a lot of teenagers without any of the parents getting particularly upset was the most artistically and financially successful of the series, making around $50 million, out of which Harlin got $100,000 and a one-way ticket to the Big Time.

Harlin, who sleepwalks and talks in his sleep, was a natural for the assignment. But he had a new take: "I suggested to them that Freddy had to become a more central element, a James Bond hero. To go for a wider audience, it should go more for surreal comedy."

As a result, the film is even more hiliarious than usual, with Freddy Krueger, the child molester turned serial murderer, firing off all sorts of witty lines such as "How's that for a wet dream?" after a teen is slain in his water bed, or "Why don't you reach out and touch someone?" as he poses menacingly with his attention-getting metallic pinkies. And, as always, there are bloodcurdling special effects: teens' shrunken heads as toppings on Freddy's pizza; a hot babe doing her aerobics who is transmogrified into a slimy insect and then squished as Freddy cackles, "No pain, no gain."

Special effects aside, part of Harlin's appeal is the speed with which he can crank out a product. He says that he storyboards every shot in his films (1,200 drawings in *Prison* alone), a habit that enabled him to start *Nightmare* at the end of February and finish in July. "I delivered the final cut two days after I stopped shooting," he says. Yablans also feels that his protégé's work habits account for much of his success.

"Is he that talented?" asks the veteran producer. "You want to know the truth? First of all, remember, they're only movies, and with the prosperity of the moment, movies are more like manufacturing than anything else. Renny is no more or less talented than about twenty-five of the other guys in this town. What makes Renny different is, he's a hard worker, and he's got a good visual sense." Okay, yes, Yablans admits, "it kind of baffled me that it went so fast. But remember, the studios are being run by executives. They have no sense of what's good or what's bad."

But they have a sense of what makes money, and *Nightmare IV* made $13 million the weekend it opened. After that, says Harlin, beaming, "everything changed. It was like a fairy tale."

On the set of *Die Hard II*, folks are chuckling about a tabloid's reporting that Bruce Willis had cheated death the previous week, when he narrowly avoided being sucked into a jet engine. Actually, the scene has not yet been shot, and the crew has not even visited that location.

Harlin, an easygoing type, seems to have a good relationship with the crew, teasing a young actor whose three lines have been cut out of the film by saying: "Cancel that letter home to your mother." He works relatively fast, shooting each scene just three or four times, but not throwing any tantrums to demand that actors spill their life's blood to deliver the best performances of their lives. This is, after all, traditional, American assembly-line cinema. Get it out by July fourth.

At one point, Harlin confers with a set designer about whether he needs to build a second elevator panel in the control tower for a subsequent action shot. "Isn't moviemaking exciting?" he giggles as the chat ends. The crew seems to think so. "Let's clear the set and make motion picture history," barks one of Harlin's assistants.

Yet relaxed as Harlin seems on the set today, Yablans recalls that this was not always the case.

"He had a big problem on *Prison* because the crew didn't like him," recalls the producer. "He's reticent, by virtue of being

Scandinavian, and they thought he was arrogant. I took him aside and said, 'They don't understand you, Renny, they think you're an asshole.' And he said, 'I'll never be like that again. I want to be everyone's friend. I want to make sure they'll like me.' "

After *Nightmare IV*, Harlin wanted to do a movie about a love affair between an American and an Italian actress in Rome in 1963 during the filming of *Cleopatra*. But then the Diceman entered his life. Harlin was also offered *Aliens III*, and is getting paid play-or-pay for developing that project, which means that he'll get paid even if the film never gets made. Finally, he will receive the $3 million for *Gale Force*. "I really am not interested in making another sequel," he sniffs.

Ford Fairlane continues Harlin's blossoming association with the legends of the silver screen—Mike Norris, Lane Smith, Robert Englund, Bruce Willis—featuring as it does not only the gay community's least-favorite standup comic, but also the multitalented Priscilla Presley and the neophyte thespian Wayne Newton. As Harlin explains: "It's like a parody of *Chinatown*. We're parodying the kind of movie Joel Silver has made." Could he be more specific? "It's a parody of an action movie; it's a parody of a detective movie; it's a parody of a comedy, and it's a parody of a musical."

Does that mean it's okay to bring Mom and the kids?

"I wouldn't go that far," says Harlin. "You have *cousins* or anything?"

Meanwhile, back in Finland, people have been whistling a different tune lately. Even Harlin's old nemeses at the Finnish Film Foundation have expressed an interest in having him return to make a film. "I would love to do it," he says, "but it's unrealistic right now."

But if he did go back, even for a short time, would he take a probing look at his roots, a sort of *Mean Helsinkian Streets*? After all, he is reminded, Woody Allen keeps going back to the old neighborhood. Scorsese keeps going back to the old neighborhood. Coppola keeps going back to the old neighborhood.

"Billy Wilder never went back to the old neighborhood," Harlin shoots back. Any more dumb questions?

How big a star can Harlin become?

"He's a harbinger of the new international phenomenon," says Yablans. "He's going to be a big, big director, the kind who makes one big film after another. He wants to amass a fortune, and drive a red Ferrari, and he makes no bones about it."

"He *really* wants to be an American," says Venetia Stevenson, adding, "His whole story is like a Hollywood cliché." At another point, she wonders, "What is it about this town that makes a guy want to go out and buy a red Ferrari?" Well, growing up in downtown Helsinki with a prison doctor for a dad might have something to do with it.

Yablans says that he once told his "protégé," "Don't go out and become a Hollywood schmuck." He adds, cryptically, "I think he's going to beat the odds." What odds? "Drugs, alcohol, the Hollywood scene. I think Renny's going to beat the odds."

But mustn't it feel strange to be this rich and this much in demand when your only claims to fame are a low-budget Part IV, a soon-to-be-released Part II, and a not-yet-even-scheduled Part III?

"A while ago, it was like looking at people on a pedestal," Harlin confesses. "In a way, now, they are my equals. Whether it's Walter Hill or Oliver Stone, it's people I talk with and share thoughts with, and it has become a natural part of my life."

One of Harlin's numerous ex-friends finds this sort of talk unnerving. "I've seen too many guys like this burn through town and then end up directing Finnish television," he jeers. "I live and breathe for the day I can say, 'Renny, you're Finnish in this town.'"

Is Harlin aware of such hostility?

"Maybe I'm just too ignorant to know it," he says, "but I feel no negative feelings coming from anywhere."

As the man who allegedly calls himself the Finnish Steven Spielberg lets me out of his red Ferrari, I ask if he brought along that copy of *Prison* that I'd had great trouble locating, even at video stores in Manhattan where they give you a complimentary lifetime membership if you can show any knife wounds. Yes, says Harlin, a trifle furtively, fetching the video from the trunk. as I take the plastic case, I notice a little sticker on the side, reading "HORROR." Oh my goodness, it's a rental from a West Hollywood video store! Harlin mutters something about not being able to find a copy in his office and suggests that I view it when I get back to New York and then mail it back.

My heavens, I think to myself; here's a guy with a four-picture, $5 million-plus gig going who just a couple of years ago was making movies so bad that even he himself doesn't keep copies of them in his office or his home. I take *Prison* back to New York and watch it twice, gritting my teeth through Lane Smith's deranged performance as the wired Watergate Warden of West Wyoming. Actually, that barbed wire through the eyeballs is a real nice touch, Renny, so I'll be keeping the movie a few extra days. And when I finally do send it back, I'll ship it without any money to cover overdue charges. You've got the $5 million, pal. You pay the fine.

12 IF YOU CAN'T SAY SOMETHING NICE, SAY IT IN BROKEN ENGLISH

In the appalling 1980 remake of the appalling 1953 remake of the appalling 1927 film *The Jazz Singer* (the first appalling talkie), aspiring rock star Neil Diamond is forced to leave home, ostensibly because of a feud with his father, played by Laurence Olivier. To the unsophisticated moviegoer, the antagonism between father and son might seem to result from the natural desire of the elderly Jewish cantor to see his son follow in his footsteps. A defter analysis of Neil's insubordination could be ascribed to the normal tensions between the Old World patriarch and the upstart immigrant kid. But each of these readings is wrong. The reason Diamond decides to leave home and abandon his cultural heritage is to escape from Olivier's horrendous accent. "I hef no son!" thunders Lord Larry at a critical moment in the film. Yes, and you probably hef no bananas, either.

Olivier's accent in *The Jazz Singer* is one of the monumentally bad accents in the history of cinema, an accent so Promethean in its awfulness that a Jewish friend of mine refers to it as "an act of unintentional yet nonetheless unforgivable anti-Semitism, virulent beyond all conception." Yet it is a testimony to Olivier, lord of the truly bad accents, that his work in *The Jazz Singer* was by no means his worst, and in many ways was the culmination of a lifetime spent honing his skills as a practitioner of the truly grotesque accent. Who can forget Olivier's odd squawking in *The Betsy*, in which his attempts to capture the inflection of an American auto tycoon end up sounding like a cross between Jed Clampett and Scrooge McDuck?

Similarly noteworthy are his frightful central European accent in the Frank Langella *Dracula*, his bizarre Sudanese accent in *Khartoum*, his terrifying Russian accent in *The Shoes of the Fisherman*, and his unjustifiably neglected, yet hilarious, French-Canadian accent in *49th Parallel*.

Of course, it is Olivier's legendarily bad German accents (*Marathon Man*, *The Boys From Brazil*) for which he is best remembered. Yet what is most fascinating about these accents is not so much that they are bad—How should I know? I don't speak German—but that they fulfill the essential criterion for a truly bad accent: They literally take a film prisoner, making it impossible for the viewer to concentrate on anything else. A bad accent is the cinematic equivalent of a festering Limburger cheese planted on a sumptuous dinner table, making it pointless for the gourmand to try thinking about anything other than that *peculiar* odor.

In the epic scope of his bad accents, Olivier has but one serious rival: the indefatigable Marlon Brando, whose vocal gymnastics have eviscerated films as varied as *Burn*, *The Teahouse of the August Moon*, *Viva Zapata*, *The Missouri Breaks*, *The Freshman*, *The Godfather*, and *Mutiny on the Bounty*, in which he concocts the single worst accent in motion picture history. (It's worth noting that some of the finest bad accents appear in remakes, as if the only way of distinguishing the sequel from the original is to imbue it with accents too horrendous to ignore.)

What distinguishes Brando from Olivier is the utterly serendipitous nature of his bad accents. Olivier has a bad French-Canadian accent in *49th Parallel* and a bad Jewish accent in *The*

Jazz Singer, but in each case he is using a bad accent in keeping with his bad role in the bad film. Not so with Brando who, in Arthur Penn's incomparably awful *Missouri Breaks*, plays the psychopathic bounty hunter Lee Clayton with a brogue so thick and attention-getting that even Victor McLaglen might have demanded Gaelic subtitles. Many critics have faulted Jack Nicholson for his diffident performance in this film, but it is my belief that the Man Who Would Be, But Was Not Yet Jack heard the Big Fella's accent during rehearsals, correctly sized this up as a no-win situation, and decided to quietly bank his paycheck and wait for the whole thing to blow over.

To this day, critics debate what Brando was up to in *The Missouri Breaks*, the conventional wisdom being that the mischievous actor took the measure of Penn, concluded that he was dealing with a cream puff, and simply decided to have himself a bit of fun as Bronco Bustin' Brendan. I disagree. It is my earnest belief that in using that diabolically wee Irish accent, Brando was attempting nothing short of a linguistic revolution: speaking, not as he imagined a nineteenth-century Irish gunslinger might, but as he imagined a nineteenth-century Irish gunslinger—and, indeed, *all* Irish people—*should*. In short, Brando was attempting to redefine the Irish accent right in front of our eyes—and ears—hoping that future generations of Irish people would speak with a brogue learned not at the knee of sweet Mother Macree or the equally sweet Rosie O'Grady, but by watching a really bad Arthur Penn film. Of course, I could be wrong about this.

Clearly, one of the great tragedies of the twentieth century is that Olivier and Brando—two of the most colossal hamburgers of all time—never had the chance to trade bad accents in a bad film together.* It is equally clear that, with Olivier's death and Brando's legal problems, there is no one on the scene who can match their innovativeness. (True, Meryl Streep does many, many

---

Since this article appeared, Brando has served up a really bad South African accent in A Dry White Season. *Olivier, of course, is still dead.*

accents, but, as is usually the case with this monotonously talented humanoid, she does them rather well.) Yet it is a mistake to think that the movie industry is completely bereft of noteworthy linguistic marauders. In recent years, Olympia Dukakis, Mickey Rourke, Meg Tilly, Al Pacino, Dennis Quaid, and Cher have each indicated a willingness to seize the torch that has tumbled from Lord Olivier's hand, and in the fullness of time may yet achieve similar immortality. Probably not in a remake of *Richard III*, though.

But to understand where we are going, let us first consider where we have been. To achieve a position in the pantheon of the immortals, to qualify for the Horst Buchholz Nine Hours to Rama Memorial Cup, it is usually necessary to play a character from an ethnic group so far removed from one's own that the baffled audience either makes the star unbelievably rich and famous or starts throwing things at the screen. Among the most celebrated of these performances are New Yawker Barbra Streisand as a nineteenth-century British aristocrat in the flashback scenes from *On a Clear Day You Can See Forever*, white-bread sitcom fugitive Dick Van Dyke as a Cockney chimney sweep in *Mary Poppins*, pioneer anorexic Frank Sinatra as a Parisian bon vivant in *Can-Can*, and professional strange human being Tony Curtis as an English medieval knight in *The Black Shield of Falworth*. Bad as they are, none are the equal of aging child actress Natalie Wood as a Puerto Rican chiquita in *West Side Story*, in which she uses an accent so endearingly stupid that she also qualifies for the Horst Buchholz Aryan Cowpoke Award, in honor of his stultifyingly bad accent in *The Magnificent Seven*.

Yet if these are the Babe Ruths and Lou Gehrigs of the Golden Age of Bad Accents, it is reassuring to note that there are some exciting Jose Cansecos and Darryl Strawberrys alive and well in the present. Foremost among them is Mickey Rourke, whose Irish brogue in the alarmingly bad film *A Prayer for the Dying* is so thick that the authentic Irish actors in the film sound like ringers from Berlitz. Rourke—who plays an IRA hit man anxious to get into a new line of work after he accidentally blows up a school bus loaded with little girls—unleashes an accent so overpowering that both the blustery Bob Hoskins and the energetic Leonid Brezhnev impersonator Alan Bates simply back off. Rourke is so gamey, so slimy, so vile in this film that even his accent seems to be wearing cheap sunglasses. Top o' the mornin' to you, cocksucka. Erin go fuckin' bragh.

A tour de force is also served up by Meg Tilly in the psychosexual thingamajig *The Girl in a Swing*. Posing similar ethical questions to those raised by *A Prayer for the Dying* (if you blow up a school bus full of cute girls, does it mean you're a bad person?), *Girl in a Swing* demands: Can a German translator living in Copenhagen find love and happiness with a British antiques dealer without first murdering her little girl?

That question would be difficult to answer under the best of circumstances, but Tilly, who always brings her own special brand of zaniness to her roles, further complicates things by speaking with a furry thick, furry sexxxy German accent. Frankly, if there's a better film about scantily attired, trilingual infanticides who mumble baby talk in German to twittish British Hummel salesmen out there, we are *all* in for a real treat.

One of the interesting things about bad accents is the serial-killer component: the certainty that actors and actresses who have resorted to bad accents in the past will almost certainly use them again. That's what happened with all-purpose, ethnic mother-in-law Olympia Dukakis—we didn't elect Mikey, so we're stuck with her—who gives the performance of a lifetime in *Steel Magnolias*. Hands-down winner of the 1990 Tony Franciosa Least Convincing Long Hot Summer Southern Accent Award, Dukakis, who looks out of place anywhere south of the garment district, literally blows away the competition, thoroughly upstaging Daryl Hannah (generic redneck), Julia Roberts (Dixie peach), and Shirley MacLaine (bayou ballbuster). This film, so strange that it seems to have been dubbed into English, has one truly memorable line, when MacLaine tells Dukakis, "You are a pig from hell." Correct.

Though hardly the equal of Dukakis, Rourke, and Tilly, there are many other young actors and actresses on the scene whose bad accents bear watching. Well, listening. Daphne Zuniga is impressively unconvincing as a Mexican slut in *Last Rites*; her accent is so bad that when she speaks, guitar music occasionally swells up in the background to lend an air of authenticity to her hot tamale delivery. Dennis Quaid, who scored big with his Cajun patois in *The Big Easy* also wins points for his loony accent in *Great Balls of Fire*, in which he plays Jerry Lee Lewis as if the Killer were a *complete* moron. Goodness gracious. And though it is late in the game for the man in the poncho, Clint Eastwood comes through a top-shelf bad John Huston accent in *White Hunter, Black Heart*, conjuring up memories of another male lead who once came down off his horse opera to ham it up: the Duke as the Khan in *The Conqueror*.

Many of the worst accents in history involve actors or characters of Italian origin: Al Pacino as a Sicilian Yankee Doodle Dandy in *Revolution*; John Travolta as a Texas-based asshole in *Urban Cowboy*; Jack Nicholson as a likable Mafia hit man in *Prizzi's Honor*; Robert De Niro as a Spanish slave trader turned Jesuit in *The Mission*; Mia Farrow as a Michelle Pfeiffer prototype in *Broadway Danny Rose*; Emily Lloyd and Peter Falk as likable thugs in *Cookie*, a *Desperately Seeking Carmine* that features *dueling* bad accents.

In virtually all of these films, actors were recruited to play characters from ethnic groups to which they obviously did not, and could not, *ever* belong: Pacino and Travolta because they do not look or sound like people whose last name is Dobbs or whose first name is Bud; Nicholson because he does not look or sound like someone named Charley Partanna; Mia Farrow becuase she hangs around with Woody Allen; Emily Lloyd because she's a limey. As for De Niro in *The Mission*: okay, he could have passed for a Spanish conquistador, but he would have had to give up the

Mott Street accent. He didn't, so what we get is *Travis Bickle in the Amazon.* That's our Bobby.

All of this leads us to one of the Crowning Rules of Bad Accents: that the actor or actress with the bad accent must always be surrounded by dozens of people who are perfectly capable of doing the accent the way it should be done, so that morons and critics in the audience will notice the accent and say things like, "Boy, you'd think she was a native Lapp, she's so much more *natural* than the rest of these clowns." Which is precisely how things turned out for the current occupant of the Michael Caine Hurry Sundown Chair, a fine actress and snappy dresser who has also won the coveted award from the Ben Kingsley Foundation, the Golden Gandhi. Yes, the peerless Cher.

Cher's work in *Moonstruck* is an example of bad accents at their very best. Surrounded by real Italians (Danny Aiello, Vincent Gardenia), and people who could pass for Italians (Olympia Dukakis), Cher logs in with an accent so fulsome, so corny, so idiotic that it almost seems self-parodying when she says—yes, she actually says it—"Whatsa matta with you?" An act of cultural genocide every bit as odious as Olivier's Jewish accent in *The Jazz Singer*, Cher's accent in *Moonstruck* inflicts more damage on proud Italian-Americans than a thousand bad Mafia movies. A million bad Mafia movies. 137,876,546 Joe Garagiola commercials. A life's supply of stale cannoli. Etc.

Obviously, in an essay of this length it is impossible to cite every truly deserving bad accent: Cary Grant as a cockney in *None But the Lonely Heart*; Nastassja Kinski as a fully clad, American virgin in *Boarding School*; Joan Plowright as a Yugoslavian immigrant hell-bent on murdering her son-in-law, Kevin Kline, in *I Love You to Death*, in part because of *his* horrible (Italian) accent. It is hardly surprising to learn than Plowright, whose thick, improbable oi vey! accent brings *Avalon* to a screeching halt every time she opens her mouth, is, of course, the widow Olivier. Oh, to have been a fly on the wall when these two meatballs were in the shower at home practicing their bad accents together . . .

For reasons of space, we must also overlook such promising newcomers as Uma Thurman, proud owner of a truly daunting New York accent in *Henry and June*, made all the more impressive because it is delivered at John Wayne speed, and Amber O'Shea, the star of *Intimate Power*, who proclaims to her not entirely convinced fellow harem denizens: "My name is Aimee Debuque DeRivery." Right, and my name is Napoleon Bonaparte.

Happily, as the foregoing makes clear, we as a people are in no danger of seeing bad accents vanish from our celluloid culture. This is largely because bad accents seem to be contagious, and actors appear to be smitten by a deep psychological need to return to the scene of the crime. It was doubtless Nicholson's exposure to Brando's bad accent in *The Missouri Breaks* that inspired his own dire cowboy accent in *Goin' South*, which then paved the way for his ludicrous mobster accent in *Prizzi's Honor*. Had Dukakis been stopped earlier in her career, her *Maud Does Memphis* turn in *Steel Magnolias* would not have been possible. And it was almost certainly Frankie's bizarre Spanish accent in *The Pride and the Passion* that inspired his show-stopping French accent in *Can-Can. N'est-ce pas?*

In the final analysis, though, it all comes back to Olivier. It was Lord Larry's demented Nazi dentist in *Marathon Man* that laid the groundwork for his Austrian Nazi-hunter in *The Boys From Brazil*. And it was Olivier's bad German accent in *The Boys From Brazil* that made Gregory Peck's bad German accent in the same film seem all the more horrible. Finally, it was being close to Peck, who had just played General Douglas MacArthur in the not-so-good 130-minute movie *MacArthur* that inspired Olivier to play MacArthur in the atrocious 140-minute movie *Inchon*. There is something almost mystical in these intertwining paths—Peck and Olivier, Brando and Nicholson, Dukakis and Cher—that assures us that many bad movies with many bad accents lie ahead of us, movies at which millions of Americans from all walks of life will stand up and say, "Two thumbs up, surely one of the year's ten-best; when was the last time you saw a movie that made you want to stand up and cheer?" They will say that, and you will say it, too. Vee hef vays of making yoo tawk.

13 THE LONELY RAGING BULL

A mook and a palooka are playing nine-ball
for $1.69 a game in a dingy Little Italy social
club. Suddenly a blonde named Carmella
dressed all in white (camouflaging the semen on
her skirt) gets out of a big yellow taxi and drops
a rosary on the ground. As an aria from
Donizetti wells up in the background, switch to
an overhead shot of a wise guy firing five
bullets, four of which miss, into the mook's
neck, while three old men named Tommy holler,
"Yo, Mikey, whatsa matter with you?" The film
now fades from color to black and white, save
for the huge red neon light in the distance
reading "JESUS SAVES."

"Hey, Joey, didn't you used to be
somebody?" the vamp asks the wounded man.

"No, that was my brother, Vinnie," he
replies.

—from *Mott Street*, an unproduced
Paul Schrader screenplay.

In 1972, Martin Scorsese directed a low-budget film
called *Boxcar Bertha*, which ends with the hero getting crucified. In 1988, Martin Scorsese directed a
big-budget film called *The Last Temptation of Christ*,
which ends with the hero getting crucified. In 1973,
Martin Scorsese directed a movie with Robert De Niro
called *Mean Streets*, which depicts two small-time
hoods growing up in Little Italy. In 1990 he will
release a film with Robert De Niro called *Goodfellas*,
which depicts two small-time hoods growing up in
Little Italy. Styles, budgets, and Harvey Keitel may
come and go, but some things stay the same.

There's been a lot of talk about Martin Scorsese lately, not only because he has a new film that purports to be the best mob movie ever, but because the people who compile things like the ten-worst, ten-best lists of 1989 have deemed *Raging Bull* the greatest film of the 1980s. This is a bittersweet tribute to Scorsese because *Raging Bull* was released in 1980, meaning that the greatest film of the decade was made a decade ago. The intervening ten years have been a turbulent period for Scorsese: the catastrophic *The King of Comedy*, the quirky *After Hours*, the financially remunerative but pointless *The Color of Money*, the idiosyncratic *The Last Temptation of Christ*, plus a couple of worthy smaller projects (*Bad, Life Lessons*). Scorsese has done some crackerjack work in the 1980s, but not the kind that rivals *Mean Streets, Taxi Driver*, and *Raging Bull*. Maybe that's why he's going back to the old neighborhood.

Still only forty-eight, Scorsese is widely thought to be the greatest American director of his generation, winning on points because Francis Ford Coppola's career is a mess, because Brian De Palma has shown us the bottom of his tiny bag of tricks, and because Woody Allen's small, egocentric films fail to address the problems of people living any further West than, say, Columbus Avenue. Another Scorsese contemporary, Steven Spielberg, has made quite a name—and an awful lot of money—for himself addressing bedrock American concerns—Are there fifty-foot sharks in the water? Are there extraterrestrials in the garage?— before wandering off to turn great books into so-so movies. All of these people are at least as gifted as Scorsese, but Scorsese is the only one who keeps making powerful, attention-getting movies by remaining generally faithful to his gloomy vision of life. So he gets the ring.

Martin Scorsese has clawed his way to the top by portraying an endless collection of poor role models for our kids.* (It should

---

Since this essay appeared, Martin Scorsese has made Cape Fear, *the sixth film in which he has cast Robert De Niro as a character who is not a good role model for the kids. The long-suffering victim is played by Nick Nolte.*

come as no great surprise that he started out working for Roger Corman and John Cassavetes.) The classic Scorsese protagonist is a jerk who, if he plays his cards right, might work his way up to being a schmuck. In *Mean Streets*, Charlie is a loser and Johnny Boy is a dope. Rupert Pupkin (*The King of Comedy*) is a schlemiel. Eddie Felson (*The Color of Money*) is a has-been. Travis Bickle (*Taxi Driver*) is a psychopath. Jimmy Doyle (*New York, New York*) is a clown. Jake LaMotta (*Raging Bull*) is a Neanderthal. Judas (*The Last Temptation of Christ*) is Judas. And Scorsese's Christ is a very, very reluctant Messiah who has a nine-to-five job making crucifixes and who would really rather not end up on one, if that could possibly be arranged. As for the women, don't ask.

Obsessed as he is with this galaxy of hangers-on, losers, and guys who are not yet ready for prime time, Scorsese has had a problematic career. The critics loved *Mean Streets*, his first major-league outing, but audiences stayed away in droves, giving Harvey Keitel the first cruel intimations of the direction his career was heading in. After that came *Alice Doesn't Live Here Anymore*, a sort of big-screen *Rhoda*, which some see as Scorsese's apology to the film industry, the money-making project that saved his career. (He *still* hasn't apologized to *us*.) Since that time, he's been in and out, making them big (*Raging Bull*) and small (*Life Lessons*), good (*Taxi Driver*), and bad (*New York, New York*), successful (*The Color of Money*), and not-so-successful (*The King of Comedy*). He's made three great movies, a couple of pretty good ones, three flawed experiments, a pair of interesting duds, and *Alice*, which flat out sucks. Grade: A –

With rare exception, the asthmatic ex-seminarian has continued to dance with the one who brung him: bozos, schlubs, plus the occasional goofball. Non–Robert Redford types. *People you couldn't care less about unless Scorsese was telling you their story.* Scorsese makes movies about the problems of troubled urban men, which explains why a lot of critics love his work, because film critics are, by and large, troubled urban men. Lacking a more universal appeal—Mom, Dad, Aunt Edith, and of course, those lovable twins, Bernie and Ernie—Scorsese has rarely demonstrated the kind of box-office pull that would induce Sony to hire him as a toy. Hell, where's the market for Jake LaMotta T-shirts?

With it all, Martin Scorsese has stayed the course, making movies that are as passionate, thought-provoking, and daring as the current system will permit. He has never gone way out on the limb like Bob Rafelson, but that's basically because he's more Sunset Boulevard than Cinémathèque Française. Though Scorsese's films may reflect the cinematographic influences of visionaries such as Godard, Antonioni, Pasolini, and the rest of that crew, the primary thematic influences are Little Italy, the Catholic Church, and the movies he saw as a kid when he was trying to avoid being suffocated by Little Italy and the Catholic Church. He is an eclectic, a fallen-away Catholic who went to film school, but he is no revolutionary. You want to be a revolutionary, you end up like Kenneth Anger.

Though on the surface it may seem that Scorsese has dipped into a number of genres (film noir, musicals, rock documentaries, romances, and even TV commercials), in reality he has been remarkably consistent in the way he makes movies and the types of movies he makes. If it worked once, Marty's credo seems to be, why not try it again? No, it is not unfair to Scorsese to say that he reworks familiar territory, sometimes because he wants to go back and get it right, sometimes because he probably doesn't even know he's doing it. *Taxi Driver* is at least partially about a man who wants to save a whore from herself, and so is *Last Temptation*. *Raging Bull* deals with a guy who doesn't mind taking a dive; ditto *The Color of Money*. *Mean Streets* profiles a hapless individual who, because he's been born into the wrong family, has an unappetizing career path cut out for him; same deal with *Last Temptation*.

Other similarities abound. The trick endings of *Taxi Driver* and *The King of Comedy* are cut from the same cloth, cynical afterthoughts that seem to tell the audience: These guys are cruds, but you're idiots. De Niro ends up getting shot several times in the neck at the end of *Mean Streets*, which is just how he ends up in *Taxi Driver*. In both of those movies, the audience is tricked into thinking that De Niro finally dies, though he doesn't. People get popped in a chaotic fight in a pool hall in *Mean Streets*, and Tom Cruise gets thumped in a scaled-down version in *The Color of Money*. Jodie Foster changes her name (Doris) because she doesn't like it in *Alice*, and she changes her name (Iris) because she doesn't like it in *Taxi Driver*. When in doubt, Scorsese always goes to an overhead shot for dramatic effect; and if something big is going to happen look for the color red in a dress, a neon light, a film credit, or a blood vessel (*Taxi Driver* only got an "R" rating after Scorsese agreed to tone down the color of blood at the end of the film). It is hardly surprising that Scorsese should be so active in the movement to preserve color film, because otherwise future generations are going to be seeing Travis Bickle oozing orange and magenta, instead of Scorsese's favorite hue: artery crimson.

More noteworthy than the recurrent scenes, themes, colors, props, amazing soundtracks, the impeccable work of his screenwriters, and the fact that all great Scorsese movies feature the talents of De Niro and/or Keitel, are the recurring relationships. Basically, Martin Scorsese makes buddy movies—Keitel and De Niro; De Niro and Joe Pesci; Paul Newman and Tom Cruise; Willem Dafoe and Harvey Keitel; De Niro, Pesci, and Ray Liotta—where women are usually an inconvenience at best. When the women surface—they are often jailbait—they usually form the third wedge of an uncomfortable triangle. *Mean Streets* centers on the relationship between Keitel and De Niro, with De Niro's epileptic cousin, Teresa, mucking things up. *Taxi Driver* has two triangles—De Niro, Cybill Shepherd, and Albert Brooks, and De Niro, Keitel, and Jodie Foster. *The Color of Money* has three competing characters—Tom Cruise, Paul Newman, Mary Elizabeth Mastrantonio. *Alice* has two triangles—Burstyn, Keitel, and Keitel's wife, and Burstyn, Kristofferson, and the kid. *Raging Bull* focuses on De Niro's suspicion that his brother has been screwing his wife. *The King of Comedy* revolves around De Niro and Sandra Bernhard vying for the affections of Jerry Lewis. In *Last Temptation*, Christ has two relationships: one with Judas, the other with Mary Magdalene. (There is a third, with God Himself, but He never appears on screen.)

Scorsese has been married four times, so he obviously has trouble with women. No, maybe they have trouble with him. It's worth remembering that Scorsese plays the thoroughly unappealing passenger in *Taxi Driver* who chit-chats with De Niro about blowing off his wife's face. After that scene, it's amazing that Scorsese has had four dates, let alone four marriages.

Given Scorsese's problems with the opposite sex and his fallen-away Catholic background, it's hardly surprising that the women in his films, almost without exception, are virgins, goddesses, or whores. The only exceptions are Liza Minnelli in *New York, New York* and Ellen Burstyn in *Alice*, and those are his two worst movies. The only Scorsese movie that ends with a solid relationship is *Alice Doesn't Live Here Anymore*, where Burstyn, no looker, improbably gets to keep the ruggedly handsome Kristofferson, who made a lot of money in the 1970s playing sensitive, caring males while Redford and Jon Voigt were busy being sensitive on some other set.

As for kids, forget it: They're either absent, irrelevant, or abandoned. The only time kids intrude are in *Alice*, where Burstyn's coy geekling is a walking justification for child abuse, and *Taxi Driver*, where Jodie Foster plays a twelve-year-old who takes it all ways. If the world had to depend on Martin Scorsese's characters to repopulate the world, mankind would be extinct in one generation. This is not what you would expect from a Roman Catholic Italian-American. But, of course, Scorsese went to NYU in the sixties.

Scorsese's movies are inhabited by outsiders, people who screw around with people they shouldn't screw around with, victims, and prisoners. Jodie Foster's Easy doesn't want to go down on every guy in town, but what's a twelve-year-old girl from Pittsburgh to do? Keitel's Charley doesn't want to be in the mob, but he got born into the family. De Niro's Jake LaMotta doesn't want to tank a fight, but that's his only route to the title. Last but not least, Dafoe's Christ would really be most appreciative if this cup might only pass from His lips, but His Father insists. This is family business, so do the right thing. Son.

Obviously, Scorsese makes disturbing, violent films, but one reassuring element is how grubby and unglamorous he can make it all seem. Unlike Coppola, whose violent scenes have a Machiavellian quality, or De Palma, whose films invariably degenerate into macabre bloodfests, Scorsese has always depicted violence as an untidy mess. The goofy fistfight in the pool hall in *Mean Streets*, where the camera goes careening around the room chasing a bunch of unathletic dimwits as they try to uncork a decent swing, is a far cry from the stage-managed, choreographed fistfights for which Hollywood is famous. The same is true of Keitel's ferocious explosion in *Alice*, the chaotic denouement in *Taxi Driver*, and even the ungainly Sandra Bernhard's deliriously idiotic pursuit of the spastic Jerry Lewis in *The King of Comedy*. The only film in which Scorsese's characters are not graceless and clumsy is *New York, New York*, his aimless hymn to movies that aren't anything like his own.

The apotheoses of Scorsesian mayhem are the two crucifixion scenes in *Last Temptation*. In the first, when Christ the crossmaker helps crucify a condemned man, Scorsese shows that back in the good old days in Galilee, crucifying people was just a job like any other, so watch out for the spurting blood. In the second, Scorsese wants to show that Christ's crucifixion was no big deal—no epic pagentry, no Cecil B. DeMille stuff, but just something the Romans did on some back street when they got pissed off at somebody and had a few spare planks lying around. There is never, ever death with dignity in the world of Martin Scorsese. There's just death.

Despite all the unpleasantness in his films, Scorsese is one of the great cutups of all time. Woody Allen may be the comedian-turned-filmmaker, but for my money, some of the funniest jokes in the history of cinema are in Scorsese's films. For starters, the scene in *Mean Streets* where the hoods manqués from Riverdale ask the two trainee wise guys if they accept checks. And for the top-drawer material, consider the strange case of Travis Bickle. If you were a gun-toting, sexually repressed psychopath who didn't want to blow your cover, could you seriously hope to find a better disguise than as a New York taxicab driver? It's also a hoot when Cybill Shepherd has to hail a taxicab to escape from De Niro's nutty-as-a-fruitcake taxicab driver in *Taxi Driver*. Finally, for real connoisseurs of mirth, how about Bickle's request for detailed information about becoming a Secret Service agent?

Actually, De Niro is the butt of some of Scorsese's best jokes, including the one in *New York, New York* where Liza Minnelli asks him if he understands the theory of relativity. And for a good running gag, try this: In *Alice*, the fight between the kid and Kris Kristofferson erupts because the teenager can't stand Kristofferson's shit-kicking music. In the very next film, *Taxi Driver*, Cybill Shepherd asks De Niro if he is familiar with the lyrics from a song by the Krisser. "Who's he?" asks Bickle. De Niro subsequently is seen purchasing a Kris Kristofferson record. De Niro/Bickle buying a Kris Kristofferson album? Where, Neptune?

Obviously, Scorsese has an abiding affection for the bedrock hokiness in American life: De Niro's stupid Hawaiian shirt (which reads "New York") in *New York, New York*; Peter Boyle's idiotic philosopher-king soliloquy in *Taxi Driver*; Rupert Pupkin's Kmart duds in *The King of Comedy*, in which De Niro blazed bold haberdasherial trails for his direct sartorial descendant: Pee Wee Herman. But Scorsese was also in top form when he chose to reject some five hours of footage featuring Bob Dylan, Eric Clapton, and Van Morrison and instead retain Neil Diamond's where-the-hell-did-that-come-from? lounge lizard act in *The Last*

Waltz. Toss in the bizarre moment when Neil Young, looking like Keith Richards on a bad day, staggers onto the stage in a semicoma and sings, appropriately enough, "Helpless, Helpless," while backstage, the thoroughly unacceptable Joni Mitchell, Young's former girlfriend, impersonates the Mormon Tabernacle Choir, belting out pure saccharine while concealed in silhouette so no one has to gaze directly at her. Is this hitting below the belt, or what?

Joni, whom the authorities have never apprehended, also takes a shot in *After Hours* when the divine Teri Garr ("Miss Beehive 1965") shows up in a tight yellow miniskirt and shiny white boots looking like she's just come back from an audition with the B-52s. With her trademark home-fried zaniness, Garr puts "Last Train to Clarksville" on the turntable while the menaced, bewildered Griffin Dunne, quite justifiably, sinks into a torpor of despair. When Dunne explains his gloom by announcing that he has just found Rosanna Arquette's corpse, Garr takes off the Monkees, puts on Mitchell's "Chelsea Morning" (the film is set in Soho), and asks politely, "There, is that better?" Marty, Marty . . .

Scorsese, like others before him, has found that film is a delightful medium for rewriting history until it comes out the way you like it. An obvious example is *Last Temptation*, which depicts Christ as a somewhat wimpy, confused, diffident guy who's really turned on by Mary Magdalene and maybe isn't all so sure about this Messiah business. That certainly isn't the way the Scriptures record it, but in making the story this way, Scorsese has succeeded in doing what every fallen-away Catholic schoolboy has always dreamed of doing: getting back at the nuns. *They* don't get to make movies.

Revisionism is also at work in *Raging Bull*, which sanitizes the legend of boxer Jake LaMotta. LaMotta, truth to tell, is not remembered by boxing aficionados because he took the title from Edith Piaf's doomed loverboy, Marcel Cerdan, but because he took a dive for the Mob so he could later get a shot at the title.

Scorsese's movie creates the impression that he was more of a fighting legend than he was. In reality, LaMotta took the title and held it a short while, but is not spoken of by boxing fans in the same breath as Sugar Ray Robinson, whom he beat once, but got pounded by several times. Say it again: The guy took a dive. It's worth noting that Sylvester Stallone and Scorsese have both made movies depicting white fighters as tough hombres that legendary boxers Muhammad Ali and Sugar Ray Robinson wanted no part of. Of course, that's bullshit; Ali and Robinson ate these guys alive. The only place white fighters ever beat black fighters is in Hollywood.

There is also a congenial brand of revisionism in *The Last Waltz*, Scorsese's brilliant 1978 documentary about The Band's farewell concert in 1976. Looking at this film today, and not knowing a whole lot about the 1970s, a viewer might get the impression that The Band was as big as, say, the Beatles. They were not. They were never as big as Whitesnake. They were a quaint, eclectic, funny little outfit who used balalaikas and fiddles and sang the kinds of offbeat songs that Bon Jovi doesn't cover. They were, in fact, the world's greatest backup band, as they demonstrate during this ebullient two-hour affair in which they intersperse their own charming but forgettable numbers with signature tunes by stars of far greater magnitude: Bob Dylan, Eric Clapton, Muddy Waters, the Neils Young and Diamond. Who else but The Band would give a farewell concert and then invite a half-dozen superstars to come over and upstage them? In short, The Band were classic Scorsese characters: a bunch of colorful guys lurking at the edge of the big time.

In *The Last Waltz*, Scorsese, who seems like a congenial fellow, tried to jumpstart the mercifully brief acting career of his friend and subsequent collaborator Robbie Robertson by putting him on center stage in a series of up-close-and-personal interviews. It was apparently Robertson's idea to splice in these chats with members of the band, giving the formerly bespectacled lead guitarist and songwriter a chance to deliver flatulent discourses about the brutal life of the rock star. "The road has taken a lot of the great ones," Robertson tells us. Well, yeah: Janis, Jimmy, Elvis, and Jim . . . but, uh, Robbie? Tragically, Richard Manuel committed suicide *after* The Band quit the road.

The result is something other than Scorsese or Robertson intended: a bug-eyed Robertson, who, as he would subsequently find out in *Carny*, has no real cinematic appeal, sounding like a white, thirtysomething Blind Lemon Jefferson, with Scorsese feeding him big, fat 45 mph hanging curve questions right down the middle of the plate. (The two would atone for their offenses in the vicious *This Is Spinal Tap*, where Scorsese is brutally parodied by Rob Reiner.) None of this changes the fact that *The Last Waltz* is a terrific movie in which the goofy, inarticulate Manuel, not the self-conscious Robertson, the terse Levon Helm, or the incommunicative Rick Danko delivers the best line, admitting that he only got into the rock 'n' roll business because of the women, adding, "I didn't *mind* the music." As for Garth Hudson . . . well, Garth is Garth.

Nobody working today can start a movie with more of a jolt than Scorsese. From the majestic opening credits of *Raging Bull* to the big yellow taxi popping out of what looks like a mushroom cloud at the opening of *Taxi Driver*, Scorsese knows how to get his hooks into an audience, and keep them there for a good, long while. But the openings sometimes write a check that the rest of the film can't cash. De Niro's schtick to Minnelli at the beginning of *New York, New York* is the high point of the film, and in many other cases Scorsese's films seem overly long and languid, as if the middle is just filler between the TNT at the beginning and the nitroglycerine at the end.* He also seems to have trouble bringing down the curtain, often because he wants more than he's entitled to. A lot of people feel that the surprise ending of *Taxi Driver*, where the murderous Travis Bickle becomes a hero, pushes the envelope. *The King of Comedy* has the same problem:

---

*This description is stolen from Henry Miller.

Having built to a wonderful climax, Scorsese wants to tack on yet another climax. *The Color of Money* is another film flawed by a disappointing and ambiguous ending. This film cries out for Tom Cruise to kick Paul Newman's ass, but, instead, Scorsese takes a page out of Stallone's book and leaves the issue undecided, creating the possibility that an outclassed has-been could perhaps whip the top gun, suggesting that we might even see a sequel to what is already a sequel. The movie did get Scorsese a nice deal with Disney, so learning all that stuff about hustling may have paid off.

Given Scorsese's problems with endplay, Nikos Kazantzakis's controversial finale in *Last Temptation* was just what the doctor ordered. Here, the audience is teased with a bogus ending in which Christ comes down from the cross, marries, has a family, and lives out his career in middle-class serenity, before the real ending takes place, with Christ crawling back up on the cross and redeeming mankind. The ending also reiterates the fundamental misogyny in Kazantzakis's worldview: that given a choice between a wife, kids, and a house in the country, men would still rather be crucified.

Scorsese's thoughts on the furor surrounding *The Last Temptation of Christ* betray a disingenuousness that has surfaced before. In a recently published book entitled *Scorsese on Scorsese*, the director expressed astonishment at how enthusiastically some viewers reacted to the bloodbath at the end of *Taxi Driver*. Hey, Marty, you've been to the kung-fu movies on Forty-second Street! Scorsese also told one writer that he was surprised that people thought De Niro died at the end of *Mean Streets*. Well, their confusion is understandable; when last seen staggering down the street De Niro *did* have six slugs in his jugular. As for Scorsese's chagrin at all the trouble he had making *Last Temptation* because of the Moral Majority, what planet is this guy on? In the first fifteen minutes of the film, Christ gets taunted by Judas, of all people, for being a traitor, helps the Romans crucify another Jew, and sits in a brothel while Mary Magdalene screws everything that moves. None of this is recorded in the Scriptures. Did Scorsese really think no one was going to complain? From the point of view of devout Christians—many of whom are, admittedly, buffoons—Scorsese was merely borrowing Christ for a 120-day shoot. *They*, on the other hand, had a proprietary interest in Jesus.

And now, a few words about the neighborhood. In *Scorsese on Scorsese*, the director notes that until he was a teenager he never really left those mean streets, never even wandering as far as New York University, which is only a few blocks to the north. That sense of isolation shows in *After Hours*, Scorsese's strange little film about a Yuppie's night in the art colony Hell of Soho. Soho and Little Italy intersect and occasionally overlap one another, yet the Soho Scorsese depicts—the artist's ghetto of gays and bikers and punks and performance artists and people like David Byrne—is, culturally speaking, four million miles away from the Little Italy it borders. It might as well be Lima. Proving that you can take the boy out of the neighborhood, but you can't take the neighborhood out of the boy. Another thing: It's five years since Scorsese made *After Hours*, but the downtown scene has only gotten worse, proving that it's going to take a lot more than cunning satire to rid us of Philip Glass and Laurie Anderson.

Like the rest of the film school squad, Scorsese is forever quoting from the movies that influenced him. Thus, scenes from *The Wizard of Oz* or *Citizen Kane* or Roger Corman's horror flicks pop up all over the place. The result is movies that are as much about other movies as they are movies themselves. Sometimes that comes in handy; if you need to make a dramatic exit from a flick, what better way than to have Robert De Niro play Jake LaMotta impersonating Marlon Brando playing Terry Malone?

Okay, it works in *Raging Bull*, but this obsessive postmodern repackaging of other people's work—the quotes, the parodies, the appropriations, the use of inside jokes that only thirty-seven other people in the whole universe are going to get—doesn't make the films any better. Nobody's going to come to see *The*

Last Temptation of Christ because you used the same setups as Roberto Rossellini or because you had the Romans played by Englishmen because that's the way Nicholas Ray would have done it. This whole thing about film school inside jokes is a tad annoying coming from a guy who ruthlessly eviscerates Soho bohos for being part of a cabal. It reminds me of the time a musician friend of mine put on a Beethoven symphony and immediately started chuckling. When I asked him why, he explained that the symphony is written in one key, but then immediately modulates into a higher key—meaning that only the opening notes are actually in the key it's supposedly written in. This was supposedly Beethoven's little joke, a joke that only people who studied composition at Juilliard could understand. That's nice, that's cute, but in all of this we miss the larger point. Who cares?

Is Marty Scorsese a great director, like Renoir, Fellini, Hitchcock, Bergman, Truffaut, Godard? Well, let's be careful about how we use the term "great." Dan Marino is a *great* quarterback; he's just not *as* great as Joe Montana. Scorsese is in the same boat: He's not one of the all-time greats, because there aren't enough colors in his palette, there aren't enough gears in his gearbox. No, he's more like the American Chabrol, a maker of lurid, disturbing films, or Herzog, a colorful eccentric. They, like Scorsese, need lots of gimmicks to make it work, and when in trouble always resort to pyrotechnics. But Chabrol and Herzog are still pretty fast company.

Scorsese himself does not seem ready for enshrinement in the pantheon; as he remarks in *Scorsese on Scorsese:* "I think all the great studio film-makers are dead or no longer working. I don't put myself, my friends, and other contemporary film-makers in their category. I just see us doing some work."

Yeah, but it's some pretty good work, isn't it? It's a personal vision, and it may not be a huge one, and it may be too much about one city, and one class, and even one ethnic group, but it's still probably the biggest we've got right now. Scorsese is a filmmaker who makes reasonably commercial, accessible films that always seem like they got started in his head, not in somebody's market research department. They're brutal and they're disturbing, but they're never stupid, condescending, or trendy, and they always make you leave the theater knowing you've spent a couple of hours in the presence of somebody who knows what the hell he's doing. If we had ten more directors like him, we'd be living in a Golden Age, But we don't, and we ain't.

14 THIRD TIME LUCKY?

People are always asking each other, "If you were marooned on a desert island, what books or records or movies would you want to bring along with you?" Excuse me for asking, but why do people always assume that they're going to get a choice? Why don't people realize that if they're unlucky enough to be stranded on a desert island, they're probably also going to be unlucky enough to be stranded there with a bunch of books by Norman Vincent Peale, a bunch of records by Abba and Kenny Rankin and the Bee Gees, and a bunch of movies starring Kate Jackson and Jan-Michael Vincent? The first thing that people unfortunate enough to get marooned on desert islands have to get through their thick heads is that room service is no longer available.

The desert island we will be discussing today is a tiny sandbar lost amidst a vast but remote archipelago in the Tasmanian Sea, several thousand miles off the coast of nowhere. For the purposes of this article, try to imagine that you are trapped on this island, that you realize that you are never, ever, *ever* going to be rescued, and that the only things you have to entertain you are a VCR and a stack of movies that are *Part III* in a series where you haven't already seen *Parts I* and *II*. The $64,000 question then: Is it worth spending your time watching these movies, or should you just find some shade somewhere and lie down and die?

The answer to this question is not as obvious as it would seem. For, although on the surface it would seem that *Part III*'s are usually the last and worst installments in series that were never very good in the first place, this is not entirely true. *Exorcist III* is better than *Exorcist II*, just as *Jaws 3-D* is better than *Jaws II*. This does not mean that *Jaws 3-D* and *Exorcist III* do not suck— they do; it merely means that when we talk about how badly they suck, we must be very careful to remember that they do not suck as much as the films immediately preceding them. *Jaws II* and *Exorcist II* really suck. Or, as they like to say on ESPN, *Jaws II* and *Exorcist II* suck big time. As opposed to ESPN. (This sort of Jesuitical nitpicking can be very helpful in whiling away the hours on a desert island.)

It is also important to remember that there have been several *Part III*'s that were actually fairly decent movies. *The Return of the Jedi* (*Star Wars III*) and *Indiana Jones and the Last Crusade* (*Raiders of the Lost Ark III*) were both pretty entertaining, as was *Aliens III*. Unfortunately, because everyone saw one or more of the early installments in these enormously popular series, we will not be including them in our Desert Island Collection. The same goes for *Back to the Future III*, *Godfather III*, *Nightmare on Elm Street III*, *Halloween III*, *Psycho III*, and *Poltergeist III*, as well as *The Return of the Secaucus Seven III*, which one studio has had the gall to market as *Peter's Friends*. Our investigation will be limited to *Part III*'s where the person trapped on the desert island did not see *Part I* or *Part II*.

For the purposes of this article, that person will be me, and since I am not now, nor have I ever been a moron (though once, in a momentary lapse of reason, I did suggest that Keanu Reeves can act), I will now state that I have never seen *Rocky I* or *II*, *Rambo I* or *II*, *Lethal Weapon I* or *II*, *The Karate Kid I* or *II*,

Police Academy I or *II*, or any of the *I*'s or *II*'s laying smooth the path for *Angel III*, *The Beastmaster III*, *Stepfather III*, *The Howling III*, *Basket Case III*, *Puppetmaster III*, *Emmanuelle III* or *Child's Play III*. And, shocking as it may seem to some readers, I have never seen *Silent Night, Deadly Night I* or *II*, either.

There are two questions that quickly pose themselves in a rigorously scientific investigation such as this. First, do movies that are *Part III* make sense in and of themselves, or do you have to have seen *Parts I* and *II* to understand what is going on? In other words, is *The Beastmaster III*, like Shakespeare's *Richard III*, a free-standing work of art that can be understood and appreciated on its own merits without any familiarity with the events that transpire in its two predecessors? Or is it just another pile of shit?

Second, is there something about *all Part III*'s that links them with all the other *Part III*'s, something that sets them apart from *Part II*'s, *Part IV*'s, or *Part VIII*'s? And if there *is* something unique about *Part III*'s that makes them different from *Part IV*'s or *Part VII*'s, is this unique feature something that also makes them better? Put another way: Is the uniqueness of *Part III*'s, as opposed to the uniqueness of *Part VII*'s, something that will make you happy to have them in your permanent—and final—video library as you sit there awaiting death on that godforsaken desert island of yours, or is it something that's going to make you wish you were stranded on a desert island with nothing but a VCR and a bunch of movies that were *Part V* or *Part VIII* in a series where you hadn't already seen *Parts I, II, III, IV, VI* and *VII*? If you can see what I'm driving at.

To answer these questions, let's take a closer look at the world of *Part III*'s, of what film historians refer to as *mundus cinematicum tertium partibus*. Generally speaking, there are two kinds of *Part III*'s. The first consists of films that are the direct descendants of *Part I*, and are thus the latest, and hopefully the concluding, installments in an epic saga where there is some kind of unifying vision. *Godfather III*, *Alien III*, *Rocky III*, *Child's Play III*, *The Stepfather III*, and *Police Academy III* all fall into this category, either because they were all directed by the same gasbag director, because they were all made by the same ego-maniacal producer, because they all feature the same ensemble of fabulously talented performers who appear again and again, or because they all maintain a consistently low level of cinematic excellence. In short, because they are films so bad that it would take a sage with the intellectual subtlety of Solomon, Ptolemy, Galileo, and Bill Moyers rolled into one to tell whether Steve Guttenberg was worse in *Police Academy III* than he was in *Police Academy I* or *II*.

The second group consists of films that are only a distant cousin, a barely recognizable niece, or the bastard grandchild—twice removed by marriage—of the original movie. Included in this group are properties such as *Jaws 3-D*, *The Howling III*, *Exorcist III*, *The Amityville Horror III*, and *Psycho III*, films that bear little or no thematic or qualitative relation to the films that launched the series in the first place. In short, films that bite the big one.

By and large, *Part III*'s are relatively easy to tell apart from *Part I*'s and *Part II*'s. In high-class *Part I*'s, when the credits roll at the end of the film, you tend to see a lot of names like "Brando," "Hitchcock," "Spielberg," and "Pacino." By *Part II*, you're already venturing into Danny Aiello and Harry Dean Stanton territory, and by *Part III* you've got Sofia Coppola on your hands. A similar thing happens in low-budget, trashy *Part III*'s. While films such as *The Howling*, which are set in California, may include names like "John Sayles" and "Patrick Macnee" in the credits, by the time you get to *The Howling III*, you're seeing names like "Imogen Annesley" and "Dasha Blahova" at the top of the bill, and instead of taking place in California, the film is shot in the Australian outback, where it's cheaper to make werewolf movies, because you can hire authentic Australian townies to play the lead roles and thus save on all that makeup.

As a form of shorthand, it is best to think of these types of *Part III*'s—low-end *Part III*'s—as funeral urns in which are encased the ashes of actresses who used to be on *Three's Company*.

Another way to look at it is this: If you turn on the TV set and a movie featuring Gregory Harrison appears on the screen, you are probably still in the relatively safe DMZ of *Part II*'s. On the other hand, if you tune in a movie and the names "Mitzi Kapture," "Tedra Gabriel," "Leigh Biolos," or "Edward A. Warschilika, Jr." appear anywhere near the top of the credits, you are probably well across the border into *Part III*–land and might even be way out there in the dreaded *Part V*–ville. This is also true if the words "Directed by Frank Henenlotter," "Special appearance by Martin Kove," "Also Starring Tawny Fere," or "Richard Roundtree as Lt. Doniger" appear in the credits. And if Jerry Weintraub's name turns up anywhere, five will get you ten that you're deep into *Part-III* territory. At which point, there is only one thing to do: For God's sake, get out of that house!!!!

The most astonishing thing I discovered in my survey of thirteen (13) *Part III* movies was the staggering thematic unity that linked the films. For example, *Lethal Weapon III*, a relatively high-budget affair, deals with the wacky exploits of members of the Los Angeles Police Department and has a lot of car chases and explosions. Similarly, *Police Academy III*, a relatively low-budget movie, deals with the wacky exploits of members of the Los Angeles Police Department and has a lot of car chases and explosions.

Other common themes abound. *Basket Case III* depicts authority figures (cops) getting eaten by monsters; *The Howling III* depicts authority figures (cops) getting eaten by monsters; *Puppetmaster III* depicts authority figures (Nazis) getting eaten by monsters; and *Jaws 3-D* depicts authority figures (lifeguards) in the same dilemma. And that's not even mentioning the garbage man who gets eaten by his own truck in *Child's Play III* or the repressive parent who gets eaten by a wood-chipper in *Stepfather III*.

Another unifying thread in *Part III* movies is the ubiquity of foiled retirement plans as a major thematic element. In *Lethal Weapon III*, Danny Glover plays an aging cop, a scant eight days away from retirement, who is tired of his violent past and just wants to sit back and take it easy, but who gets talked out of it by a wisecracking buddy with whom he goes way back. In *Rambo III*, Sylvester Stallone plays an aging commando who is tired of his violent past and just wants to sit back and take it easy, but who gets talked out of it by a wisecracking buddy with whom he goes way back. In *Rocky III*, Sylvester Stallone plays an aging boxer who is tired of his violent past and just wants to sit back and take it easy, but who gets talked out of it by a wisecracking buddy with whom he goes way back. And in *Basket Case III*, some guy you never heard of plays a mass murderer who is tired of his violent past and just wants to sit back and take it easy, but who gets talked out of it by an old buddy with whom he goes way back: a mutant pustule that was attached to his chest at birth, but which got surgically removed against both parties' will in *Part I*. This repugnant creature, the hapless moviegoer eventually learns, is actually the mass murderer's disturbed, nonidentical twin brother, a Siamese twin who happens to be a large, viscous growth. And you thought *your* family was dysfunctional.

There are many other themes that appear over and over again in *Part III* movies:

• In *Child's Play III*, a cute little kid named Andy is pursued by a serial killer everyone else mistakes for a harmless toy. In *Stepfather III*, a cute little kid named Andy is pursued by a serial killer everyone else mistakes for a harmless stepfather.

• In *Rocky III*, a short Italian-American who cannot act and cannot fight is depicted as the greatest boxer in the world. In *Karate Kid III*, a short Italian-American who cannot act and cannot fight is depicted as the greatest teenaged karate champion in Los Angeles.

• In *Rocky III*, Sylvester Stallone plays a champion whose

aging mentor refuses to work with him anymore because his
protégé has gone soft and will get himself annihilated by a
challenger who is a million times more talented than he is. In
Karate Kid III, Ralph Macchio plays a champion whose aging
mentor refuses to work with him anymore because he has gone
soft and will get himself annihilated by a challenger who is a
million times more talented than he is.

• In *Rocky III*, Sylvester Stallone makes a fool of himself in an
L.A. gym before achieving catharsis on a California beach and
whipping the piss out of his opponent. In *Karate Kid III*, Ralph
Macchio makes a fool of himself in an L.A. gym before achieving
catharsis on a California beach and whipping the piss out of his
adversary.

Other than that, the pictures have nothing in common.

Part III's are also characterized by a predilection for mutants
that suddenly and unexpectedly emerge from parts of the human
body where most viewers would probably prefer that they not
emerge, at least not while the family is huddled around the TV
set eating Chinese. In *The Howling III*, which is as fine a film
about the ecological threat posed to the western Australian
marsupial werewolf community by a cynical, environmentally
callous, totally unsympathetic public as has ever been made, the
vastly underrated Imogen Annesley gives birth to a cuddly
werewolflet that explodes from her loins and then crawls up her
lower abdomen and wriggles into a pouch cleverly concealed in
her stomach. *Charming.* This is pretty much the same thing that
happens in *Basket Case III*, where a horrible monstrosity suddenly squirms loose from a deformed woman's stomach, and then
is followed by a dozen siblings. Hey, the more the murkier.

The unorthodox lifestyles and dearth of interpersonal skills
that typify these horrid monstrosities invariably culminates in
their being persecuted by close-minded humans. Indeed, this
leads to another theme that unites most *Part III* movies: that
werewolves, sharks, psychopathic puppets, and serpentine mu-

tants suddenly exploding out of a female's bowels only appear to be monsters to unsophisticated observers, when in reality they are our friends. This is the theme of *Jaws 3-D*, in which perky marine biologist Bess Armstrong pleads with environmentally insensitive Sea World owner Lou Gossett, Jr., to refrain from killing a great white shark that may have eaten one of his employees, because Science will benefit from studying it. It is also the theme of *Basket Case III*, where the director seems to feel that if the rest of us would only refrain from prejudging the hideous mutants around us, we would probably come to like them, to accept them, and perhaps even to invite them into our homes to work off the books as nannies. In other words, to know, know, know them is to love, love, love them. Even if they do appear to be nothing more than festering carcasses of putrefied hog excrement.

This conciliatory theme is repeated in *Puppetmaster III: Toulon's Revenge*, a film contending that the Third Reich might never have been toppled were it not for the intercession of a crack squadron of short, homicidal, anti-Nazi puppets. (Actually, the puppets are far more believable in their roles as enemies of the Gestapo than is Melanie Griffith, cast as an American spy working behind enemy lines during World War II, in *Shining Through*. I am willing to believe that there were short, wooden creatures active in the anti-Nazi underground in Berlin during the Second World War; I am even willing to believe that some of them are still on the CIA payroll. But I am not willing to believe that there have ever been any women like Melanie Griffith active in any antiwar movement anywhere. Though, if the U.S. did use spies who talked like Betsy Wetsy back in the forties, this might explain why it took us so long to win the war.)

The theme of the Misunderstood Monsters Among Us also surfaces in *The Howling III*, whose message is: If the rest of us will only back off and leave the western Australian marsupial werewolf community in peace, its members will probably end up doing what other normal people do: go to Hollywood to get jobs in the movie business. The only movie in which weird creatures given to unprovoked, sadistic outbursts resulting in extensive carnage are treated unsympathetically is *Child's Play III*, in which the murderous toy who goes by the name of Chucky is basically depicted as a sick fuck.

Are there any other themes that unite the various *Part III*'s that I watched? Yes. *Rambo III*, *Rocky III*, *Lethal Weapon III*, *Karate Kid III*, *Child's Play III*, and *Police Academy III* all revolve around white leading men (Sylvester Stallone, Mel Gibson, Steve Guttenberg) or white leading boys (Ralph Macchio, Justin Whalin) who have ethnic sidekicks (Sasson Gabail from *Rambo III*, Carl Weathers, Danny Glover, Pat Morita, Jeremy Silvers from *Child's Play III*, Bubba Smith). Los Angeles Police Department vehicles get destroyed in *Lethal Weapon III*, *Angel III*, and *Police Academy III*, while unscrupulous businessmen who will do anything for a buck, even if it means endangering the lives of small children, appear in *Child's Play III*, *Lethal Weapon III*, *Angel III*, and *Jaws III*. Moreover, *Lethal Weapon III*, *Angel III*, *Basket Case III*, *Rambo III*, and *Rocky III* are all movies in which the murderers have a lot of facial hair. This is also the case in *The Howling III*, where the murderers have a lot of facial hair on nights when there is a full moon.

Are *Part III*'s in fact self-contained, free-standing, individual works of art that can stand on their own merits and be understood without having seen *Parts I* and *II*? Or do you have to backtrack and watch a bunch of earlier films starring Drew Barrymore to make any sense out of them?

The answer to the first question is a qualified yes, and the answer to the second question is a qualified no. While it is generally true that *Part III*'s are unbelievably stupid movies that boggle the mind, they are usually not all that hard to follow, even if you haven't seen the unbelievably stupid movies that inspired them. Through the judicious use of flashbacks, dreams, old snapshots, or prescient comments by Joe Pesci, the directors of

Part III's usually make it fairly easy for the audience to get up to speed.

We thus return to the original question: If you happen to be stranded on a desert island with nothing but a VCR and a bunch of movies that are *Part III* in a series where you haven't already seen *Parts I* or *II*, is it worth watching the movies—or should you just lie down and die? The answer: Flip a coin. It's probably worth watching *Child's Play III*, *Stepfather III*, *Rambo III*, *Puppetmaster III*, and *The Howling III* for laughs, and since you know you're going to be dying anyway, it can't hurt to watch *Rocky III* and *Lethal Weapon III* first. *Basket Case III* I would advise against, however, because it is so disgusting that it will give you nightmares after you die. As for *Karate Kid III*, *Angel III*, *Lethal Weapon III*, and *Jaws 3-D*, no, I would not recommend postponing your death simply to watch them. Pull the plug now.

Police Academy III is the single case where I would make an exception: This movie is so bad it will make you glad that you'll soon be dead, glad that you'll soon be going on to your eternal reward. Because once you get to Paradise, you'll realize what the term "eternal reward" actually means: a billion years in a place where there are no people like Bubba Smith and George Gaynes. And you'll also find out what they mean by the term "beatific vision": a place where as far as the eye can see there are no Steve Guttenberg movies, and, better still, no Steve Guttenbergs.

There is one other matter to discuss here. If you happen to be stranded on a desert island and the last *Part III* movie you still have left to watch is *Beastmaster III*, make sure that it's really *Beastmaster III* before you put it in the VCR. The night I set aside ninety-three precious minutes to watch Deathstalker do battle with Troxartes—the evil wizard and ruler of the Southland—while the winsome Princess Carissa looked on, I was really anxious to find out if Deathstalker would be able to protect the enchanted jewel, one of three which hold the key to the fabled city of Erendor. Imagine my fury and disappointment when the film came on and in the place of Deathstalker was a young, anemic Tim Robbins ogling a girl in a skimpy bikini through a telescope. Yes, the overworked youth at my local video store had put *Fraternity Vacation* in the *Beastmaster III* box, and I had to wait until the following day to find out how Deathstalker fared against the undead Warriors From Hell.

The moral: If you're stranded on a desert island and the only movies you have to watch are a pile of *Part III*'s in series where you haven't seen *Parts I* or *II*, make sure that the people who maroon you on the desert island at least put the right flick in the box. Conversely, if you're cast adrift on a desert island where you only have a VCR and a bunch of frat-house movies, make sure the people marooning you don't put *Beastmaster III* inside the *House Party II* box. *Beastmaster III* doesn't have *any* babes in underpants.

One final question many readers will want answered: After watching thirteen *Part III* movies from series where I hadn't already seen *Parts I* or *II*, did I develop a sixth sense about these things enabling me to tell, just by glancing at the screen, whether I was watching a *Part III*, a *Part IV*, or even a *Part VII?* Absolutely. The last day of my research, I had my wife load up a bunch of sequels on the VCR so I could guess whether they were *Part III*'s. I watched five films and was right on target in four cases. Right off the bat I spotted *Emmanuelle V* as a *Part V*-er (If Yaseen Khan is in a movie, it has to be at least a *Part IV*), and I also hit a bull's eye with *Star Trek V, Inside Out IV* and *Nightmare on Elm Street VI.* The only film that I struck out on was *Silent Night, Deadly Night IV,* where the appearance of Maud Adams, star of *Angel III,* beguiled me into thinking I was watching *Silent Night, Deadly Night III.* But, hey, nobody's perfect.

At this point, readers may find themselves wondering: If this guy went to all the trouble of watching *Basket Case III* and *Puppetmaster III,* why didn't he go the whole nine yards and watch *Leatherface III, Critters III, Ghoulies III,* and *Delta Force III?* The answer is simple: I still have standards. What's more, I think most readers of this essay still have standards. I am willing to contemplate a situation in which one of my readers might be stranded on a desert island with nothing but a VCR and a bunch of movies like *The Stepfather III* and *Rambo III*. But I am not willing to contemplate a situation in which one of my beloved readers would be stranded on a desert island with nothing but a VCR and a bunch of movies like *Leatherface III* and *Ghoulies III*. Anyone who would voluntarily watch movies like *Leatherface III* and *Ghoulies III* actually *deserves* to be stranded in the middle of a remote, desolate, culturally petrified wasteland where there is nothing to do but watch movies like this, or die.

I believe they call that place Los Angeles.

15 MISS CONGENIALITY

tatistically speaking, it should be possible for someone somewhere to write a story about Susan Sarandon
without mentioning her incredible breasts. Here goes.

Susan Sarandon is in high spirits these days because *Bull Durham* was a critical and financial success, because the industry admires her trouperlike
behavior after Cher absconded with her part in *The
Witches of Eastwick,* because she just finished shooting a low-budget antiapartheid movie in Zimbabwe
with tubby recluse Marlon Brando, and because her
latest release, *January Man*, which also stars Kevin
Kline, came off without a hitch.

"I play a complete, calculating, out-and-out bitch,"
says Sarandon, smiling. "It was just a breeze."

It has not always been thus. Sarandon almost got to
play opposite Brando in *The Missouri Breaks*, but, as
she puts it, the director "decided to buy a brown suit
instead of a blue suit." She got killed off early in the
not-so-great *Waldo Pepper*, a film-wrecking decision
that screenwriter William Goldman still rants about.
Sweet Hearts Dance bombed so quickly no one heard
the explosion. And *Pretty Baby* was not the smash it
might have been because "people couldn't accept the

fact that the only person in the film who had it together was this twelve-year-old hooker." Especially when the person was played by Brooke Shields.

There have been other setbacks. *The Hunger* looked like a can't-miss project, with Catherine Deneuve seducing Sarandon while David Bowie caught some zzzs in his sepulcher, but the movie, she says, turned into "one of David Begelman's thrift-shop productions, starting out as the 'Six-Million-Dollar Film' and ending up as 'The Two-Million-Dollar Film.' " Nor did the Long Island periodontic whodunit *Compromising Positions* prove to be Sarandon's ticket to stardom.

She has not always gotten the respect she deserves; halfway through a 1983 *Interview* interview, Andy "Mr. Class" Warhol wandered off to look at some of Julian Schnabel's sketches, leaving Sarandon to be quizzed by one of his minions. He returned later only to confess that he didn't remember Sarandon's unforgettable role in *The Rocky Horror Picture Show.* (We'll all miss you, Andy.) But she has not always showed respect; she and Joan Baez once got Johnny Carson so ticked off during a 1976 *Tonight Show* episode that he turned over the last twenty-five minutes of the show to Eubie Blake, an affable if unrepentant ragtime pianist whose performance that evening probably exhausted any residual goodwill America may have felt toward that insidious musical idiom.

"Johnny got up at the end of the show and stormed off the set," Sarandon recalls. "Freddy DeCordova came up to me and said, 'Could you please go and talk to him?' But Johnny's secretary said, 'He's busy.' So I wrote him a note. But I didn't go on the show again for quite a while." (*The Tonight Show* disputes Sarandon's version of these events.)

Careerwise, things eventually reached such an impasse that by 1986 Sarandon actually had to read for the part of Annie Savoy in *Bull Durham*, or, as she puts it, "grovel completely," flying into L.A. in the dead of night from her Italian villa to get the part. As it turned out, it was worth the flight.

Because of these ups and downs, articles about Susan Saran-don have often focused on the question: "Why aren't you as famous as Meryl Streep and Goldie Hawn?" A more pertinent question would be: "Gee, isn't it great not to be Valerie Perrine?" After all, as up-and-down careers go, this hasn't been a bad one. Though the box-office success of *Bull Durham* may have been long overdue, Sarandon has been making entertaining films in which she fuses sex, grit, sass, and smarts for more than a decade. What's more, she does so in a way both women *and* men find appealing. This sets her apart from Streep of the Arctic, who, despite her thespian skills, is the only actress on the planet who can play a woman whose child has been killed by wild Australian dogs and can actually have you rooting for the dingoes.

Sarandon has always been a hard worker. She recalls that when she made her first film, *Joe*, which started shooting five days after she arrived in New York, "the director didn't even know what drugs we were supposed to be taking. We were 'on some-thing,' but nobody knew what; they were completely generic drugs. So I actually went out and tried to figure out what kinds of drugs we were taking."

This fastidious attention to detail stood her in good stead when she showed up on the set of *The Witches of Eastwick* and found out that Cher had annexed the role she assumed she had. This meant that Sarandon had to cook up her ditzy, frumpy cello teacher on the spur of the moment.

"These people [the director et al.] didn't have a clue, but after my three weeks of humiliation, I think I fared better than anyone else in the film," remarks Sarandon. "The advantage of playing a role that doesn't exist is that you can make up anything you want."

On the other hand, Sarandon does admit to some concern about all the time Eva, her three-year-old daughter by Italian director Franco Amurri, spent on the set of *The Witches of Eastwick* with Jack Nicholson.

"Jack was so sweet with my daughter; he'd have us for lunch

all the time, and he even gave her a 'Baby Witch of Eastwick' jacket. But after Jack, I don't know how she'll make the adjustment to ordinary men."

Though commercial releases like *The January Man* pay the bills, Sarandon has done a number of artsy projects—*Pretty Baby*, *Atlantic City*, the new antiapartheid flick—and would like to do more. "Foreign films don't count," she explains. "It's like a woman making love to another woman. If you do a movie in Europe and it doesn't work, nobody holds it against you."

Speaking of having things held against you, Sarandon's views on *The Hunger* underscore the radical differences between movie stars and lay people. To Sarandon, *The Hunger* is a morality play about how much women have changed in the past few centuries, because the character she played "would rather die than live life as an addict"—an attitude Catherine Deneuve's three-hundred-year-old non-feminist lesbian bloodsucker obviously cannot relate to. But to the uninitiated, *The Hunger* looks like a *Revenge of Vampirella* T&A project in which a luscious, middle-aged French actress gets it on with a comparably luscious young American. This is not intended as a criticism.

Speaking of incredible bodies, how about Brando's? Sarandon says that she agreed to "work for practically nothing" on the antiapartheid film *A Dry White Season*, which will be released sometime in 1989, because of her left-wing political beliefs, but also because she was supposed to get to play a scene with Marlon Brando, who has apparently not parted company with his talent, nor his breadbasket. But the scene never materialized.

As for her beliefs . . . like many people who have villas in Italy, apartments in New York, and good jobs in Hollywood, Sarandon espouses innumerable political causes. These include women, homeless women, homeless people in general, victims of Central American political repression, AIDS victims, Nicaraguan mothers, the poor, and various combinations thereof. Environmentally insensitive readers, or manatee buffs ired by the immense amount of press coverage more colorful aquatic species seem to get, will be heartened to know that at no point during the interview did Sarandon express any concern about the whales.

Speaking of children, Sarandon is now pregnant for a second time, this time by *Bull Durham* costar Tim Robbins. The thought did occur to ask Sarandon whether the infant will get to suckle at the breasts that interviewers can't stop asking about, the "noteworthy bosom" that *Playboy* once voted Celebrity Breasts of the Summer, the breasts that Burt Lancaster couldn't take his eyes off during the memorable lemon-juice, peeping-Tom scene in *Atlantic City*, the breasts that Sarandon herself has repeatedly described as overrated. But that kind of stuff is just too, too tacky, and this reporter is not going to sink to it.*

---

*Since this essay appeared, Sarandon has starred as a truckstop babe on a rampage in Thelma and Louise, *as a white trash waitress in* White Palace, *and as Mom in* Lorenzo's Oil, *a film about how cruel life can be. Though Sarandon veils her physical charms throughout long stretches of* Thelma and Louise *and* Lorenzo's Oil, *it should be noted that the videocassette container for* White Palace *depicts an enthusiastic James Spader burying his head in her ample bosom.*

The long-suffering dad in Lorenzo's Oil *is played by Nick Nolte.*

16 BY THE TIME I GET TO PHOENIX, YOU'LL BE WRITHING OR YOUNG GUMS

When I started writing this story, Tom Cruise, Julia Roberts, Kiefer Sutherland, Laura Dern, River Phoenix, Emily Lloyd, and Christian Slater were all young movie stars who seemed to have a reasonable chance of being around for a while. By the time I finished writing this story, at least one of them seemed to have hit the skids, and by the time you finish reading it, several of them may have been superseded by a new generation of Kiefers and Phoenixes. It depends on how fast you read.

This is not necessarily a reflection on the seven actors and actresses, for, with the notable exception of young Kiefer, they all seem to be reasonably gifted performers, with fine teeth. But with no studio system to nurture their talents, to develop sturdy projects on which they can cut their baby teeth, there seems to be little logic to their careers as they carom from one dubious project to the next, hoping that a *Rain Man* will obscure the memory of *Cocktail* and *Legend*, that a *Heathers* will rescue one from a lifetime of penal servitude in films like *Gleaming the Cube* and *Young Guns II*, that a *Blue Velvet* will win one widespread critical acclaim while *Fat Man and Little Boy* pays the bills. Building a career like this is building a career on quick-sand: You could end up like Brandon de Wilde or Sandra Dee—Christian Slater and Julia Roberts in a previous lifetime.

Ever since Hollywood started making movies, young stars have faced a number of serious problems. For one, they are locked into an autocannibalistic system that will eventually consume them. By and large, the Christian River Cruisers are young people being asked to play even younger people in movies aimed at even younger people. They are regularly cast as characters from a strange netherworld—not quite old enough to be adults, but not quite teenagers, either. They are basically People Who Are Too Old to Be Sent to Their Rooms. Unfortunately, the kids who pay to see their movies do eventually grow up, and part of growing up is turning against the things you enjoyed when you were a kid. Queen. David Lee Roth. Quaaludes. Once teens grow up, they're ready for serious actors—like Kevin Costner or Danny De Vito. The teens who have replaced them are ready for new Toms, new Julias. Bye-bye, Kiefer.

All of these actors—with the notable exception of Kiefer Sutherland—have made at least one decent movie, some two. But the good films they have made are not the films the public associates them with. Emily Lloyd had a full-blooded role in *Wish You Were Here*, but if the public knows her at all it is for her mugging in *Cookie* and bouncing around in a tanktop in *In Country*. Tom Cruise's best movies are *Rain Man*, *The Color of Money*, and *Born on the Fourth of July*, but those aren't the movies that made him rich and famous. They're the movies he made to show that there's more to him than we saw in *Top Gun*, *Risky Business*, *Cocktail*, and *Legend*. But Hollywood didn't create Tom Cruise so that he could do *Rain Man* and *Born on the Fourth of July*. Hollywood created him to make twelve *Top Guns*, and it will replace him if he doesn't.

Repackaging the same product over and over again is what this industry is all about; with few exceptions (*Mosquito Coast*, *Wild at Heart*, *Blue Velvet*), the fifty or so films these stars have made are interchangeable, life-affirming, rah-rah pulp dealing with one of the following themes:

1. You Can Make It if You Try.
2. You Can Make It if You Try, Even if You're from the Wrong Side of the Tracks.
3. You Can Make It if You Try, but You Might Need Help from Some Blind or Deaf Person or Somebody with a Horribly Disfigured Face.
4. Sooner or Later, Love Is Gonna Get Ya.

Over and over again, the same theme emerges: I May Be an Outsider or an Underdog, but I Will Triumph over Adversity Because I Have a Will of Steel and Incredible Teeth. Tom Cruise has done the wrong-side-of-the-tracks routine in *All the Right Moves*, *The Outsiders*, *The Color of Money*, and *Cocktail*. Julia Roberts did it in *Mystic Pizza*, *Satisfaction*, and *Pretty Woman*. Emily Lloyd did it in *Wish You Were Here*, *Cookie*, and *Chicago Joe and the Showgirl*. Kiefer Sutherland did it in *Young Guns*, *Promised Land*, and *The Lost Boys*. Christian Slater did it in *Tucker: The Man and His Dreams*, *Heathers*, and *Gleaming the Cube*. Laura Dern did it in *Mask*. River Phoenix did it in *Stand by Me*, *Running on Empty*, and *A Night in the Life of Jimmy Reardon*. It is amazing to think that in a society this wealthy, there could still be this much adversity for teens to overcome. It's not like they're black or something.

Bear in mind that, although the seven actors being discussed here have appeared in many, many bad films, they are by no means the worst films being made today. By and large, the Phoenix Christians stay away from slasher movies, cop movies, and movies that require peering through a keyhole to watch cheerleaders in their underwear. If you appear in movies like that, you get nowhere *fast*. But if you make a habit of appearing in movies like *Cocktail*, *Cookie*, *Young Guns*, *1969*, *A Night in the Life of Jimmy Reardon*, *Satisfaction*, *Gleaming the Cube*,

Chicago Joe and the Showgirl, *Legend*, and *Crazy Moon*, you'll probably get nowhere slow. But you'll still get nowhere.

Now, a case-by-case evaluation of the stars:

CHRISTIAN SLATER: Lots of people have commented upon Slater's Jack Nicholsonesque acting style, while ignoring his equal, and perhaps surpassing, debt to Leonard Nimoy. Yes, when Slater gets those hyperactive eyebrows going, it's like Vulcan Night at the Lido: All Patrons Accompanied by a Dr. Spock Impersonator Get in Free. This is the sort of tic that no normal person would notice right off the bat, because no normal person would sit and watch *Gleaming the Cube*, *Heathers*, *Young Guns II*, *Tucker*, and *Pump Up the Volume* in rapid succession. But I noticed it, and once Slater starts making movies that reach a wider audience, it's only a matter of time before influential critics with larger thumbs than brains start to notice it, too. Better get clamps or something, Christian. And stop slapping your forehead every time you want to emote.

Slater is a good-looking, affable sort who has survived a number of bad movies to win mild critical acclaim in *Heathers* and *Pump Up the Volume*. He was utterly useless as a trainee monk in *The Name of the Rose*, where he did a lot of vacuous eye-rolling in the footsteps of the equally miscast Sean Connery, who tried to recycle an earlier performance as Robin Hood in Winter into the role of a medieval sage. Better luck next Inquisition, Sean. Slater had an inconsequential role in *Tucker*, somehow managing to avoid being blinded by Jeff Bridges's high-beam smile, and was utterly absurd in *Gleaming the Cube*, a sort of skateboard version of *Valdez Is Coming*. In *Young Guns II*, he was what you would expect: a Young Gun II.

Slater's reputation, such as it is, rests on his roles as rebellious teenagers in *Heathers* and *Pump Up the Volume*. In the former, he turns up the Jack Nicholson act full blast, providing a nice counterpoint to Winona Ryder's performance as a confused high school girl torn between social acceptance and mass murder. But he really came into his own in *Pump Up the Volume*, last year's highly entertaining saga of a repressed teenager with an illegal radio station in an Arizona high school. The only troubling element here is Slater's split personality: When he plays the talk-hard deejay who rips into parents, police, the authorities, etc., he carves out a nifty, brash persona for himself. But then, when he reverts to being a shy geek, donning eyeglasses, hunching his shoulders, and digging his hands into his pockets—he resembles no one so much as River Phoenix. You can't build a major career by aping River Phoenix. One other thing: *Pump Up the Volume* got ecstatic reviews from adult critics who admired its message about twisted high school kids, but not enough to make it a hit; they were all over in the next plex, watching *Young Guns II*.

LAURA DERN: Until David Lynch worked his special brand of magic, Laura Dern had a dewy, girl-next-door charm that posed baffling genetic questions, given that she's the daughter of veteran fruitcake Bruce Dern and scenery-chewing belle Diane Ladd. That charm first manifested itself in *Smooth Talk*, the fine 1985 adaptation of a surprisingly readable Joyce Carol Oates short story about a teenager crossing the line between being a child and being jailbait. Dern did a lot of frowning and wincing and lip-biting in this film while trying to decide if it was a good idea to take a spin with Treat Williams (it is *never* a good idea for a young girl to take a spin with a man named Treat, or even a man being played by an actor named Treat), and herein defined the essential persona she would play in one film after another: the passive cupcake who does a lot of wincing and frowning and lip-biting.

Bear in mind that although Dern appears in David Lynch's creepy *Blue Velvet*, she has the only normal role in the film, as The Girl. And although she starts off at a pretty torrid pace as Nicholas Cage's slinky associate in *Wild at Heart*, she eventually gets burned to a crisp by the orthodontically dysfunctional Willem Dafoe in one of the most memorable seduction scenes ever to take place in a puke-stained motel room. Ultimately, she winds up as a typical American mom, raising a kid, waiting for that man of hers to come home. Germaine Greer, she ain't.

Want more evidence? In *Mask*, the 1985 Peter Bogdanovich tearjerker about a teenager who triumphs over having a horribly disfigured face *and* Cher for a mom, Dern plays a blind cherub with a Sunkist smile. And in *Fat Man and Little Boy*, she actually plays a goddamned nurse. So this is a very problematic career: fine work in a low-budget artsy movie where she plays a troubled teen; a nothing performance as the Girl Next Door in the artsy *Blue Velvet;* a red hot performance as a roving sex machine in the artsy *Wild at Heart*. Having exhausted the possibilities of virginity, Dern seems ready for a career as a hot tramp, à la Sarah Miles or Charlotte Rampling. The USA Network is waiting.

JULIA ROBERTS: Julia Roberts is the distaff Tom Cruise, a competent actress who, if she plays her cards correctly, should be able to parlay her remarkable good looks into a major career. If you're one of those people who think that she only has the lips, the figure, the hair (which she foolishly decided to chop off last summer), take a look at *Satisfaction*, the 1988 Justine Bateman vehicle that Justine successfully drove right over the cliff. Hemmed in by three horrible actresses and one man named Liam, Roberts makes the best of a bad situation, as she does in *Steel Magnolias*, acting in a perfectly professional fashion while Daryl Hannah, Olympia Dukakis, and Shirley MacLaine hang from the chandeliers. This girl is no dummy.

Of the five Julia Roberts films in captivity, three deal with girls from the wrong side of the tracks. In addition to *Satisfaction*, where she plays a white trash bassist in an all-girl band so bad they would embarrass Wilson Phillips, Roberts plays Portuguese white trash in the romantic comedy *Mystic Pizza*. She was not especially convincing as a poor kid from a Connecticut fishing village, but she was a lot more convincing than Annabeth Gish, who looks like she was part of Sarah Lawrence's prenatal registration program. *Mystic Pizza*, for those who have not seen it, is one of those small, tough, honest movies that deal with ordinary people in ordinary settings in an ordinary way. You know: horseshit.

Pretty Woman is the film that made Roberts a star, in part because only someone as vivacious as she could breathe life into the cadaverous Richard Gere. Roberts is not terribly convincing as a prostitute with a heart of gold—prostitutes find it very difficult to keep their teeth that white—but she's a hell of a lot more convincing than Gere as a corporate raider with a heart of gold. Personally, I can't decide whether *Pretty Woman* is the last really stupid film of the 1980s or the first really stupid film of the 1990s—but none of it is Roberts's fault. The film is a fairy tale, and she is perfectly cast as a damsel in distress.

Most recently, Roberts appeared in *Flatliners*, a so-so thriller about Young Doctors in Love and Death. As always, Roberts did her number with those lips, lips so big they make Mick Jagger's seem unobtrusive. It remains to be seen whether her lips will remain bankable as long as Jagger's have. She shouldn't have cut her hair.

RIVER PHOENIX: As one would expect from a person named River Phoenix, River Phoenix does not look like he grew up on the north side of Chicago, the west side of Philadelphia, or the south side of anywhere. Starting out as a rapscallion (*Stand by Me*), progressing to a heartthrob (*A Night in the Life of Jimmy Reardon*), Phoenix has lately been cast as a mildly dweebish teen in a series of relatively decent films (*The Mosquito Coast, Running on Empty, Indiana Jones and the Last Crusade*). The problem is: Unless you're looking for him, you hardly notice that he's there. He's a moody little guy who frets and frowns, and though he seems to choose his roles with some care, he's basically like wallpaper: pretty, expensive wallpaper. In both *The Mosquito Coast* and *Running on Empty*, he is completely overshadowed by overbearing dads (Harrison Ford, Judd Hirsch), and in both films he is completely overshadowed by Martha Plimpton, a real corker. In the more recent *I Love You to Death*, he plays a goofy zit, no better or worse than the rest of the cast, with the exception of Kevin Kline, who's both better *and* worse. River Phoenix is a mildly talented young actor whose name has written a check that his body can never cash.*

EMILY LLOYD: One minute she was hot; the next minute she was making Kiefer Sutherland movies. What happened? Back in 1987, then sixteen-year-old Lloyd got lots of attention when she debuted in *Wish You Were Here*, David Leland's tawdry tale of a girl who uses sex as a weapon in the dreary England of the 1950s. But she immediately misfired by appearing opposite Peter Falk in *Cookie*, a bad *Married to the Mob*, and got involved in another crime against nature when she teamed with veteran bomb detonator Kiefer in *Chicago Joe and the Showgirl*, a tale of sex and crime in the dreary England of the 1940s. In addition to the radioactively hammy Falk and the catatonic Sutherland, Lloyd also worked with the useless Bruce Willis in *In Country*. This dull, obvious film, which faithfully captured the nuance of Bobbie Ann Mason's dull, obvious novel, afforded Lloyd numerous chances to shimmy in jogging shorts while trying to come to terms with her father's death in Vietnam, but other than that I can't imagine what the point was. Of course, I can't imagine what the point of Vietnam was, either.

It's ironic that Lloyd, who is English, handles a Dixie accent better than Willis and a Mob accent better than Falk. Of course, *she* can act. But handling accents isn't enough to ensure success, and a couple more films with the likes of Falk and Sutherland, and Lloyd could find herself on the next plane back to Stonehenge.

Since this essay was written, River Phoenix has appeared in My Own Private Idaho, *in which he portrays a Seattle-based, narcoleptic male hustler who has a habit of falling asleep in the middle of the highway. Phoenix was quite believable in the role, as was the highway.*

TOM CRUISE: Tom Cruise is the male Julia Roberts, only more so. He has a big, huge, sparkly smile, expressive eyes, an appealing swagger, and can read his lines. Half of the movies he makes are idiotic, and half of the movies he makes are not, which seems like a very high ratio when compared to his peers (Sylvester Stallone, Arnold Schwarzenegger, Mel Gibson). In this sense he resembles Michael Douglas: He is not the world's greatest actor, but he does manage to occasionally involve himself in a halfway decent project when he could have just gone out and made fifteen consecutive *Days of Thunder*.

Cruise started out as a generic heartthrob in *All the Right Moves, Risky Business*, and *Top Gun*, but has since profited from the widely held notion that appearing in *Rain Man* and *Born on the Fourth of July* demonstrated a willingness to stretch. It is a measure of how spectacularly infantile the movie industry has become to suggest that making a film with either Oliver Stone or Barry Levinson constitutes a stretch, since all we are talking about is *Of Mice and Men Goes to Vegas* and a wheelchair *Platoon*. Still, it's a start.

Cruise has the teeth, the smile, the bod, the *attitude* to carry a whole picture, as he has done again and again in *Top Gun, Days of Thunder*, and the ingratiatingly moronic *Cocktail*. Still, years from now, when people look back on the 1980s, they will puzzle at films about superstar bartenders, peacetime pilots, and boys who wreck their dad's Porsches. And while it was a nice idea for Cruise to do some heavy lifting in *Born on the Fourth of July*, if you're looking for an actor who makes a real impression, it's Willem Dafoe, who beats Cruise hands down, in or out of a wheelchair. The same is true of *Rain Man*, where Cruise delivers a good performance as a badass, but clearly plays second fiddle to full-time actor Dustin Hoffman. Even in *Risky Business*, Cruise is outgunned by Rebecca de Mornay, who, at that time, looked like she might have a career. Tragically, God, who created woman, can also destroy her—though Roger Vadim and movies like *Feds* will do it faster.

Tom Cruise has perfected a persona that the American people will pay to see again and again and again. Sometimes the character is a bit smarmy (*Cocktail*), sometimes a bit shady (*Rain Man*), but in the end he's a true-blue, wave-the-flag, let's-go-for-it-on-fourth-and-inches, clean-cut American kid. In short, not Nicolas Cage. But Cruise's meal ticket is still films like *Top Gun* and *Days of Thunder*, and those kinds of movies don't make you the next John Wayne or Gary Cooper. They make you the next Burt Reynolds.

KIEFER SUTHERLAND: There is a wonderful moment in the film *Young Guns*, when Brian Keith, a grizzled bounty hunter, disappears into an outhouse in the middle of a gunfight with Charlie Sheen, Lou Diamond Phillips, Emilio Estevez, Kiefer Sutherland, and several other very young, very bad guns. Though Keith is no longer visible, he continues to dominate the action while relieving himself, eventually killing Sheen. But it is not merely as a bounty hunter that Keith dominates the action; he also dominates it as an actor. Let's be clear about this now: Brian Keith—never mistaken for Laurence Olivier—packs more of a dramatic wallop while invisible in a shithouse than Lou Diamond Phillips, Charlie Sheen, Emilio Estevez, and Kiefer Sutherland when they are fully visible on the screen.

This is really embarrassing.

Sutherland's entire career is embarrassing. Of all the actors treated in this survey, Sutherland is the only one whose sustained ability to find work is a source of amazement. Sutherland, who has been churning out one bad film after another since his debut in 1984, has probably made more bad movies at a younger age than any actor in history. These include the sappy *Bay Boy*, a 1984 Canadian-American production showcasing seasoned victim Liv Ullmann; a second Canadian disaster entitled *Crazy Moon;* the horrendous *Promised Land;* the imbecilic *Bright Lights, Big City;* assorted *Young Guns;* and the lethal *1969*. Sutherland, in his brief career, has appeared in a movie whose best performance was supplied by Mariette Hartley (*1969*); a movie whose best performance was supplied by Joe Don Baker (*The Killing Time*); and a movie whose best performance was supplied by one guy named Corey, and whose second-best performance was supplied by another guy named Corey (*The Lost Boys*). This is really embarrassing.

Kiefer's big problem—aside from the fact that he isn't very good—is that he can't decide what sort of roles not to be very good in. He's passable as a teen vampire in *The Lost Boys*, mostly because of his Billy Idol Goes to Montreal Smile, and he's okay as Michael J. Fox's drug-snorting sidekick in *Young Fact-Checkers in Love* (*Bright Lights, Big City*). But young Kiefer wants to be loved, and so we get such abortions as *Young Guns*, where he plays a poetic gunslinger; *Promised Land*, where he plays a pussy-whipped geek; *Crazy Moon*, where he plays a dweeb with a mannequin companion who is rescued from ennui by a cute mute (does this remind you of any other film?); and *Chicago Joe and the Showgirl*, where he plays a malleable Yank soldier lured into a brief life of crime by an unscrupulous British tart. The schizophrenia in Sutherland's career—Should I be a leading man with a goofy smile or a villain with a goofy snarl?— is typified by his work in *Flashback*, where he is believable as a bland FBI agent for the first half of the film, but then makes a fool of himself when he lapses into his child-of-nature role as the hippie child Free. "Free" should be the price of admission to his films.

Sutherland has appeared in numerous movies where he receives acting lessons from his betters: Dennis Hopper in *Flashback*; Jack Palance, Brian Keith, and Terence Stamp in *Young Guns*; Baker and Beau Bridges in *The Killing Time*; Meg Ryan in *Promised Land*. But he has also been fortunate enough to appear in several movies where there are other people on camera so horrific that Sutherland's dreary work escapes closer attention. For true connoisseurs of bad acting, *Young Guns I* is a must-see. First off, it features Emilio Estevez, who is too short and scrawny to play Emilio Estevez, let alone Billy the Kid. Second, it features Charlie Sheen, the least plausible cowboy since Klinton Spilsbury in *The Legend of the Lone Ranger*. Third, it features Kiefer in a transcendantly asinine performance as a Young Gun on peyote. Lastly, and most memorably, it features Lou Diamond Phillips as a Native American psychopath. Down through the history of motion pictures, scores of actors have had the audience rolling in the aisles as they delivered the obligatory "The Pony Soldiers Came in the Morning and Cut the Squaws to Pieces" speech. But no one, no one, no one has ever been more ridiculous in the role of the Long-Suffering Indian than Lou Diamond Phillips. He's really something special.

Anyway, Kiefer. At a select group of video stores across the nation, aficionados of the cinema can rent a film called *1969*. This mesmerizingly awful antiwar movie showcases the limited talents of Sutherland—whose father is a talented actor and made one of the great countercultural movies of the 1970s (*MASH*), Bruce Dern, who used to make countercultural movies in the 1960s and 1970s, and Robert Downey, Jr., whose talented father once made the kinds of innovative, risk-taking, nonidiotic movies that *1969* is not. The film, nightmarishly stupid as it is, perfectly summarizes the state of the art today: terrible movies with retro sixties era soundtracks relying on blockheaded scripts acted out by third-rate actors who are the children of first- and second-rate actors that deal with rebellious teenagers from the wrong side of the tracks fighting against the Establishment, rich kids, Society, blah, blah, blah. Luckily, Bruce Dern has Laura to carry on for him. Donald's only got Kiefer.

This is really embarrassing.

17 TALK DIRTY TO ME

In 1988, Oliver Stone made an extremely important, and in many ways prophetic, movie about the danger posed to this society by psychologically dysfunctional talk-radio hosts. In the film, cunningly entitled *Talk Radio*, the resourceful monologist (monologists, for the unitiated, are standup comics who sit behind desks so that no one will notice that they aren't as funny as standup comics) Eric Bogosian played an abrasive, amoral, unprincipled, pretentious, condescending, conceited, mentally ill, bug-eyed talk-show host who continually provokes his pathetic Dallas listeners with idiotic rants about politics, religion, and sex.

By the end of the film, a grimy, frothing, hirsute, orthodontically challenged member of a neo-Nazi group shows up at the radio station and blows him away. Although the neo-Nazi killed Bogosian for all the wrong reasons—because he was Jewish, because he was an urbanite, because he'd probably gotten more than 1200 in his SATs, because Zog said to do it—the audience comes away from the film relieved that at least somebody had the good sense to drive downtown and gun down this colossal asshole.

In *Talk Radio*, Oliver Stone had issued a clarion call about one of the greatest social problems of our times: the tragic fact that all across this great nation hundreds of thousands, perhaps millions, of desperately lonely human beings spend their free time phoning talk-radio stations, seeking a bit of friendly advice, a smidgen of balm for the soul, and instead end up talking to some fuckhead like Eric Bogosian. If you, like me, view movies not as facile diversions, not as fluff, not as the celluloid equivalent of a banana fudge sundae, but as subliminal expressions of a society's deepest neuroses, then *Talk Radio* marks the first public expression of the growing conviction among ordinary Americans that talk-radio hosts, having miserably failed in their anointed function as amateur psychologists, surrogate clergymen, and shamans, deserve to die.

Just as *Dracula* is really about heterosexual males' fear that they're going to get AIDS; just as *Deliverance* is really about heterosexual males' fears that sooner or later they're going to get butt-fucked by mountain men; just as *Fatal Attraction* is really about heterosexual males' fears that they're going to get caught; and just as *Fried Green Tomatoes* is really about heterosexual females' fears that they're going to end up like the women in *Steel Magnolias*, *Talk Radio* is really an expression of the deeply rooted, though rarely articulated, belief that talk-radio hosts are ruining life for the rest of us, and thus deserve to be killed.

This conviction has only solidified in the four years since *Talk Radio* appeared. In that time, we have witnessed such major releases as *The Fisher King*, a movie about a talk-radio host whose cynical wisecracks lead directly to a mass murder; *Pump Up the Volume*, a movie about a high school student with a pirate radio station whose cynical wisecracks lead directly to a suicide; and *Straight Talk*, a movie about a talk-radio host whose cynical wisecracks lead directly to another bad James Woods movie. In each of these films, the subtle message is identical: Our beloved country is being overrun by a plague of talk-radio personalities who are ruining our lives. So let's get rid of them.

If this message were being imparted merely in high-class projects such as Terry Gilliam's clever *Fisher King*, Oliver Stone's cerebral *Talk Radio*, Allan Moyle's sincere *Pump Up the Volume*, and Barnet Kellman's whimsical *Straight Talk*, we could dismiss it as the generic, paranoid bellyaching of the cultural elite, as the predictable terror of people who are scared of their own shadows and who have an innate, clinical aversion to anything that working-class people (i.e., losers) enjoy: radios, ice hockey, polyester, Steven Seagal. But once that message begins to surface in films emanating from the cultural demimonde inhabited by the likes of Shannon Tweed and Lisa Hartman, it's time to take a closer look at the phenomenon and admit that something much more serious, much more *primal* is going on out there in the hinterland.

This is precisely what has happened in the past year. At the very moment that Paleolithic mammalians such as Howard Stern and Rush Limbaugh have achieved their greatest notoriety, a whole slew of low-budget Hollywood productions has appeared, all driving home the message that talk-radio hosts do not have the best interests of this society at heart and must be put to the sword in a reasonably expeditious fashion if the rest of us have any hope of surviving. This is the message that comes through loud and clear in Adam Simon's bracing *Body Chemistry II*, a film in which a sadomasochistic talk-radio hostess seduces a caller who enjoys rough sex, and then ends up murdering him. It is the message that comes through loud and clear in A. Gregory Hippolyte's superb *Night Rhythms*, a film in which a raunchy talk-radio host is sought by the police for murdering a bisexual call girl he was harpooning live on the air during one of his groundbreaking broadcasts. It is the message that comes through loud and clear in *Sexual Response*, the absorbing Yaky Yosha film in which the versatile Shannon Tweed plays a sex-talk radio therapist who is seduced by a caller who happens to be her stepson. In each and every one of these films, the message is the same: Our country is being overrun by a plague of talk-radio personalities who are ruining our lives. So let's get rid of them.

It is hardly an accident that most of the films in question deal primarily with sexual problems. A country that confers the official designation "heartthrob" on ungainly, plain-looking women such as Madonna or short, smiley Scientologists such as Tom Cruise is plainly having problems beneath the national loincloth and needs all the help it can get. Accordingly, many ordinary people have been calling talk-radio programs seeking sexual advice. But at what cost! For as each of these films demonstrates, the last person you would want to call for advice about your love life is a psychologically dysfunctional talk-radio host.

Consider the predicament of the confused young dweeb named Edwin who phones Jack Lucas (Jeff Bridges) in *The Fisher King* and discusses whether it is advisable to visit a fashionable Manhattan watering hole named Babbitt's to pick up girls. Edwin is obviously a perplexed individual—a jerkoff, if you will—who clearly needs to be treated with kid gloves. So what is Lucas's response?

"Edwin, hey, come on now. I told you about these people. They only mate with their own kind. It's called Yuppie inbreeding. That's why so many of them are retarded and wear the same clothes. They're not human. They don't feel love; they only negotiate love moments. They're evil, Edwin. They're repulsed by imperfection, horrified by the banal—everything that America stands for, everything that you and I fight for. They must be stopped before it's too late. It's us or them."

Edwin promptly goes out and blows away a roomful of Yuppies with a shotgun. To be fair, everything that Lucas says about Yuppies is absolutely true: They are scum, and they do deserve to die painful deaths. But telling things like that to a person like Edwin is like yelling "Muslim!" in a roomful of Hindus. Or "Fire!" in a roomful of anybody else.

It just isn't done.

Another instance in which a lonely individual seeking a guiding hand is cruelly rebuffed occurs in the delicate Kristine Peterson vehicle, *Body Chemistry II*. In the original *Body Chemistry*, Peterson plays a sex researcher (Hey, aren't we *all* sex researchers in our own little way?) who is so obsessed with sadomasochism that she eventually murders the married co-worker she has lured into Helmut Newtonland. Seeking a new life in a small West Coast town where her unconventional résumé will not impede her career, Dr. Archer lands a job as a sex counselor on a local radio station (1-800-SEX-TALK). Her program, derived from her philosophy that "pain defines pleasure," is remarkably successful, and before long the station owner has an offer to take the show national. Meanwhile, Dr. Archer has resumed her zesty personal life by seducing a former police officer who, because of his fascination with rough sex, has been fired from the Los Angeles Police Department (this is the only defect in an otherwise plausible plot). Archer even goes so far as to handcuff her victim to a pick-up truck and give him a blow job in the gas station where he works. His protests are meek and not entirely credible.

Alas, Dr. Archer's unseemly past ultimately comes back to bite her in the ass, as it were, when the radio station's owner, played with *élan* and nuance by trash TV pioneer Morton Downey, Jr., discovers that his top deejay is actually a murderer. "What's a major-league lady like you doing in a Triple-A town like this?" Downey says to his star employee, outlining the terms of blackmail he insists that she agree to. But Mort—the French word for "death"—soon must pay the piper when Dr. Archer, who shows up at the studio decked out in a dominatrix outfit, binds him, gags him, forces him to wear a lady's wig, tortures him with a feather, whips him, and murders him.

Whatever her other qualities, Dr. Archer is not the sort of person a lonely lass should be calling on a crisp fall evening seeking advice about dealing with an abusive boyfriend. Yet this is precisely what happens when Dr. Archer receives a call from a tormented young female named Peggy who tearfully recounts her suffering at the hands of her violent boyfriend.

Caller: Why does he hit me?

Archer: Because it's the natural way. Fighting is linked to sex in many species—uh, fish, lizards, elk, deer, rabbits, mink, moose, monkeys . . . and men.

Caller: I never thought about it that way.

Archer: Yes, well, consider yourself lucky, Peggy. The male mink often bites right through the pelt of his lover's neck, severing all of the neck muscles and arteries before copulation is even through.

Caller: Really?

Archer: Really. At least your boyfriend cares enough to hit you.

The recurring theme of talk-radio hosts as morally defective human beings providing extremely unhelpful advice over the airwaves surfaces again and again in these films. In *Pump Up the Volume*, pirate deejay Christian Slater has an ongoing conversation with a lonely, alienated high school chum named Malcolm Kaiser who informs him that he plans to commit suicide. Does Slater thereupon tell the sexually repressed youth to call the Suicide Hotline, dial 1-900-EX-YOUTH, or contact a nonsectarian clergyman specializing in human salvage jobs, regardless of the caller's color, creed, or sex? No, he tells the kid to write a note so that at least everyone will know why he did it. Magic, Christian.

Frequently the subject of sex comes up even when the callers are phoning in to discuss entirely noncarnal matters. Consider the poor old lady in *Talk Radio* who phones Bogosian to complain about her pension program.

Poor old lady: I changed my name and didn't have any trouble getting social security. . . . My birth certificate has my name spelled differently and I . . . hello?

Bogosian: Yeah, yeah, it's very interesting. What's your view on lesbian priests?

Poor old lady: My view on what?

Bogosian: How about masturbation, you got any view on that?

Poor old lady: Well no, I don't . . . I . . . I . . .

Bogosian: How about that law in Arizona where it's a felony to go around with an erection in your pants? What do you think about that?

Poor old lady: Well, I'm not really calling about that. If they want to do it, then let them do it.

The sexual no-man's-land into which all of this smut and kinkiness inevitably leads is exposed in all of its meretricious seaminess in Yaky Yosha's adroit Shannon Tweed vehicle *Sexual Response.* Unhappily married to a middle-aged Australian jerkoff with a pony tail, the gamey Tweed makes her living by hosting a talk-radio program specializing in sex. Not all of her advice is bad—"Go out and buy yourself a vibrator," she counsels a woman whose boyfriend beats her—but, clearly, Tweed's standards as a psychologist fall considerably short of the ethical benchmark for her profession. Why else would she end up sleeping with one of her callers: a young, deviant, biker sculptor named Edge who likes to play with butcher knives and guns and who leaves a naked statue of Tweed on her front lawn, right where her husband can see it?

"You have a lot of unresolved issues," she tells Edge.

He has a lot of unresolved issues?

The Edge of night spends a lot of time smearing whipped cream on his girlfriend, playing around with her husband's guns, sucking her nipples, and delicately broaching the subject of murdering her husband and making it look like an accident. Tweed tells Edge that the relationship is going nowhere and throws him out. Shortly thereafter, the otherwise invisible Catherine Oxenberg discovers that Tweed's ponytailed husband is actually an Australian murderer who killed his own wife years earlier. As luck would have it, he is survived by a son named Edge. Coincidence, you say. Edge impales his dad on his own artwork, then apologizes to his stepmother for his aberrant behavior in the early phases of their relationship, particularly all that Oedipal stuff involving his tongue and her breasts. Tweed, whose name in the film is Eve, tells Edge that she likes him because he's "honest about his feelings." She concludes the film by staring at the mike as he fades out of her life forever and sighing, "Thanks for listening."

Are any of the protagonists in recent films involving talk radio capable of soothing the savage breasts in the bosoms of their listeners? No, they are all complete assholes. The closest any of them comes to dispensing useful advice occurs in *Straight Talk* when the likable moron that Dolly Parton plays, and probably is, remarks: "Having an affair is like shooting pool on two tables. You may have the balls, bud, but you're gonna wear out your stick."

Actually, this depends entirely on how old, how long, and how well maintained one's stick is. Parton is similarly wide of the mark when she tells a caller: "A bird and a fish can fall in love, but where do they make a home?"

Why, Roman Polanski's house, of course.

The movies we have discussed here are so similar in style, treatment, and content that the viewer occasionally suspects that they were written and directed by the same person. After all, *The Fisher King* deals with a maverick talk-radio host whose personal life is destroyed when his wiseass remarks lead to a mass murder; just as *Talk Radio* deals with a maverick talk-radio host whose personal life is destroyed when his wiseass remarks lead to a murder; just as *Pump Up the Volume* deals with a maverick talk-radio host whose personal life is destroyed when his wiseass comments lead to a suicide; just as *Sexual Response* deals with a maverick talk-radio host whose personal life is destroyed when her wiseass comments lead to a murder; just as *Night Rhythms* deals with a maverick talk-radio host whose personal life is destroyed when his wiseass comments lead to a murder; just as *Body Chemistry II* deals with a maverick talk-radio host whose personal life is destroyed when her wiseass comments lead to a murder. Only *Straight Talk* deviates from the pattern. This bold, pace-setting, iconoclastic film deals with a maverick talk-show host whose personal life is destroyed when her wiseass comments lead to a divorce and to her own near-suicide, but not directly to any murders that we know of. Unless we count moviegoers as victims.

There are many other similarities between this group of films. In *Talk Radio*, the male callers despise Eric Bogosian, viewing him as a threat to civilization. In *Night Rhythms*, the male callers despise Nick West, viewing him as a threat to civilization. They view him as a threat to civilization because so many of his female listeners say things like: "Oh, Nick, you do things to me on the phone my husband doesn't even do in person." Really? Like what? Tele-enemas?

Other similarities? *Body Chemistry II* includes a scene where a person is murdered on the air while having kinky sex. *Night Rhythms* includes a scene where a person is murdered on the air while having kinky sex. *Straight Talk* features a scene where the talk-radio hostess admits to her listeners that she is a complete asshole. So do *Pump Up the Volume*, *The Fisher King*, and *Talk Radio*. *Sexual Response* has a pivotal scene where the talk-radio hostess confronts her confused lover on the air. *Talk Radio* has a scene where the talk-show host confronts his confused lover on the air. In *The Fisher King* Jeff Bridges gets his career going again after a pivotal meeting with a complete lunatic. In *Talk Radio*, Eric Bogosian gets his career going again after a pivotal meeting with a complete lunatic.

Oh, the similarities go on and on! *Sexual Response* stars Shannon Tweed; *Night Rhythms* stars Tracy Tweed. *Talk Radio* deals with a foul-mouthed psychopath who wants to take his grubby radio show national; *Body Chemistry II* deals with a foul-mouthed psychopath who wants to take her grubby radio show national. *Sexual Response* stars Catherine Oxenberg. *Night Rhythms* doesn't, but seems like it does.

There is one other characteristic that these movies share. In bygone areas, in films involving radio personalities, it was the person armed with the telephone who posed the threat to society. This was the case in the 1978 film *Martin,* which dealt with a teen vampire who continually phones in details of his misadventures to a radio announcer who thinks he's making it all up. And who can ever forget the horror wreaked on the hapless Clint Eastwood by the demented Jessica Walter in *Play Misty for Me?* In both of these cases, it was the deejay, not the caller, who was the victim.

Those days are gone. As the tidal waves of films we have discussed make clear, the Republic now finds itself menaced by people on the other side of the phone: the talk-radio hosts themselves. What right does Nick West, the talk-radio host of *Night Rhythms,* whose lesbian producer strangles her bisexual girlfriend on the air and makes it look like West did it, have to give women advice about their sex lives? How are we to take Bogosian seriously after he tries to talk a serial rapist caller out of attacking his next victim by saying: "The last time we spoke, you said that jogging helped you." "I feel like I'm a magnet, but I attract shit," moans Jeff Bridges in *The Fisher King.* Well, yeah.

As is usually the case, the brilliant director Alan Rudolph saw all of this coming years ago. In 1984, Rudolph directed an ominously prescient film entitled *Choose Me,* in which the fabulously gifted Genevieve Bujold plays a talk-radio sex therapist named Dr. Love. Dr. Love has regular phone chit-chats with a retired prostitute and bistro owner played by Lesley Ann Warren, who has not been able to find the man of her dreams. Unaware that her new roommate is a regular caller to her program—"The Love Line"—Dr. Love rents a room in Warren's house. Meanwhile Lesley Ann has taken up with an ex-poetry professor, CIA spy, air force officer, and killer played with passion and gusto by the human sarcophagus Keith Carradine. Although Carradine adores Lesley Ann, in a momentary lapse of reason he goes home with a barfly convincingly played by Rae Dawn Chong, whose boyfriend is a psychopath who regularly calls Dr. Love, who is now screwing Keith Carradine even though Carradine is really in love with Lesley Ann Warren and is screwing Rae Dawn Chong in a momentary lapse of reason. Carradine asks Dr. Love to drop everything and go to Las Vegas to get married, but Dr. Love doesn't think this is such a good idea, so after many beatings and attempted murders and phone calls and momentary lapses of reason, Carradine goes to Vegas to marry Lesley Ann Warren.

It is clear from Warren's facial expression in the final frames of the film that this relationship is not going to work. Yes, all the way back in 1984, the clairvoyant Alan Rudolph had foreseen the coming of an age in which neurotic talk-radio callers would destroy their personal lives by taking extremely bad advice from people like Genevieve Bujold. Foreshadowing the scene in *Body Chemistry II* in which an abused woman is told she should be gratified to have a boyfriend who cares enough to beat her, *Choose Me* contains a scene where Rae Dawn Chong, sporting a huge black eye, remarks: "I love him. I really do . . . even though he roughs me up. At least he cares enough to do it." Eight years before Shannon Tweed would play a nutcake sex maniac named Eve in *Sexual Response*, Lesley Ann Warren would play a nutcake sex maniac named Eve in *Choose Me*. Eight years before David Carradine played a shady character with female troubles in *Night Rhythms*, brother Keith played a shady character with female troubles in *Choose Me*. I think, in his own small way, Alan Rudolph was trying to warn us all: Blow up that fucking radio before it kills us all. But as is usually the case with Alan Rudolph, we did not listen, and now we must pay the price.

18 OH, YOU BEAUTIFUL DOLL OR ARE SEAN YOUNG'S DAYS NUMBERED?

On or about the night of August 16, 1988, somebody left a grotesquely disfigured doll on the doorstep of actor James Woods. Sean Young, who costarred with Woods in *The Boost*, and who reportedly had an affair with the actor during the filming of the movie (both parties deny the allegation), says that it wasn't she. She also says that it wasn't she who made threatening phone calls to Woods's girlfriend, Sarah Owen; that she didn't make an early exit from *Wall Street* because she was widely loathed on the set; and that the note Charlie Sheen pinned on her back describing her as "the biggest @#*#! in the world" was really just a joke.

"This stuff would bother me if I was a really shitty actress," says Young. "But I'm not."

Sean Young is, unfortunately, becoming better known for her offscreen exploits—or alleged exploits—than for her work as an actress. Some parts of her growing legend she admits to—such as giving the finger to the softball team from *Wall Street* while they were playing ball in a Long Island park one night after shooting. But she says she only did it because the guys waited too long to let her pitch. In any case, after some prodding, Sean Young eventually agrees to discuss these matters, but first she has a little matter to attend to: her weekly algebra lesson.

"That's very good, that's perfect," says Ron Lulov, a young man who teaches high school in New York City but who moonlights as a tutor. His student has just given a correct answer while seated in the kitchen of her Greenwich Village apartment, and Lulov is pleased. "You see, you *have* to express it as a polynomial."

Actually, Sean Young doesn't *have* to do anything. Affluent, talented, and remarkably beautiful, Young made a big impression in 1987 as Kevin Costner's doomed but leggy lover in *No Way Out*. She recently gave another intense performance in *The Boost*, in which she and Woods illustrated in graphic fashion why you shouldn't take drugs, or at least why you shouldn't take as many as they do. She currently can be seen in the movie *Cousins*, the American version of *Cousin, Cousine*.

All of which pays for a lot of algebra lessons.

"The next time you negotiate a contract," says Lulov, "say that you'll take half the amount, but you want it to the tenth power!"

This is good advice, considering how fast the contracts have been coming in. Young, who has been in nine feature films (including *Stripes*, *Blade Runner*, and *Dune*), has a small part in Woody Allen's newest movie, and is angling for such roles as Blaze Starr, the famous stripper, and Tess Trueheart, Dick Tracy's wife, in the upcoming Warren Beatty flick. She was supposed to play Batgirl in Tim Burton's *Batman*, but fell off a horse, broke her collarbone, and was replaced by the more durable Kim Basinger, who survived *9½ Weeks*.

Before her breakthrough in *No Way Out*, Young's biggest shot at stardom was her role as Michael Douglas's wife in *Wall Street*. But she got left on the cutting-room floor, either because she got fired (reportedly) or because "that part was only three days shooting in the first place" (her version). As for the note Charlie

Sheen pinned to her back during the shoot, Young, twenty-nine, laughs it off.

"You have to understand," she says patiently, "Charlie is so *young*."

Nevertheless, Young admits that her exit from *Wall Street* could have been more decorous. "You know the scene where Daryl Hannah is with Charlie in the stable, and he says something about a racehorse, and she says, 'It's a jumper, Bud, not a racehorse'? Well, that was my line. One morning I came into the stable, and everyone is standing around shooting this scene, and I start edging my way around, and Daryl is saying *my* line. I can just see myself saying it. So I asked why Daryl was saying my line, and Oliver said, 'That line has been changed for months.' 'Well, how come nobody told me?' I said. 'I mean, I don't think I should be doing this scene if I don't get to say that line.' "

Stone seemed to agree. Exit Sean Young.

Young is no stranger to unpleasantness, having inexplicably incurred the wrath of local female bullies when she was growing up in Cleveland, the daughter of magazine writer Lee Guthrie and a retired public relations executive. "These girls were big and ugly and fat and mean," she says. "They used to throw French fries at me. I begged my mom to send me to Interlochen (a boarding school for the performing arts in Michigan)."

After graduating from Interlochen, Young moved to New York and became a successful model. She then got into movies, and within a few years was seducing Kevin Costner in the backseat of a limo and being sued by James Woods for leaving a mutilated doll on his doorstep. Savaged by the media as a comely but perhaps sinister human being, Young has now retreated to the reassuring sanity of the quadratic equation.

"I like algebra because it's finite, it's not up for interpretation," she says. "It doesn't change. I can count on it."

It may also have aided her in portfolio management during the Crash of '87. "I invest in small midwestern life insurance companies and government securities," she explains, insisting that she lost no money when the stock market took its biggest nose dive ever. "They don't make a lot of money, but they don't lose a lot, either. They're very conservative."

No one is ever going to say that about Young. Take the mutilated doll incident. According to James Woods's attorney, Dale Kinsella, "On or about the night of August 16, 1988, a disfigured doll was left on the doorstep of Mr. Woods. Subsequently, a note was left by an anonymous individual saying that they [*sic*] had been put up to this by Sean Young. And that she was upset because they were supposed to hang it by the neck, not just leave it on the doorstep."

Young denies this allegation (she *was* questioned, however, by the Los Angeles Police Department and will give a deposition in the near future). In fact, Young retains a great deal of respect for Woods, saying, "He's really smart; he keeps coming at you with these ideas and observations—just like a machine gun." She says the problem is "that Jimmy just never said goodbye. He never closed the circle."

She regrets that she and her costar parted company under unfortunate circumstances—after take twelve of a scene that required her to devour what she recalls as a very unsavory chili dog.

"I went around the corner to puke my guts up," she says, "and when I came back, they said, 'It's a wrap.' And he was gone."

Young is upset by the way she has been treated by some people in her profession. For example, she says that Cher snubbed her at last year's Academy Awards ceremony ("All right, I'm young and I'm beautiful, but you don't have to hate me"). But if her current notoriety does ruin her movie career, she still has several things to fall back on. Tap dancing, for example. Yes, in addition to her burgeoning mathematical skills, Young is an avid tap dancer who dreams of one day being in a big Broadway musical like *42nd Street*.

A member of the American Tap Dance Orchestra, Young expresses great admiration for Ruby Keeler, who, she claims, helped Al Jolson extricate himself from the clutches of organized crime when he was being leaned on by the mob many years ago. She recounts this story in a restaurant in Little Italy, where a patron at a nearby table—who seems just old enough to have done some of the learning—is listening with great interest.

Speaking of restaurants, yes, Sean Young eats food: linguine, olives, bread, you name it. Some people have speculated that Young may not be eating regularly, that she may be drifting into anorexia. But in person, Young is . . . okay, okay, maybe a tad skinny, but, nonetheless, more beautiful than anyone else in the immediate solar system, and could easily do for anorexia what Diane Keaton once did for stupid-looking hats.

And think what a role model she could be for future mathematicians! Young is so serious about her algebra that she actually offers to fly back from Los Angeles a day early so that she won't miss her next class. Lulov notes that the next class is scheduled for December 26, Christmas Monday. But Young seems all set to catch the red-eye if it will hasten her understanding of why X to the tenth power is not equal to 10X.

"I want to learn geometry, too," Young beams. "I know that I'm going to teach someday."

As this week's algebra lesson breaks up, conversation turns to the subject of Lulov's name. "It's a Jewish name," he explains. "It's the Hebrew word for *palm*. Like in Palm Sunday."

"I was just confirmed!" Young interjects excitedly. "My confirmation name is Esther. It's amazing how much the Jewish and Catholic religions are tied in." She elaborates. "Jesus was a Jew."

Wasn't he, though? And, truly, there is something endearing in all this, something elfishly reassuring that in an era where many starlets want to impress strangers with how much they learned in college, Young is willing to reveal how much she didn't learn in high school.

Yet, if Young entertains serious dreams of becoming America's most fetching algebra teacher, she's going to have to start hitting the books. Lulov concedes as much when he tells his pupil that she is still having trouble "translating verbal phrases into algebraic concepts," as when he asks: "If you want to buy a dress for C dollars, and I give you a discount of D dollars, how much are you going to pay for the dress?"

"I don't know," she confesses.

"Think of it this way," he says. "Seven minus three does not equal three minus seven."

"So C minus D is not the same as D minus C!" says Young enthusiastically.

"Right!" says Lulov.

Study hard, Sean. Study hard.

19 THE MAN WHO DID NOT LOVE WOMEN

In an early, and not especially good, Alfred Hitchcock movie entitled *Secret Agent*, Peter Lorre goes on a rampage when he learns that the British Secret Service has not provided him with a delectable female companion. Whereas leading man John Gielgud gets to amuse himself with the comely Madeleine Carroll, the extremely unattractive Lorre, here cast as a mysterious sleazeball nicknamed the "Hairless Mexican," goes positively bonkers when he finds out that "headquarters" has not issued him a blond playmate.

"This is too much, really too much," Lorre seethes, pounding the walls with his fists. "For you, beautiful women, and what for me? What for me?—nothing!"

Well, that pretty well sums up Hitchcock's own career: an extraordinarily unattractive man who spends his adult life working in close proximity to the most beautiful blondes of his era—but who has to suffer in silence as they snuggle up on the laps of good-looking guys named Grant or Stewart or Olivier or Gielgud, none of whom ever had to lose 100 pounds just to get down to a more manageable 265.

As Donald Spoto has observed in his insightful if dreary book *The Dark Side of Genius: The Life of*

Alfred Hitchcock, the director often developed an obsessive relationship with his female leads, going so far as to tell Tippi Hedren whom to date, and having Edith Head design personal wardrobes for both Hedren and Vera Miles. Other critics have dwelled on Hitchcock's fascination with blondes, even suggesting that Janet Leigh's brutal murder in the shower scene in *Psycho* may have been Hitchcock's perverse little way of getting back at Grace Kelly for abandoning him for the more dashing and, no doubt, less demented Prince Rainier of Monaco, and also punishing Vera Miles (demoted to the second string in *Psycho*) for throwing away her chance to be the next Kelly by going out and, of all things, having a baby. The slut.

Of course, it is possible to make too much of all this, to go too far with the amateur psychologizing, and I think that's exactly what we should do here. If anyone deserves to be subjected to a bit of Monday morning psychoanalysis, it's Hitchcock; he himself was an amateur psychologist who always went overboard with this stuff. It's hard to look at *Spellbound* today without chortling at its pop Freudianism, and the same is true of *Vertigo*, *Rebecca*, *Notorious*, and *Suspicion*, all of which are wonderful motion pictures whose abiding appeal is not diminished by the fact that they are, at heart, really quite ridiculous stories. So is *Gone With the Wind*. Just ask black people.

Alfred Hitchcock made fifty-three movies, of which about forty are available in video. No one watching these videos over a two-month period of time, as I have, could fail to notice certain recurring elements. The most obvious ones, which do not need to be discussed here, are the claustrophobia, the ambivalent feelings toward policemen, and the fixation with churches, trains, tunnels, heights, and Mom. The elements that will be discussed here include Hitchcock's willingness to subordinate plot, theme, and character to his passion for visual effects; his penchant for preposterous story lines drawn from trashy paperbacks; his childlike view of politics; his brilliant sense of self-parody; and, most important of all, his obsession with blondes that would become a *complete* obsession by the early 1950s.

No one could fail to notice that as the years go by Hitchcock really likes to put the girls through the wringer. Kelly is nearly strangled to death in *Dial M for Murder,* and again flirts with disaster in *Rear Window.* Kim Novak plunges to her death in *Vertigo,* Leigh is hacked to pieces in *Psycho,* and Hedren is very nearly pecked to death in *The Birds.* After that, Hitchcock gave it a rest, but having spent the better part of a decade feeding the girls into the meat grinder, he had certainly made it clear that, at least when he was in the neighborhood, blondes did not have more fun.

Of course, it wasn't just blondes who didn't have fun. In *Notorious,* Ingrid Bergman spends two hours being psychologically brutalized by Cary Grant, and Joan Fontaine signed on for two years before the mast on the *H.M.S. Hitchcock.* In *Rebecca* Fontaine plays a character who is ignored by her husband, preyed upon by her malevolent housekeeper, haunted by the specter of her husband's deceased first wife, belittled by her employer, and humiliated by her servants. In *Suspicion* she plays a character so barmy that she finally decides to simply drink what she believes to be a poisoned glass of milk and get the misery over with.

One of the most interesting things a viewer picks up after watching the full gamut of Hitchcock films is that when the girls wouldn't go along with the gag, they were not invited back. Hitchcock may have treated most of his players like cattle, but Tallulah Bankhead certainly didn't get pushed around in *Life-boat,* nor did Marlene Dietrich in *Stage Fright,* and Hitch never worked with either again. Hitchcock seems to have given Carole Lombard a dry run in his unsuccessful *Mr. and Mrs. Smith,* decided she wasn't docile enough, and moved on to more fertile fields. Had Kelly and Hedren not decided to pursue other interests, there's really no telling what Hitchcock might have had in store for them. Chainsaws? Famished rodents? Obstetrical equipment?

Vertigo, in which a trashy brunette is transformed into an elegant blonde, who then goes back to being a trashy brunette and is again transformed into being an elegant blonde—before meeting her unpleasant fate—is probably Hitchcock's most autobiographical film. At the very end of this *Pygmalion the 13th,* an unhinged Jimmy Stewart shrieks at Novak: "You played the wife very well, Judy. He made you over just like I made you over, only better. Not only the clothes and the hair, but the look and the manner and the words. . . . And then what did he do? Did he train you? Did he rehearse you? Did he tell you exactly what to do? And what to say? You were an apt pupil, too, weren't you? You were a very apt pupil. But why did you pick on me? Why me?"

It is not at all clear what Novak made of all this, much less Prince Rainier. But coming as it did in 1958, three years after Amazing Grace had concluded her trio of great films (*Dial M for Murder, Rear Window,* and *To Catch a Thief*) only to desert Hitchcock, and just one year after Vera Miles's debut in *The Wrong Man,* it's not hard to figure out what was going on in the director's mind. Hell, it was right there on the screen. *The Ladies Vanish.*

Was Alfred Hitchcock a sadist? Yes, so now let's get on to the next question: What kind of a sadist was he? Certainly not a sadist of the traditional British variety; otherwise we would have seen Bergman and Kelly in white knee socks and frilly knickers hauled over stern teachers' knees for firm, well-deserved spankings. No, Hitchcock camouflaged his fascination with seeing women suffer by channeling it into conventional, acceptable sadomasochistic practices: butcher knives in the abdomen, school ties coiled around the neck. Had he gone in for canes or whips (he did have a bit of a thing with handcuffs), people would have said he was a trifle kinky. Butcher knives and neckties were more acceptable. Still are. And in a pinch, try seagulls.

We mustn't forget that Hitchcock choreographed his heroines' predicaments so as to suggest that the girls had brought some of their misfortune upon themselves. With the exception of the unnamed wimpette in *Rebecca*, Hitchcock usually depicted his female victims as ladies of, if not the evening, certainly the late afternoon. In *Notorious*, Bergman is a party girl who has slept around while Dad was busy being a Nazi, and who is persuaded by secret agent Cary Grant to sleep around some more, marrying the authentically creepy Claude Raines, also a Nazi. In *Vertigo*, Novak is a willing accomplice to a murder. *Dial M for Murder* opens with Kelly cheating on her husband with Robert Cummings. (For you symbolism buffs, she is seen wearing red.) The obsessive naughtiness of these doomed dollies reaches its apogee in *Psycho*, where Leigh, who has embezzled $40,000 from her employer, atones for her fiscal indiscretions by having a transvestite fruitcake hack her to ribbons. The moral of all this is clear: Bad girls will be sent to their rooms. And the rooms will be in the Bates Motel.

Hitchcock's treatment of Kelly gives the whole show away. The very idea of enlisting the audience in her murder (the camera approaches her neck from behind the murderer's shoulder, making the viewer a coconspirator in the attack) is bad enough, but more to the point, what kind of audience really and truly wants to see Grace Kelly—the quintessence of 1950s quintessitude—with her eyes bulging out and her tongue turning purple? Probably the same folks who would have liked to see Shirley Temple boiled in hot pitch.

Strange as *Dial M for Misogynist* may be, *Rear Window* takes the cake for sexual perversity. This is the film in which Jimmy Stewart frankly admits that he doesn't want to marry Kelly because she's "too perfect." Yes, every man's nightmare. What Stewart does enjoy is checking out the derriere on the surprisingly full-figured ballerina across the courtyard, whose volatile wiggling as she peers into the refrigerator may have inspired the film's title. To ensure that Stewart cannot consummate his unconventional relationship with Kelly, Hitchcock has him start the movie with one broken leg and end the movie with two. (Play-on-word buffs should note that the film concludes with Kelly perusing the magazine *Harper's Bazaar*—as in "bizarre." Grace wears a huge smile.)

At the time of his death, Hitchcock enjoyed a huge but curiously muddled reputation. To the American public he was the master of shock, a reputation that probably derived more from *Psycho*, *The Birds*, and his enduringly clever television programs—most of which he did not direct—than from the rest of his movies. To serious critics—no, not you, Roger and Gene—he was either an incomparable technician who failed to address truly important issues, or a vastly underrated genius. It should be noted, however, that François Truffaut and Claude Chabrol were the guys who got the Hitchcock-as-vastly-underrated-director bandwagon rolling, and Chabrol *is* and Truffaut *was* French.

The ominous implications in this cannot be ignored. French people, after all, think Jerry Lewis is a genius. French people think Frank Zappa and Carlos Santana are geniuses. French people hold Don Siegel Film Festivals. French people, when they learn that you are an American, immediately start asking questions about Richard Brautigan and Chester Himes, whom they think are geniuses. French people are very impressed by heartless technicians, which is why they produce gifted but sterile musicians like Claude Bolling and Jean-Pierre Rampal, but have never produced a single rock star of any consequence. French people think that anyone who pokes fun at policemen or the CIA is really a subversive at heart, because the French, subversives at heart, collaborated with the Nazis even though they really didn't like them, which made it okay. French people are *very, very* strange.

Yet, the truth is, all of these people—the French, the public, the hard-core artsy types who never really liked Hitchcock—were on to something. Alfred Hitchcock made visually stunning works that packed moviehouses for years. He not only struck a nerve, but he kept on striking it for four decades until he burned out midway through *The Birds*. He knew that people lived in fear—of the government, of each other, and of themselves—and he knew that no matter how many times he went to that same well, it would never run dry.

On the other hand, did he absolutely, positively have to keep on going to that same well? Wasn't he ever tempted to make a great movie about a broader theme: injustice, class warfare, anti-Semitism, the betrayal of one's youthful ideals, politics? Politics is an especially baffling one, because, although Hitchcock made a whole slew of films with some political component, the treatment is uniformly sophomoric. *Secret Agent, Sabotage, The Thirty-Nine Steps, North by Northwest, The Man Who Knew Too Much, Saboteur, Torn Curtain, Foreign Correspondent,* and, yes, even the abysmal *Topaz* all deal with spies, but the political component is, without exception, merely a mechanism to get the manhunt underway. To make a real political film like *The Conversation, Z,* or *The Conformist,* you have to have genuine political beliefs, to believe that the Right is bad and the Left good, or vice versa. Hitchcock had no such beliefs. The closest he ever came to making a political movie was *Lifeboat,* in which he seemed to admire the Nazis because they made the boats run on time. This was one odd chap.

On the other hand, so were Pasolini, Arthur Conan Doyle, Oscar Wilde, Roman Polanski, Georges Simenon, Ambrose Bierce, Edgar Allan Poe, and H. P. Lovecraft, the artists Hitchcock most resembles. To a man, these were strange guys with a highly personal, idiosyncratic view of the world, artists who were largely contemptuous of conventional, bourgeois values. "There's nothing like a love song to give you a good laugh," Hitchcock has Bergman say in *Notorious.* Frank Capra he wasn't.

So, yes, Truffaut was right, Hitchcock was a great artist and a great moviemaker, one of the twenty-five greatest of all time. But almost certainly not one of the five greatest. Why? Frankly, because he let his talents run away with him, constantly focusing on technical matters to the detriment of other elements: character, plot, theme. Look at his subject matter. Most serious moviemakers will move heaven and earth to get to the point in their careers where they can film the important works of Western literature: *Jane Eyre, The Grapes of Wrath, Madame Bovary, The Last Temptation of Christ.* Hitchcock started out with writers like Daphne du Maurier and worked his way down. His dalliances with the masters were few, far between, and futile: a very bad version of Sean O'Casey's *Juno and the Paycock* in 1930, and a clumsy if reasonably faithful rendering of Joseph Conrad's *The Secret Agent.* But *The Secret Agent* was a bad Conrad novel, unlike *Lord Jim, Heart of Darkness, Nostromo, The Secret Sharer,* or *Almayer's Folly.*

Well, of course, it was bad, because bad books were what Hitchcock made his good movies from. Hitchcock was always and forever in the alchemy business, taking what the English call "penny dreadfuls"—heavily plotted, convoluted thrillers— and turning them into visual masterpieces. Why did he like them? Because they were easy for the audience to sink their teeth into. They had people getting hatpins stuck in their eardrums, or having their eyes pecked out by seagulls. They had contrivances that could scare the pants off the viewing public. Bad fiction writers churn out plot, plot, plot, replete with tricks, gimmicks, mistaken identities, subterfuges, endless contrivances to keep the action moving. You can film that stuff. Good novelists rely primarily on character development and language, which puts directors in a pickle. Where the hell is the plot development in *Pride and Prejudice, The Wings of the Dove,* or, for that matter, *Anna Karenina?*

But Hitchcock's decision to give the masterpieces a wide berth may have been a wise one, for, with rare exception, the great books have stymied the great directors. That's because it is virtually impossible to externalize internal psychological activity, as David Lean found out in his elegant but unsuccessful *A Passage to India.* John Huston made a bunch of great movies, but *Moby Dick* is not one of them. *Moby Dick* is a mess. So are *The*

Castle, *The Scarlet Letter*, Polanski's *Macbeth*, and any number of *War and Peace*s.

To his everlasting credit, Alfred Hitchcock made movies that were supposed to be *looked at*. Watching those two-score films I was amazed by how many specific *scenes* from Hitchcock's movies are riveted inside my brain, including movies I had not seen in twenty years. They include the belltower scenes from *Vertigo*, the strangling in *Dial M for Murder*, the shower scene from *Psycho*, the playground scene from *The Birds*, and the Mount Rushmore scene from *North by Northwest*. Of course, if you want to rivet visual images inside people's heads, it helps if you use Cary Grant and Eva Marie Saint hanging off Mount Rushmore. With Ralph Meeker and Donna Reed dangling from the Sears Tower, it might not have worked.

Hitchcock started off by making visually arresting silent movies and he kept making them the rest of his life. Oh, the dialogue was great—superb, hilarious, pick your kudo—but it's what the viewer *sees* that makes these films so unforgettable. Thus, all that Freudian chatter in *Spellbound* doesn't amount to a row of beans next to the Salvador Dali dream sequence or the scene where Gregory Peck drinks the milk while holding a razor blade. In fact, there is genuine irony in the fact that Hitchcock hired Dali for those dream sequences, because Dali enjoys much the same reputation as Hitchcock: a stunning visual artist with an aggressive self-promotional streak who has always been criticized for pandering to the masses by going heavy on the special effects but light on the subject matter.

The visuals were ever so important because they got the audience over some of the rough patches. The plots, for example. Yes, one aspect of Hitchcock's movies that has not received sufficient critical attention is the fundamentally idiotic nature of his stories. If you were Ingrid Bergman and your boss, the head of the Green Manor loony bin, told you that he was stepping down and handing over the reins to a famous psychoanalyst no one had ever met or even seen a photograph of, wouldn't you find that a bit strange? (It certainly created an embarrassing moment when Gregory Peck, with no formal training as a physician, was called upon to perform surgery.) If you were a comely young woman who had just spent fifteen minutes chatting with the decidedly quirky Norman Bates, would you then strip to your black slip and brassiere and take a shower? If you were a timid dumpling being slowly driven insane by a psychotic housekeeper with overtly lesbian tendencies, mightn't it have occurred to you to corner Laurence Olivier and say, "Look, honey, if it's all the same to you, couldn't we just can that bitch?" And while we're on the subject, whose idea was it to cast Montgomery Clift and Karl Malden as English-speaking denizens of French Quebec in *I Confess*?

No, it's all quite mad, isn't it; and yet so devilishly clever. Hitchcock simply had no equal in making the most absurd plot lines seem plausible, perhaps even *realistic*. Of course, we mustn't overlook the distinct possibility that Hitchcock himself thought it was all one big joke. It's well documented, for example, that Hitchcock started off with the idea of having people dangling off Mount Rushmore long before he had any plot for the movie. His philosophy seemed to be: Let's set up an amazing, thrilling visual sequence and then work our way back to a story line. For example, I'm still trying to figure out what Suzanne Pleshette was thinking of when she told the kids to march out of the school-house—where they were perfectly safe—and run down the street—where they were not—with a legion of blackbirds pursuing them. On the other hand, I have two small children.

Nor should we forget that Hitchcock was a master of self-parody; his very last film, *Family Plot*, is a small jewel of self-mockery, largely centering on the fact that Bruce Dern has to keep going to work as a taxi driver. But there are many other moments of gleeful winking. When Claude Rains's mother (*Notorious*) lights a cigarette after learning that Ingrid Bergman is a spy, Hitchcock gave us one of the crowning Oedipal shots of all time: Jocasta with a Lucky Strike. (She was one of the few blondes Hitchcock didn't get to rough up.) In *The Thirty-Nine Steps*, when Mister Memory, who knows just about everything, appears before the audience, the question that keeps getting hollered out is: "How old is Mae West?" In *Rear Window*, when one of Stewart's neighbors discovers that her dog has been killed, she delivers a hilarious soliloquy, concluding with the lines, "Why would anyone want to kill a little dog? Because it knew too much?" And for major-league chuckles, how about the scene in *Lifeboat*, where, after the Nazi captain has blown up an unarmed vessel, torpedoed the lifeboats, caused a baby to freeze to death and its mother to commit suicide, and murdered William Bendix, one character wonders, "What do you do with people like that?"

Hitchcock also knew that his movies were going to be seen more than once, and that the jokes people didn't get the first time around would be hootfests the second. "There are plenty of motels in this area," the menacing state trooper tells Janet Leigh when he finds her dozing in her car early in *Psycho*. "Just to be safe." And let's not forget Anthony Perkins's remark to his doomed guest: "My mother . . . she isn't quite herself today."

Alfred Hitchcock was one sick pup. Nevertheless, he had the goods, because when God gives out talent, He doesn't care whom He gives it to. Hitchcock was so good, and was good for so long, that his achievement calls, and will continue to call, into question the very notion of what art actually is. Because, no two ways about it, looking at those thirty-six movies for two months was a whole lot more uplifting than locking myself in with the complete works of Merchant and Ivory or Michelangelo Antonioni. But what does it all mean? When unknown actresses get slashed to ribbons in *Friday the 13th* movies we recognize the films have low production values. When hack directors butcher females in slasher movies, it's called garbage, but when Hitchcock does it with style in *Psycho*, it's called art. And it *is* art. It's weird, creepy art. It taps into something primal: the need to have the bejesus scared out of us, the need to be reminded that this is a very strange planet where strange, unexpected things can happen. As Tippi Hedren says to Rod Taylor after the first brutal avian onslaught on the kids in *The Birds:* "Mitch, this isn't usual, is it?"

It was in Alfred Hitchcock's neighborhood.

20 THE DARK SIDE OF THE MOON

In the town where I live there are two video stores. One is the kind that carries Melanie Griffith movies and one is the kind that doesn't. Oh, all right, they *both* carry Griffith's mainstream flicks, *Working Girl* and *Something Wild.* But if you want to see vintage Griffith, prime Griffith, the *Ur*-Griffithiana, that made Melanie the remarkable actress she is today—movies like *Cherry 2000*, *Fear City*, *Joy Ride*—you have to visit the video store in the rundown part of town. The other video store doesn't cater to *that* kind of clientele.

This kind of hoity-toity attitude is unfair to Melanie, of course, but more to the point, it's unfair to her legions of fans, to those of us who have been with her since the beginning. Unlike those Johnny-come-lately aficionados who try to parse and pare the Griffith oeuvre—to act as if her career begins with Jonathan Demme's quirky 1986 hit, *Something Wild*, and Mike Nichols's 1988 let's-bash-Sigourney film, *Working Girl*—those of us who have been keeping an eye on Griffith, or, at least, an eye on certain parts of Griffith (the part with the tattoo) for a long time, see her films as a continuous, seamless body of work.

What we see is a Melanie Griffith who, from her

very earliest days, from her first electrifying performance as a horny nymphet in *Night Moves* to her riveting performance as a horny nymphet in *The Drowning Pool* to her stunning performance as a horny stripper in *Fear City* to her show-stopping role as a horny stripper in *Body Double* to her mesmerizing role as a call girl who is not especially horny in *Stormy Monday*, has given shape and voice and body and soul to that quintessential American archetype: the culturally and politically disenfrancished bimbo. The type of girl who, as Griffith puts it in *Working Girl*, has "a mind for business and a bod for sin." Not necessarily in that order.

From the middle 1970s until the present, no American actress has shaken her bootie with as much verve, passion, and regularity as Melanie Griffith. Yet, unlike more vulgar, opportunistic performers, Griffith has injected these roles with pathos and compassion, evoking crocodile tears from enthusiastic audiences filled with men and women who have known, or have themselves been, bimbos, and who recognize a performance that rings true. In the kingdom of the bimbo, Melanie Griffith reigns supreme, making ersatz bimbos like Valerie Perrine seem like pikers or, for that matter, ersatz bimbos. As she once told *The Los Angeles Times:* "There's a bit of a stripper in every woman." Well, maybe not my wife.

Melanie Griffith is, and has always been, a survivor. The daughter of actress Tippi Hedren and a socially prominent film producer named Peter Griffith, Melanie has had to overcome wealth, celebrity, Catholic boarding school, being in Robby Benson movies, receiving a plastic coffin with a tiny replica of her mother inside as a gift from the ever-thoughtful Alfred Hitchcock, a friendship with Warren Beatty, and the staggering pressures of growing up on a 180-acre ranch with a bunch of wild animals on it, as opposed to, say, East Los Angeles. Well, maybe that's not such a good example. Anyway, among living Americans, only George Herbert Walker Bush—who had to deal with the stigma of being born into a wealthy family, named captain of the Yale baseball team, and being the grandson of the first president of the United States Golf Association—has had to rise above more prejudice. It is a credit to Griffith that she has been as successful as she has in overcoming what must have seemed at times like truly insurmountable odds.

Griffith did not grow up wanting to be a famous actress whose sexual charge, in the words of the English magazine *Time Out*, "could pick up confetti on a comb and turn a man's saliva to gravy." In a 1975 interview with *Seventeen* magazine, she explained that she wished to attend the Sorbonne and study philosophy. But then at age eighteen she got married to Don Johnson, a good-looking actor eight years her senior who had never told *Seventeen* or anyone else that he wanted to study at the Sorbonne. At the time, Johnson was a virtually unknown vegetarian who could not get any good parts in movies, probably because directors and producers alike thought he would make a lot of bombs and lose them a lot of money. Imagine.

With the Sorbonne and philosophy temporarily on the back burner, Griffith devoted herself to her *craft*, working hard to become one of the finest actresses of her generation. The road would not be easy. There would be bouts with drugs and alcohol, estrangement from Johnson, more bouts with drugs and alcohol, another marriage, motherhood, reunion with Johnson, many, many leg waxes, and articles in *People* magazine unfairly dwelling on those bouts with drugs and alcohol. Griffith, who, in addition to being married to Johnson twice, has been mauled by a lion once, has clearly seen the dark side of the moon—as have those who have watched her movies. But all through the dark times, Griffith never allowed personal misfortune to interfere with her art. Throughout her hegira in the artistic wilderness, when she could not get parts in films like *Working Girl* or *The Milagro Beanfield War* or *Pacific Heights* or *Bonfire of the Vanities*, Griffith worked hard to hone and polish a screen persona that is as unique in its way as the larger-than-life screen personas of John Wayne, Bette Davis, Greta Garbo, and Fred MacMurray. That persona is the instantly recognizable Griffith Girl: a trashy babe in black underpants and matching garter belt with a squeaky voice, a butt that is not to be trifled with, and a heart as wide as Asia. Breast size and tattoo configuration may vary from film to film.

Obviously, not everyone is a Melanie Griffith fan. "How could anyone live with a woman who has a voice like that?" is the question my wife asked when she saw me watching *Working Girl* one evening. It was a legitimate inquiry, and yet in its casual cynicism it reminded me only too well why my wife is an English chartered accountant with two small children and not a handcuff-toting lollapalooza who has turned men's saliva into gravy in an endless succession of torrid flicks. Because, frankly, it's just *too easy* to pick on Griffith's voice and make remarks like, "She sounds like a three-year-old."

The fact is, Griffith's infantile voice is part and parcel of her appeal. Some observers have labeled the voice kewpie-dollish, while others have pinpointed an almost Betty Boopish quality. Personally, I find Griffith's voice and her curiously studied inflection—witness the almost phonetic fashion in which she reads her lines in *Cherry 2000* in a style reminiscent of Charles Bronson's French-speaking roles in movies such as *The Mechanic*—not unlike the pitch and delivery of those talking dolls that were so popular when I was growing up. The way I see it, Griffith's appeal to the male moviegoer probably derives in large part from the fact that, deep down inside, every redblooded American man has at one time in his life harbored a secret desire to go to bed with Chatty Cathy.

Griffith's seemingly infantile voice must also be considered in light of her relationship with Don Johnson, whom she recently married for a second time. Whereas Griffith possesses a high-pitched, butter-wouldn't-melt-in-my-mouth, little-girl voice that does not seem to go with her robust physique, Johnson/Crocker has an artificially deep voice that seems out of place in what seems to be a thoroughly magnificent but nonetheless normal-sized body. Were the two voices grafted together, the pair would at least have one normal speaking voice between them. This symbiotic need to drown out each other's physically incongruous voices and create a choirlike effect is almost certainly the reason they chose to remarry and appear in public together. That and the fact that her body can turn men's saliva into gravy.

Physically, Griffith is capable of the most protean of transformations imaginable, being her generation's female equivalent of Paul Muni and Lon Chaney—the men of a thousand faces. For example, in Abel Ferrara's vastly underrated *Fear City*—perhaps the finest film ever made about the largely unspoken bond between New York strippers and their booking agents—Griffith bears a striking resemblance to Cheryl Ladd, with perhaps a slightly larger bottom and a slightly smaller brain. In *Body Double* she does a very fine impersonation of Victoria Principal, until she tosses away the wig and makeup and reverts to the Billy Idol look. In *Cherry 2000,* another unjustifiably neglected film, Griffith sports a striking shock of reddish hair, and looks not entirely unlike Ronald McDonald. In *Something Wild* she does her Louise Brooks routine, and in the more recent *Stormy Monday*, her spiky reddish hair makes her look like every female who grew up in London or New York City from 1976 to 1985. Everypunk.

As noted above, Griffith's bosom may vary in size from film to film, but her derriere—which, after all, pays the bills—does not. Not since the days when Josephine Baker took Paris by storm has one single part of a female's anatomy been so pivotal to her success. Though Griffith has occasionally managed to keep her clothes on for extended periods of time in films such as *She's in the Army Now* and *One on One*, this is generally not the case, and in many of her films, the audience is treated to extended cinematographic homage to her physique, with particular attention rendered to those edifying glutes.

Sometimes this occurs quite early in the film, as if the director wanted to warn the audience to get out their combs so that

Griffith's sexual charge can attract confetti to them. For example, *Fear City* opens with Griffith performing a torrid striptease culminating in some rather dynamic rotation of her buttocks, and, of course, Griffith's bottoms-up bondage scene with the game but overmatched Jeff Daniels in *Something Wild* is now legendary. She does some nice ensemble work in panties and brassiere with Alec Baldwin and Joan Cusack in *Working Girl*, but her finest moment—indeed, her finest *hour*—are the extended scenes in Brian De Palma's *Body Double*, where she taunts and teases Craig Wasson with a buttock-gyrating masturbation scene that he watches through a telescope, not without amusement. Too bad Jimmy Stewart wasn't around for *that*.

In fact, it is the distinctive gyration of her immensely photogenic posterior that enables Wasson to track her down after she chucks her wig and sunglasses; while casually viewing a local porno channel, Wasson notices a pair of buttocks rotating in a disconcertingly familiar fashion, ultimately enabling him to get to the bottom of this rather strange murder mystery. It is no disservice to Melanie Griffith to say that the frequency and enthusiasm with which she activates her nether regions, coupled with her more conventional thespian charms, is the reason she may yet have a bigger career than, say, Mary Steenburgen. One can only imagine what she might have done as Paul Newman's bump-and-grind tootsie in *Blaze*, if she hadn't passed on that worthy project to have Don's baby.

Again, as previously noted, there is a tendency among critics to dismiss virtually all of the Griffith canon up until her liaison with Demme, Nichols, and, most recently, Mike Figgis: to act as if it's all Class-B trash. I think this is a mistake. For one, I do not think it is possible to understand Melanie Griffith the Actress without serious appraisal of films such as *Fear City* and *Cherry 2000*. But more to the point, I think that films such as *Fear City* are terribly underrated, and yet terribly important works, movies that subsequent generations of critics will almost certainly treat with more reverence and wonder than the hatchet men who review films today.

Fear City is an amazingly *daring* work, a stylistically innovative project that not only showcases Billy Dee Williams but actually looks like one of his Colt .45 commercials. As the uncharacteristically informative liner notes on the back of the videocassette package note: "All the glitter, glamor and wealth of New York City's 'flesh pot' district—a world inhabited by young and lovely girls who undress themselves for a living and the men who are involved with them—is breathlessly stripped away in *Fear City*." It is, it is.

The notes continue: "*Fear City* is the story of a handsome but unhappy ex-boxer and his suave partner who live amid this sea of neon, hot-blooded dancers, strippers, cops and club owners. These two former street kids have powerful friends in the underworld, and, via their thriving Starlight Agency, command the hottest review of strippers in the city.

"The good life starts to fade when, out of the depths of New York's night life, emerges a self-righteous, sadistic killer who is out to punish the evil elements of mankind. The suspense-filled sequences that follow as the partners hunt the sick and twisted killer for the final fight-to-the-finish confrontation are action-packed and guaranteed to keep hearts pounding."

Also guaranteed to keep hearts pounding is Griffith's bravura performance as a junkie stripper who seeks to re-establish an emotional liaison with her estranged lover and booking agent Tom Berenger, but who resents the fact that he does not talk enough about the things that really matter in life because he is always having depressing daydreams about a boxer he killed in the ring, and because, let's fact it, he probably feels a bit guilty about being this tight with the Mafia.

Incapable of going to work because of fear that she will be sadistically butchered by a demented sex maniac—a legitimate reason for calling in sick to just about any job—Griffith stays at home shooting smack in her underwear. In this harrowing portrait of a girl from the wrong side of the tracks who can only get ahead by screwing her good-looking boss, Griffith evokes harrowing proletarian themes that will find their fullest resonance in the masterful *Working Girl*.

Another Griffith film that deserves closer attention is *Cherry 2000*, the futuristic tale of a Yuppie whose gorgeous robot girlfriend—the "Ultimate Robotic Love Machine"—goes on the fritz when he tries to bang her on the kitchen floor, only to have the suds from the dishwasher overflow and short out all her circuits. Unable to get her repaired, and unwilling to accept what seem like perfectly adequate substitutes—the Bambi 400 or Cindy 990 models, whom the salesman describes as top-shelf products from the era "when Detroit still cared"—the hero hires veteran tracker Griffith to take him to the Badlands where he can find a brand-new model identical to his old girlfriend, in whose brain he can simply insert the microchip containing the personality of Cherry 2000. But first they must defeat a veritable legion of villains, who shoot arrows through men's faces at parties but also mistreat women.

This strangely affecting film, complete with the most affecting Ennio Morricone music this side of Ennio Morricone, affords Griffith the opportunity to wield rocket launchers, chuck hand grenades, blow up all manner of vehicles, and generally behave in a Rambo-like fashion (an especially convincing moment occurs when Griffith has to repair a biplane). It also allows audiences to see the large but not especially lithe Griffith sprint about 100 yards across open terrain as machine guns spray bullets at her feet; not since the Washington Redskins used to hand John "Riggo" Riggins the pigskin on fourth-and-three has the fun-loving American public been treated to the sight of so much indefatigably determined beef on the hoof.

Despite its grisly elements, *Cherry 2000* is suffused by a delicately overriding moral vision. At the very end, after Griffith has helped the hero locate a replacement robot, she selflessly abandons the plane in which the three of them are seeking to escape, recognizing that the fragile aircraft is carrying too much weight. As soon as she gets out, it takes off like an eagle. The hero initially flies off with his bimbo robot honeypie, but then has a crisis of conscience, reverses direction, asks Cherry 2000 to fetch him a Pepsi, and roars off into the sky with Griffith in tow. The moral? When faced with a choice between Melanie Griffith and a woman made out of silicon chips, opt for the creature with less silicon in her.

Melanie by a hair.

A more recent film that has not received the acclaim it deserves is Mike Figgis's brooding *Stormy Monday*, an *Internal Affairs Goes U.K.* This dreary, gloomy film noir, set in the dreary, gloomy northern industrial city of Newcastle, England, casts Sting as a dreary, gloomy nightclub owner menaced by dreary, gloomy hoods dispatched by Tommy Lee Jones, who plays a dreary, gloomy American businessman who is obviously a crook. Newcastle is the town where Eric Burdon & the Animals ("We Gotta Get Out of This Place") grew up.

At least part of Sting's gloomy dreariness can be explained by the fact that he books acts such as the Cracow Jazz Ensemble. But even more can be explained by the fact that Sting is the only man in the movie who doesn't get a shot at Griffith, who plays a gloomy, dreary refugee from Minnesota who doubles as a high-priced call girl and a low-priced waitress. Included among Griffith's admirers is one of Tommy Lee Jones's thuggish associates, who tries to run his hand up Griffith's dress and in return gets his testicles scrunched in her trash compressor fist. You can bet your bottom dollar that *his* saliva turned to gravy.

Because Griffith has played so many nymphets, sexpots, hookers, strippers, party girls—or what *The New York Times* calls "sirens"—and because of the unflattering portrait of her that appears in Pamela des Barres's *I'm With the Band: Confessions of a Groupie*, an unsophisticated moviegoer might find himself or herself asking the question: Is Melanie Griffith herself a bimbo? Clearly, there are bimbonic qualities to her personality; she talks like an idiot and does not always give the impression in interviews that she is participating in the Massachusetts Institute of Technology's Directed Readings Program. And anyone who beats out professional porn film stars such as Annette Haven for a role as a professional porn film star—as Griffith did in *Body Double*—has clearly been spending more time in nightclubs than, say, the Sorbonne.

Yet, there is a curious double standard in such an accusation. Does anyone accuse Sylvester Stallone of being a tall, musclebound moron simply because he plays tall, musclebound morons? No, because Sylvester Stallone is short. For similar reasons, no one accuses Meryl Streep of being a dog hater just because dingoes ate her baby in that movie about Australia. Griffith's problem is guilt by association: Because she has been married twice to Don Johnson, who has never been mistaken for Soren Kierkegaard, there is a natural propensity on the part of the press to brand her as a dim bulb.

This is not fair to her, and it is certainly not fair to Johnson. Don Johnson once dated Barbra Streisand, producer, director, and coauthor of *Yentl*. Streisand is not the kind of woman who goes out and dates a man who would marry a bimbo twice. Also, she has made records with Neil Diamond.

Case closed.

What we have in Melanie Griffith is a cunning actress who masquerades as bimbos in order to draw attention to the plight of the bimbo. Yet, as she demonstrates to majestic effect in *Working Girl*, just because you're a squeaky-voiced airhead from Staten Island whose best girlfriend (Joan Cusack) looks like Vampirella and whose boyfriend (Alec Baldwin) talks like Danny Aiello doesn't mean you can't grow up to be an investment banker. You don't have to stop being a bimbo. You just have to stop dressing like one.

The message of Melanie Griffith is a message of hope. But it is also a message of defiance. It is the message of a girl who's been cheated, been mistreated, been made blue, been lied to, and who quite justifiably wonders, "When will I be loved?" But it is also the message of a girl who is not afraid to throw down the gauntlet, of a girl who is not afraid to stare a man dead in the eyes and tell him flat out the rules of the game. As she declares in the climactic sequence of *Body Double* in which she spits out perfectly clearly the precise parameters of her relationship with Craig Wasson: "There are some things I like to get straight right up front so there are no misunderstandings later on. I do not do animal acts. I do not do S&M or any variation of that particular bent. No water sports either. I will not shave my pussy. No fist-fucking. And absolutely no coming in my face."

A girl has to draw the line somewhere.*

---

*Since this essay appeared, Melanie Griffith has starred as a bimbo in Bonfire of the Vanities, *as a terrorized landlady in* Pacific Heights, *as a nice Jewish girl from Queens who infiltrates the Nazi high command in* Shining Through, *as a New York cop who goes undercover among the Lubavitcher Hassidim in* A Stranger Among Us, *and as a grieving, working-class mother who has recently lost her child in* Paradise. *This continues to be the most inexplicable career in the history of motion pictures.*

21 SECOND THOUGHTS

ast summer the movie industry reached its most sublimely creative moment, with the virtually simultaneous release of *Robocop II*, *Back to the Future III*, *Another 48 Hours*, *Die Hard II*, and *Gremlins II: The New Batch*. All of these films were follow-ups to phenomenally successful originals, and virtually all are likely to beget at least one more sequel. To moviegoers who are still reeling from the aftereffects of *Caddyshack II* and *Poltergeist III*, the prospect of yet more sequels to sequels is very daunting indeed. In fact, market researchers have coined a new term to describe a consumer dysfunction called *preemptive serial dissonance*, in which moviegoers quizzed by pollsters automatically begin complaining bitterly about films that have not yet been made, much less released.

I am not one of these people. Mindful of the financial constraints under which studios operate in this age of Guber & Peters, Simpson & Bruckheimer, Alda & Ringwald, I understand perfectly well why we see so many sequels on the screen today. Actually, what I *cannot* understand is why we don't see *even more* sequels. Up until now, sequels have usually been

limited to the action, comedy, or horror genres—films that tend
to get released during the summer. Foolishly, this marketing
strategy ignores the blockbuster potential in sequels to touching
women's films (*Steelier Magnolias*); films that evoke a Heartland
That Is Still Out There if You're Willing to Go Look for It (*The
Trip Back From Bountiful*); films with subtitles translated from
Punjabi (*Back to the Sa'laam Bombay III*); and all the other films
that do not have Whoopi Goldberg in them. In short, films that
tend to get released in the fall. In the following paragraphs I have
set down brief plot synopses of a few works that fit this category:
worthy, eminently bankable projects that major studios are urged
to rush into production.

Baby Seals in the Mist. Bryan Brown reprises his role as the
environmentally sensitive photographer that Sigourney Weaver
(as naturalist Dian Fossey) fell in love with in *Gorillas in the Mist.*
Depressed by the news of his ex-lover's murder, Brown heads
straight for the Arctic Circle, where he defies hunters, poachers,
antagonistic government officials and right-wing editorial page
writers to take award-winning pictures of the dwindling numbers
of baby seals that inhabit this desolate, godforsaken part of the
world. An upbeat, life-affirming film that also stars Dennis
Weaver, Fritz Weaver, and Pete Seeger (formerly of the folk group
the Weavers) as Sigourney's long-lost, environmentally sensitive
cousins, all of whom work for Greenpeace, *Baby Seals in the
Mist* warms the cockles of the heart the way only films directed
by Ron Howard can.

The French-Canadian Lieutenant's Woman. An English tramp
and a seedy Canuck officer enter into a thoroughly acceptable
romance in nineteenth-century Quebec that doesn't raise any
eyebrows or cause any trouble at all. There is no film within a
film, no contrasting relationship set in contemporary times, no
screenplay by Harold Pinter, and no arty direction by Karel
Reisz. Meryl Streep, who could have avoided a whole lot of
trouble in the first film by simply emigrating to Canada, where
nobody gives a damn about who's fucking who or what class you

belong to or whether you're married or any of that stuff, gets tired of waiting for Jeremy Irons—who seems to turn up in an awful lot of fall films—and hops the next tramp steamer to Newfoundland, and sets up house with Gerard Depardieu, whereupon everyone lives happily ever after. Directed by Denys Arcand, or any other internationally renowned French-Canadian director.

Kiss of the Spider Man. John Hurt and Ruben Blades play two prisoners who live in the next cell down from William Hurt and Raul Julia, and who start to develop a similar relationship after spending all that time listening to William Hurt rhapsodize about trashy Hollywood flicks. Not being terribly familiar with third-rate American movies, John Hurt, an apolitical homophobe with a phenomenal interest in popular culture, harangues his fellow prisoner with meticulously detailed plot recapitulations of the Spanish-language versions of Marvel Comics he used to read as a child. Blades hires a death squad, whose phone number he found in a guide to Buenos Aires nightlife, to murder his neighbor. Based on the sequel to Manuel Puig's novel, *French Kiss of the Spider Monkey*. John Waters directs.

Kramer vs. Kramer vs. Kramer. It's eleven years later, and divorcees Dustin Hoffman and Meryl Streep—who seems to make an awful lot of fall movies—are back in court. This time they're being sued by their precocious son, Hilton, who's finished Yale Law School in record time, and has slapped them with a RICO suit for conspiracy to deprive him of his civil rights, plus mail fraud for using the United States postal system to send him misleading information: Christmas cards expressing emotions they never really felt. Directed with verve and passion by Stanley Kramer.

Dad II. Having finally loosened up at the end of the tearjerking original in which she costarred with doomed septuagenarian airhead Jack Lemmon, aging bitch/widow Olympia Dukakis re-marries and tries to bring a little night music into the life of a man rapidly entering his twilight years. But new husband Walter Matthau turns out to be even more of a blintz-brain than his predecessor, and ends up breaking his hip while skating on Lemmon's lava-colored skateboard. Pleurisy sets in and he too must learn to come to terms with death, which seems to be a whole lot easier to do if you're married to Olympia Dukakis. Ted Danson, having blown his career as an M&A specialist because of all that time he had to spend getting to know Jack Lemmon in the first film, never really warms up to his stepfather and simply lets the old coot suffocate. The uplifting message of Garry Marshall's brainchild, the first film with a truly nineties ethos, is: If you want to wreck your career by taking a lot of time off from work to get to know the father you never really knew, fine. But a stepfather? Screw the bastard. You owe this guy *nothing*.

More Ordinary People. In this film, again directed by Robert Redford, Donald Sutherland must come to terms with his feelings about his suicidal grandson, played by Kiefer Sutherland, who has fallen in love with his estranged wife's (Mary Tyler Moore) manic-depressive stepdaughter, played by Julia Roberts. The various family members try to cope with their angst by consulting psychiatrist Judd Hirsh (star of the forthcoming *Running on Empty II*), but you can imagine how much help he is. Eventually, Donald Sutherland gets fed up with this pack of whiners, belts a few people around the way he should have way back in *Ordinary People*, and while everyone might not live happily ever after, they at least keep their goddamn mouths shut while he's around.

Children of an Even Lesser God. It's five years since William Hurt—who seems to turn up in an awful lot of fall films—broke up with his deaf girlfriend (Marlee Matlin). A broken man, he heads back to that zonked-out school for the deaf where it all began, hoping to recapture his zeal for signing, or, at the very least, hit on another audiophonically challenged babe. This time out, Hurt falls in love with a deaf, dumb, blind janitor confined to a wheelchair, who hates his guts. After a few frantic underwater episodes, plus a scene where Hurt uses Braille to explain to the girl what Ray Charles sounds like, he agrees to wear a blindfold, earplugs, and a gag at their wedding. The Matlin character resurfaces, tells Hurt's fiancée that she always felt there was something a little bit kinky about this guy, and the wedding is called off. Well, not actually *called*.

Pelle the Conqueror II. In 1989, art houses the world over were blown away by *Pelle the Conqueror,* the electrifying story of incredibly interesting Swedish immigrants trying to make ends meet in scintillating, let-the-good-times-roll, rural, nineteenth-century Denmark. At the time, this seemed like a fairly tough product to market, and its success must have come as a big surprise to the moviemakers. They may be in for a similar surprise with *Pelle the Conqueror II,* which recounts how young Pelle, speaking only Swedish and broken Danish, sets off for America, but takes the wrong boat and winds up in Brazil. Incapable of making himself understood, he spends the rest of his life in abject poverty, finally winding up with Sonia Braga, who gives birth to his son, Pixote, named after an interesting art house movie he had once seen. Pixote runs away from home and winds up in the streets of São Paulo, ultimately getting a job as the star of *Pixote II,* a Hector Babenco movie dealing with poor kids in Brazil who have no future whatsoever, in part because they speak Portuguese with a Danish accent.

There are, of course, many other possibilities. *Agnes of God II. Pee Wee's Bigger Adventure. Punchline II: The New Gags. The Whales of Late August. The Manatees of September.* And, of course, *Plenty II,* starring Meryl Streep, who seems to appear in a lot of fall films. Or, *The Mission II: The Re-Mission,* starring Jeremy Irons.

One final sequel possibility is *The Jagged Box.* The very first dual sequel in history, this flick would save Joe Eszterhas all the trouble of having to write two separate screenplays for sequels to films that were, after all, virtually identical: *Jagged Edge* and *Music Box.* In this innovative double sequel, a seemingly wonderful man (Kurt Russell, or some other actor who gets parts only after Jeff Bridges has turned them down) is accused of torturing and/or murdering a series of seemingly wonderful women. He is defended by an attractive female attorney (some fortyish blonde with curly hair) who stands by him through thick and thin, never wavering in her undying faith and affection. Only at the very end of the film does the heroine realize that the man she has been defending is the scum of the earth, the quintessence of slime, the most repulsive creature to ever walk the face of the earth, and not at all the type of person you would want to go horseback riding with five or six times in the same movie, much less be related to. Directed by sequel wunderkind Renny Harlin, *auteur* of *Die Hard II, Nightmare on Elm Street IV,* and *Ford Fairlane I.*

22 IS THIS ANY WAY TO RUN A CAREER?

Early in her career, Jessica Lange made two volcanically unpleasant movies—*The Postman Always Rings Twice* and *Frances*—in rapid succession. At this point, her friend and *Frances* costar Kim Stanley suggested that she accept a role in "the first comedy you're offered." That was *Tootsie*, for which Lange won an Academy Award as Best Supporting Actress. The question, then, is: Where has Kim Stanley been since then? Where was Kim Stanley when Lange was getting ready to make *Far North*? Where was Kim Stanley when Lange was gearing up for *Sweet Dreams*? Where was Kim Stanley when Lange was reading the script for *Everybody's All-American*? Where was Kim Stanley when Jessica Lange *really needed her*?

One thing you can say for Lange—and there are lots of good things you can say for her—is that she seems to have a pretty good idea of where her films fit into the history of American cinema. Asked if she expects to see any sequels to her movies in the theaters any time soon, Lange whimsically shakes her head and sighs, "No." No, there will be no *Country II*, no *Far North by Northwest*, no *Sweeter Dreams*, no *First Blood: Crimes of the Heart, Part II*. Indeed, Lange doesn't even want to think about where Jewel Ivy and her beleaguered family from *Country* are today.

"Don't even ask," she sighs. "They lost the farm, probably, and they're making do the best they can in some small town." She says this while sitting in an inn in Charlottesville, Virginia, not far from the farm where she lives with Sam Shepard and their three kids. It is also not far from Thomas Jefferson's ancestral abode, Monticello. It is ironic that Lange should be discussing a highly praised but not terribly lucrative film abut the plight of well-meaning farmers who couldn't make a go of it, because Thomas Jefferson was a highly praised, well-meaning farmer who couldn't make a go of it, ending up $1 million in debt. Of course, Jefferson, like Lange, had other qualities.

The more obvious of Lange's qualities were on display in *King Kong*, in which an ape dwarfed in size only by Dino De Laurentiis's ego, put the finger on her. After excavating herself from that artistic crypt by showing that she could act like hell—in *Postman* and *Frances*—Lange hauled down an Oscar with an adroit performance as an ethereal bimbo-who-wants-to-grow in *Tootsie*. Since then, she has spent the better part of a decade making movies that are definitely not shoring up the fragile financial infrastructure of the film industry, even if she does keep getting good reviews.

Yes, Lange has mastered the art of giving solid performances in a series of bombs, near-bombs, "little" films, and projects involving her husband. These include the charming but unnecessary *Sweet Dreams*, the loopy *Crimes of the Heart*, the idiotic *Everybody's All-American*, and the unfathomable *Far North*. Her unflagging ability to do good work in works that aren't too good may be artistically admirable, but if Yo-Yo Ma kept giving virtuoso performances of Chuck Finnegan's Cello Concerto No. 103 with the Albuquerque Philharmonic, people might start to complain.

Lange is now trying to extricate herself from these mid-career doldrums by appearing in two new movies. Typically, there have been problems getting them off the assembly line. *Men Don't Leave*, finished in 1988 but shelved ever since, is th... first film *Risky Business* director Paul Brickman has made in six, going on seven years, so it's anyone's guess how it will do. A wry, compact drama with comic overtones, it's about a newly widowed mother of two boys who tries to start a new life in downtown Baltimore—always a dodgy proposition.

And *Music Box*, completed in early 1989, marks a comeback of sorts for Constantin Costa-Gavras, the earnest but heavy-handed leftist filmmaker whose last project was the abysmal *Betrayed*, an implausible neofascist/FBI love story. Lange, who always gives good, often great performances, needs to get some points on the scoreboard, but it remains to be seen whether roles as a suddenly widowed lower-middle-class mother trying to cope, or a Hungarian-American barrister forced to defend a father accused of monstrous war crimes is what the doctor ordered. As yet, there is no sound of movie-viewing America gunning the engines of their station wagons to get to the early show.

The decision to make what one pundit calls "movies that matter" probably began with *Frances*, but reached its fullest expression in *Country*, the 1984 film about a doomed Iowa farming family which Lange coproduced. This searing indictment of Jimmy Carter's grain embargo, Ronald Reagan's ruthless economic policies, the Federal Farm Home Loan Board, the United States Department of Agriculture, the American banking community, modern civilization, and anything else that happened to get in the line of fire was a microcosm of Lange's career: a well-acted, well-scripted, well-directed movie that never seriously challenged *Gone With the Wind* for box office supremacy. Lange, who subsequently made headlines by testifying about the plight of the farmers before a congressional subcommittee with quite a bit of time on its hands, is still pretty upset about the way Touchstone handled her pet project.

"The weekend it was released, the man who'd been the champion of the film at Touchstone got replaced," she recalls.

"In came a new regime: Katzenberg and Eisner. Just those names—Katzenberg and Eisner—sound like a cartoon strip. It makes me chuckle when I think of it."

The chuckle chuckled, she proceeds.

"The new crew just wanted to dust *Country* under a rug," she says. "There was no advertising, and you can't open a movie like that without a certain amount of support." Even though it was praised by critics and earned Lange yet another Oscar nomination, the movie didn't do a whole lot better than the farmers it lionized.

Having once been snakebitten by rural America, you might think this ravishing Minnesota native would have had the good sense to stay off the prairies. But no, in 1988 she was back with *Far North*, the unforgivable directorial debut by her husband and frequent costar, Sam Shepard, a far better actor than director, and, quite possibly, a far better actor than playwright. *Far North* is a dreary, artsy affair in which bedridden patriarch Charles Durning spends eighty-eight minutes trying to persuade daughter Lange to shoot an aging horse that has incapacitated him. An ambiguous finale leaves the viewer confused as to whether:

1. The horse kills Durning.
2. Durning kills the horse.
3. All the women have a big birthday party and let the horse and Durning sort things out for themselves.

The confusion is not diminished by a puzzling fadeout in which what appears to be Charles Durning and what appears to be a horse amble off into what appears to be a mist, but could be an afterlife. Or maybe they'd just gone out gunning for Shepard.

Lange doesn't have a whole lot to say about *Far North* other than "I wanted to work with Sam" and "It didn't do a whole lot of business." That isn't surprising, because as soon as the opening credits run, the viewer knows he's in big trouble. Epic windbags like Jean-Luc Godard, Robert Wilson, David Byrne, and Ettore

Scola know that if you're going to be pretentious you'd better do it in exotic locales and on a monumental scale. Unlike them, Shepard shot the entire movie in the semiarctic regions of northern Minnesota with a very tiny, predominantly frostbitten cast. Thus, from the moment the paltry opening credits appear, the viewer realizes that he's going to have to spend the next eighty-eight minutes watching Charles Durning and a menaced horse duke it out somewhere to the north of Duluth. Not even Lange, preening in high heels, can compensate. Not *that* far north.

"There are worse places than Duluth," snaps Lange.

"Like where?"

She thinks about it.

"Philadelphia."

Okay, forget Duluth, let's head south. Do tell, how could a movie combining such awesome talents as Lange, Sissy Spacek, Diane Keaton, Bruce Beresford, Sam Shepard—not to mention the formidable Dino De Laurentiis and Burt Sugarman—turn out as bad as *Crimes of the Heart*? "Actually," says Lange, *Crimes* was "one of the best experiences I ever had." But this seems to be more because of her sunny mood at the time (she'd just had another baby) rather than because of anything in the film, whose only redeeming feature is its exposure of Beth Henley's play as the flabby corn pone it is, Pulitzer or no Pulitzer. Although Lange enjoyed making the film, she decides that her work wasn't very good in it (though it was), and that she was "too fat" (though she wasn't).

"I was just really happy," she explains. "Sometimes I work better when I'm not really happy. Sometimes, if I get happy I just want to sit around and nurse my baby." She thinks about it some more. "I was just being kind of lazy."

Diane Keaton wasn't, acting up a down-home storm in that frock and those ridiculous white anklets, careening around the backyard smacking Tess Harper's bottom with a dust broom, while Sissy Spacek checked in with her usual ditzoid performance: *Carrie Goes to Chattanooga.*

And let's not forget Beresford. When Bruce Beresford made *King David*, there were people who felt there was no way he could top the ludicrous scene in which Richard Gere squat-dances, Cossack-style, into Jerusalem. But Beresford was just getting warmed up, easily topping *King David* with the scene in *Crimes* where Spacek, having unsuccessfully attempted to hang herself from the upstairs chandelier, staggers downstairs with the chandelier still wrapped around her neck and sticks her head in the oven—only to have caring sibling and codependent Keaton intervene.

"We just gotta find a way to get through these bad days," purrs Keaton soothingly, perhaps fearing Spacek will try the chain saw next. No, Diane, we just gotta find a way to get through these bad movies.

While that scene was being shot, Lange is asked, wasn't there anyone in the general vicinity who could have told Beresford and Spacek to knock it the hell off?

"You mean like the Taste Patrol?" she giggles. Now that she's coming clean, Lange admits that *Crimes of the Heart* was in trouble from the word go.

"I had difficulties with Beresford," she says. "He didn't give us any direction. I suggested when we were in so-called rehearsals that if we could just establish the relationship these three sisters had between them already that we'd be so far ahead in the story. It occurred to me that we might do that with improvisation. I suggested that to Beresford, and he said, 'I once knew an actor in Australia who liked to get prepared for a role by dressing up in a clown suit. I never could understand that.'" Lange sits back and sighs. "So he thought improvising was getting dressed up in a clown suit." Her eyes narrow. "We were out there all alone."

Lange hasn't had to spend much of her off-screen life alone: Liaisons with Bob Fosse, Jack Nicholson, and Mikhail Baryshnikov, by whom she had her first child (she has two others by

Shepard)—have all been well chronicled. Here's hoping that Sam's having a better time of it in their marriage than most of Lange's fictional mates do in her films. Obviously, Lange is not a classic ballbuster in the Meryl Streep or Glenn Close tradition: Those two can torch any man within fifty yards with their incendiary performance. But even if Lange has little of the fury or sheer power of Close or Streep, in her own charming little way she tends to take her male counterparts and grind them up into tiny little pieces.

Shepard alone is batting 0 for 3, having taken his lumps as the failed, juicing farmer in *Country*, the ditched lover in *Frances*, and the goofy, gap-toothed rustic whom cockteaser Lange flirts with in *Crimes*. Add to that list Durning's invalid father in *Far North*, Dustin Hoffman's cross-dressing neurotic in *Tootsie*, Frederic Forrest's outgunned government prosecutor in *Music Box*, Ed Harris's drunken wife-beater in *Sweet Dreams*, and Dennis Quaid's washed-up gridiron great in *Everybody's All-American* and you've got an impressive string of candidates for the Emasculation Hall of Fame. Remember, it all started with the Konger himself, who gets blown to smithereens as soon as he foolishly releases Lange's hand. The last male to hold his own in the ring with Jessica was Jack Nicholson, and even there Lange first betrayed her outclassed husband and then helped Jack polish him off. No wonder Fosse cast her as the Angel of Death.

Lange is amused by the notion that she leaves men high, dry, and wasted in her films.

"I don't choose roles for that reason," she explains. "I always choose the part because of the arc of the character, because of the exciting journey it can take you on. And if it's a woman's film, the chances are the female character is going to be the strongest."

The only time Lange gets testy is when the subject of *Frances* comes up. After all, the 1982 film *was* the story of an independent-minded ingenue who started out making dumb blonde movies, then moved east to have an affair with a pretentious playwright, and then saw her career go slightly haywire.

"I don't see any similarities in our lives at all," says Lange. "I played the part because there was a great arc to her character."

That arc again. And, in truth, though certain surface comparisons may suggest themselves, Clifford Odets never manifested the polo-playing prowess of a Sam Shepard, nor is there even the slightest indication that Lange is likely to undergo a lobotomy and end up hosting a talk show somewhere in the Midwest. That career path is staked out for Sean Young.

One movie whose autobiographical elements are not in dispute is Fosse's occasionally amusing, though fundamentally dreadful, 1979 film *All That Jazz*. Lange brushes that one off, saying she made it "just because of Bobby." Asked what it was like making a movie about a talented director and choreographer who is killing himself with booze, stress, nicotine, and sex, filmed by a man who several years later would kill himself with booze, stress, nicotine, and sex, she says: "People live with such tremendous unhappiness. Bob was so incredibly talented, so genuine, so sweet. But there was a flip side to that. He had a real dark side."

Lange has warm feelings about *Sweet Dreams*, an engaging, if not entirely indispensable, chronicle of the life and times of legendary country singer Patsy Cline. Despite fine performances by Lange and Ed Harris, this is essentially a hard-driving-woman-tries-to-save-hard-drinking-man romance, and like virtually all movies about pop stars, it ends in vehicular tragedy. Lange says that director Karel Reisz deliberately set out to make a love story, not *Coal Miner's Daughter*, though she seems to find the Ed Harris character—who gives Lange a pretty nasty beating toward the end of the film—more sympathetic than he really is. But the film lacks any real tension or overall thrust: Cline was a tough, feisty girl who could belt out a mean tune, and then she died in a plane crash. Should Emmylou Harris or Linda Ronstadt meet an untimely fate in the suddenly unfriendly skies, you could probably make touching movies about them, too. But would Michelle Pfeiffer take those roles? Cher?

Asked to identify directors she has enjoyed working with, Lange cites Sydney Pollack, Bob Rafelson, Paul Brickman, and her husband. She also loved working with Costa-Gavras because he was "so intelligent." This is not a characteristic she ascribes to Taylor Hackford, who directed the inane *Everybody's All-American*, the only movie in recent years that can seriously compete with *Silverado* for sheer volume of cinematic clichés.

"I despise that film," says Lange, curling her lips with the Jack Palance–like venom she displays in *Crimes of the Heart* and *Music Box* once she gets really riled up. "It was the worst experience of my life."

For those of you who got to the video store and found all thirty-six copies of the film rented for the weekend, *Everybody's All-American* is a churning, hokey Cuisinart clunker about the travails of a once-famous LSU football player and his ex-Magnolia Queen wife. Lange says that she loved the original script, which answered the question: "What do you do for the rest of your life when you've peaked at nineteen or twenty?"

"It asked you: What is the basis of their love?" says Lange. "It was a great love story. But Taylor just didn't get it. He somehow thought it was a football movie. I wouldn't have taken the role if I thought it would end up like that. I'm not about to do a supporting role in *The Knute Rockne Story*." She hesitates, then gets back into high gear. "It's just a stupid film. I was up in New York doing one of those press blitzes, and when I saw it I was so infuriated that I went back home the same night. I'd been writing letters and notes to Taylor for months, but he cut out the underbelly of the story." She eventually calms down. "It was just a poorly made film by a mediocre director."

Does Lange ever go back and look at her films?

"I look at them at a rough-cut stage," she replies, noting that "sometimes you can effect changes. After that, I don't want to see them. They just don't interest me anymore."

What does interest her? A role as a villainess? A part in a Claude Chabrol film? Would she like that?

"Yes," she responds, "but I think if you'd asked me that five or ten years ago I would have been more motivated." Lange, who takes parenting seriously, repeatedly rescheduling interviews because of her children's violin lessons, adds: "I've made ten movies in ten years. That's certainly all I want to do."

Lange is not especially generous when it comes to fellow actresses. "You see good movies—*Sea of Love*, *The Fabulous Baker Boys*—and they're well made, well acted, but there's nothing to them. It's all about mundane relationships; there's nothing very profound about them. It's slick, but so what? The story doesn't stick with you, the characters don't stick with you, the movie doesn't stick with you."

She also wonders why the women in *Dangerous Liaisons* got all the good ink, while John Malkovich got dumped on for his idiosyncratic performance as an almost simian eighteenth-century fop.

"I thought Malkovich was brilliant; I thought Malkovich dominated the entire film. I was stunned that Malkovich didn't get honored for his performance." She pauses. "Is my perception so far out of the mainstream?"

Apparently. But enough of Malkovich's past; what about Jessica Lange's future?

"The only thing that interests me is doing something different," says Lange. "I'm not disheartened, I haven't lost interest in acting, but I don't want to repeat anything." But she also says: "This isn't a great time for directors; it isn't a great time for scripts."

It also isn't a great time for studios that get films out on time. This month, Lange can be seen in two new films, both of which have been sitting on the shelf for quite some time. And both were directed by individuals who could use a hit. Paul Brickman made Tom Cruise a household name in 1983 with *Risky Business*, then didn't make another film until 1988. And Costa-Gavras, famous for such classics as *Z*, *State of Siege*, and *Missing*, stumbled badly the last time out of the chute with *Betrayed*, a movie only Debra Winger could love. So here we have the intrepid Jessica trying to bounce back from the worst experience of her career in the company of a director who's just made the worst movie of his career and another director who made the best movie of his career and then went AWOL for six years. Is this any way to run a career?

Still, things could pan out. Maybe it was seeing one too many films with people named Bridges or Bottoms or Quaid or Sheen in them, but *Music Box* struck this viewer as the genuine article, the real McCoy. A chilling account of a young woman's gradual realization that her Hungarian papa is not the man she thinks he is, *Music Box* draws its power from the fact that everybody in the audience—even the folks unfamiliar with Costa-Gavras's sledge-hammer approach—can see what's coming from a mile away. Drawing from Hitchcock, Costa-Gavras uses endless plot twists and unexpected detours to tantalize the audience with the question: When will the heroine realize what everybody in the audience already knows—that back in the old country Lange's poppa used to kill Jews for a living?

And although the frail, pallid Lange is not altogether convincing as a lawyer, and even less convincing as a Hungarian-American, this may be her finest performance ever. *Music Box* is a brutal, disturbing film about an unendurable truth: that some of us are the parents of fiends, that some of us are the children of monsters. Lange's talents are never better arrayed than in the scenes where she clutches her father in a silent embrace; the moment she gazes through a window with a face that seems a thousand years old; the sequence when she staggers down a flight of stairs in Budapest after seeing a photograph she never should have seen. That's where Lange's ace in the hole—her beautiful face—comes in handy. She doesn't look so beautiful after she's gazed into the abyss.

This is not Demi Moore territory; this is no place for Daryl

Hannah. This is chilling, depressing stuff, the sort of thing the sinister John Malkovich character in Sam Shepard's *True West* derisively refers to as a "film," rather than a "movie." Well, it's a good one, a domestically made foreign film that achieves the rare distinction of telling us something about the Holocaust that we *don't* already know. Thus, Lange gets her wish, making a dire, memorable motion picture that has a ghost of a chance at the box office. It beats working with Taylor Hackford. It beats making movies in Duluth.

23 THE YOUNG AND THE RESTLESS

Keanu Reeves has earned his reputation by portraying confused adolescents who toss their hair and arms around a lot, don't shave or change their clothes very often, like to hit the sauce, and seem to have trouble expressing themselves with anything other than their hands. No one meeting Keanu Reeves for the first time would get the impression that this is all an act.

The deal with Keanu—much like the fidgety teens he has been portraying in a string of top-shelf films—*River's Edge, Dangerous Liaisons, Parenthood,* and yes, even, *Bill and Ted's Excellent Adventure*—is that he just can't get settled down. Although he has enlisted the services of a top-flight public relations agency to juice up his image ("I can only afford these guys for a couple of months"), Reeves clearly doesn't enjoy being interviewed, photographed, or doing anything else that requires staying in one place for more than a few minutes at a time. This could be a real problem, because Reeves may be in the process of becoming a big star, and big stars *have to* sit still.

Stuffed into clothes that look a size too big, perched on a chair that looks a size too small, Reeves is working his way through a steak in a twee Franco-

Manhattan restaurant that doesn't look like it gets much business from people named Keanu. All the while, Reeves is doing the Keanu Shuffle with the arms, the hair, the shoulders, *the body*. He's spent an hour-and-a-half giving clipped, confusing, bizarre, or unfathomable answers to what seem on the surface like reasonable questions ("Do you go to many Knicks games?" "What do you think of William Hurt?"), and now he's starting to worry that the interview isn't going so well.

"Are you the guy who wrote that story about Sean Young?" he asks, alluding to a recent *Rolling Stone* piece focusing on the colorful but perhaps unemployable starlet's perverse fascination with quadratic equations, logarithms, and James Woods. "Oh, man, I can already feel myself being raked over the coals."

At which point, young Reeves has to be told, "Relax. Relax. Everything's going to be just fine."

Because everything *is* going to be just fine. When you've made as many good films as Reeves has at this point in his career— he's only twenty-four—you really have to pull a Sean Penn-or-Young to screw up your gig. Ignoring a couple of trashy flicks Reeves made when he was getting his feet wet, Keanu has banged out a string of superb movies about important subjects—love, death, murder, suicide, betrayal, getting your high school diploma—and it sounds like two more are in the tank: an adaption of *Aunt Julia and the Scriptwriter*,* based on the novel by Peruvian novelist and erstwhile presidential candidate Maria Vargas Llosa, and Lawrence Kasdan's *I Love You to Death*, a comedy in which he appears with William Hurt. Keanu's doing real good work here, work an actor can be proud of, work you can build a major career on. You getting all this, Kiefer?

All that said, Reeves is obviously an actor who only enjoys the work, and not the self-promotion that comes with it. He's also a little bit embarrassed about the interviews he has given in the past, concerned that some of his more effervescent remarks

The film was eventually released under the rubric Tune in Tomorrow.

could come back to haunt him. He asks if his interviewer saw
the article in which he expressed a nagging concern that he
might show up for a big date with fecal matter visible in his
underwear. His interviewer did, in fact, see that article. He asks
if his interviewer saw the article in which he expressed an
interest in fucking Meryl Streep, because "even if I wasn't good,
she could fake it the best." Yes, his interviewer saw that article,
too, an article in which Reeves also drew attention to the
infrequency with which he bathes, and to the efforts he has made
to squelch groundless rumors that his interest in personal hygiene
has grown. At this point, Keanu does one of his trademark
backpedals, whacking his forehead in his boyish way, eyes
rolling.

"Oh, that was Keanu in fine form," he hoots. "Yes, that was
Keanu in *fine* form."

If that was Keanu in fine form, today's Keanu is on his best
behavior. Friendly, not at all menacing with his knife and fork,
and ever so cheerful, the actor can not quite bring himself to
have what linguistics experts call a "conversation." His responses
to questions are civil but curt, punctuated by frequent non
sequiturs. ("Hey, if it's William Hurt being a tree, then it's
William Hurt being a tree.") Many of his answers consist of one
short sentence; paragraphs still seem beyond his ken. But he *is*
young.

And he *is* amusing. Though he doesn't have a whole lot to say
about his upcoming movie, *Aunt Julia and the Scriptwriter*, other
than to express admiration for costar Barbara Hershey and to
voice his opinion that Maria Vargas Llosa will soon be killed by
Peruvian drug lords, he does make an interesting remark about
the accent he uses in the film. Noting that the setting has been
moved from Lima, Peru, in the 1950s to New Orleans, Louisiana,
in the 1950s, he says that he used a hybrid accent to get the job
done.

"There is no New Orleans accent," he explains. "There are
New Orleans *accents*, but I didn't use one. We shot sixty days in

North Carolina and two days in New Orleans. So when I started talking, everybody asked if I was from Kentucky."

This is pretty impressive knowledge of American geography, considering that Reeves is from out of town. Born in Beirut, Reeves spent time in Australia before moving to Toronto with his mother. Dad is apparently out of the picture, and has been for some time. His name "Keanu" comes from his grandfather, and supposedly it's Hawaiian for "cool breeze over the mountains," though since Keanu's the one supplying the information, it might actually be the Hawaiian word for "Keanu."

Reeves grew up in Toronto in a neighborhood "where you could still be out playing at eleven-thirty at night," and drifted in and out of a series of high schools. Screwing up in high school laid the groundwork for his roles as a tortured youth in *River's Edge*, a tortured youth in *Parenthood*, a tortured youth in *Permanent Record*, and a tortured youth, albeit a bonehead, in *Bill and Ted's Excellent Adventure*. At the age of seventeen, Reeves enrolled in a night-school drama class, then started working on a local TV show called *Hanging In*, as well as in such not-so-memorable plays as *Wolf Boy*.

Eventually, he decided to abandon the Great Canadian Indoors for the Great American Outdoors, auditioning in the States for a role in a Disney TV movie. He didn't get it, but he did get hooked up with a big-time agent in Los Angeles, and, as he reports it, drifted west with $3,000, an ancient Volvo, and his stepfather's address. It didn't take him long to get work—he landed a small part in one of Rob Lowe's vehicles on his continuing Voyage to Nowhere, playing a French-Canadian goalie in *Youngblood*.

"It's an awful movie," says Reeves acidly of the Lowe point in his career.

Still, with the exception of the unnecessary and unseen teen comedy *The Night Before*, released in 1988, *Youngblood* was the last overtly bad project Reeves has been associated with—no mean feat in this age of sludge. Since 1986, Reeves has been appearing in a bunch of films that always manage to get attention, either because they're good, strange, loony, twisted, or because John Malkovich and Glenn Close are in them too.

First came *River's Edge*, the cult classic about a bunch of real-life northern California high school students who suppress the evidence that a deranged classmate has strangled his girlfriend. As is usually the case, Keanu plays a confused, alienated adolescent, one who initially colludes with his classmates and then realizes, Jesus, this is nuts, and goes to the police.

Reeves is outstanding in the film, and holds center stage in a scene that says more about what's wrong with contemporary American society (we can't tell right from wrong) than any other scene in a film of recent memory: He has to persuade his nine-year-old brother that it's not really such a good idea to blow him away with the .38 he stole from drug dealer and all-purpose lunatic Dennis Hopper. "Come on, man, I'm your brother." That disturbing, unforgettable scene is the moral high point of this disturbing, unforgettable movie.

Reeves, who is generally generous toward other actors, is still impressed by Crispin Glover's performance in *River's Edge*, one regarded by many critics as the very definition of "over the top." For those who have not seen the film, suffice it to say that *River's Edge* is the only known motion picture in which Dennis Hopper gives the *second* weirdest performance. Glover plays an unhinged character named Lane, a sort of townie Axl Rose, who becomes obsessed with the idea of protecting his murderous classmate by getting rid of the corpse. From the moment he upbraids the killer for only giving him a Budweiser after he disposes of the body— "I thought it was at least worth a Michelob"—the audience knows that it is in for a long, wild ride with one sick pup. "Crispin was amazing," says Reeves.

But did Reeves and the rest of the cast know how unsettling a movie they were making at the time, without the eerie sound-track, without the grainy film quality, without seeing the whole package all at once?

"No way," says Reeves. "I saw the script and I didn't get it. I knew it was going to be funny, but no, I had no idea."

Using a word he has used in the past, Reeves says that if he had done the Glover role, "my Lane would have been a lot more pedestrian." Then comes the touchy subject of morality, of whether the Reeves or the Glover character is more representative of young Americans today. In other words, is Glover's demonic Lane an archetype of sorts, or just a sick fuck the actor dreamed up to put the fear of God into people?

"It's there," Reeves intones. "It's there. It's surprising what's out there." He adds decisively, "There *are* Lanes."

After *River's Edge*, an instant favorite with critics, came *Bill and Ted's Excellent Adventure*, a spectacularly stupid film about two teen meatheads who can only avoid flunking out of high school by going back in time and kidnapping Socrates, Napoleon Bonaparte, Billy the Kid, and Beethoven, and persuading them to appear in a show-and-tell end-of-term report in the school auditorium the following day. Reeves delivers an exuberantly idiotic performance as a Valley Boy so dumb that even Dick Clark would think twice about letting him appear on *American Bandstand*.

"It was a pretty solid film," says Reeves, who, unlike many others in his line of work, doesn't mind talking about money, since he's making a lot of it. "It cost $10 million to make, and it made $43 million."

Did it make him a teen idol?

"Yeah, I think so. Girls like it; guys dig it."

Does getting typecast as a bozo worry him?

"It's not like I'm Robert De Niro in *Raging Bull*," he fires back. "But if that's going to be my claim to fame, that's going to be my claim to fame."

Bill and Ted was followed by *Permanent Record*, a potentially good film that went off the rails. Reeves, a master of having mixed feelings about things, definitely has mixed feelings about this tale of high school seniors forced to cope with the Boy Most

Likely to Succeed's decision to jump off a cliff. Keanu plays the doomed boy's best friend and does a real good job, but the film blows up about two-thirds of the way through. *Permanent Record* starts out with the same gritty quality as *River's Edge*, but then gets all mushy at the end. (The finale is a hokey standing ovation when the Girl Most Likely to Succeed performs an impromptu a capella version of the dead boy's last song at a school production of *H.M.S. Pinafore.* Please.)

In the past, Keanu has been quoted as saying nice things about the play and its director, Marisa Silver; he has also been quoted as saying that the studio sabotaged the film, wrecking what had otherwise been his most pleasant acting experience to date. He is politely asked which are his real feelings about the film?

"All of these things," he says. "It's just, I couldn't believe it when it happened."

When *what* happened?

"When everybody stood up and clapped at the end," he says. "It was pretty cheesey."

Since *Permanent Record*, Reeves has starred in the so-so *Prince of Pennsylvania*, in which he plays—guess what?—a rebellious teenager, and has also delivered a sparkling performance as Steve Martin's wired but likable hot-rodding nephew-in-law—a rebellious adolescent—in *Parenthood*. In the first real stretch of his career, he also turned up as a "mawkish youth" in *Dangerous Liaisons*, a remarkable film that seems all the more remarkable because just about everyone in it seems miscast. Although it was a terrific idea for Reeves to go out and get himself a role as an eighteenth-century pretty boy in a Stephen Frears film, and although Reeves does a whole lot more with the role than *E.T.* alumnus Henry Thomas in *Valmont* (*Dangerous Liaisons, Part B*), he was even more miscast for the role than some people say Malkovich was for his. The trademark clumsiness was actually his only saving grace; he is most convincing when floundering around in the snow dueling with Malkovich, least convincing when he asks Uma Thurman if she does not, in fact, find the opera "sublime," a word that Reeves's tongue does not seem entirely comfortable with. Nice try, Keanu, but *Ted Goes to Toulouse* ain't gonna make it.

Reeves admits to being surprised that he got the part in *Dangerous Liaisons*, considering the inauspicious circumstances of his audition.

"It was just a rag-tag thing: There I was riding my bike, and showing up late, with no pants and no shirt, just my cutoffs, and I do my thing for these two guys who are *very* English and they say, 'Thank you, but could you be a little bit less American?' I was, like, the classic American goombah," he says. Then he asks, "What's a goombah?"

I tell him we'll get back to that, and ask what it was like working with Malkovich.

"Malkovich was . . . inspiring," he says. "I only had two scenes with him, but wow. I walked up to him one day and slapped him on the back and said, 'Man, you're the greatest.' It was the classic young actor-older actor scene . . ."

How did the "old" actor react?

"He smiled. He laughed."

Although appearing in the film was a good idea, breaking the string of badly dressed adolescents getting Fs in trig that Keanu was playing, Reeves does not seem terribly happy with his performance in *Dangerous Liaisons*.

"My Danceny . . . if you compare it to the book . . . it's awful," he concedes.

Setting aside his foppish role in *Dangerous Liaisons*, you could argue that Reeves has been doing the same schtick for five films running. In *Permanent Record*, *Bill and Ted*, *The Prince of Pennsylvania*, *River's Edge*, and *Parenthood*, he's always played a disoriented kid with hair. But if you look at the markets for these respective films, you can see that something unusual is going on with his career, that he's actually tailoring that role to four different markets. *Parenthood* is a mainstream comedy, the kind that comes to a better theater near you and stays all summer. *Dangerous Liaisons* is geared more toward the Ebert-and-Siskel crowd, the kind who leave *The New Yorker* lying around the guest bedroom to impress the visitors from Ohio. *River's Edge* appeals to people who can name five Jean-Louis Trintigant movies, folks who like the Kronos Quartet, *Eraserhead*, and not much else. And *Bill and Ted* is for people who either are, or wish they were, still fourteen. Similar roles; entirely different markets. This guy's no dummy.

But if you try to get Reeves talking about this stuff, you're out of luck, because he insists that he is just taking whatever roles come down the pike, that there is no method to his madness. For example, when asked which roles he has turned down recently, Keanu mulls it over, then volunteers brightly: "I turned down *The Fly II*."

Why?

"I didn't like the script."

"But you really can't do movies like *The Fly II* at this point in your career, can you? Not after doing *Dangerous Liaisons* and *Parenthood*?"

Keanu nods his head.

"No you can't do *Fly II*." Then, brightly, Ted-style, he volunteers, "But I'd do *Evil Dead III*."

"You would?"

"Sure."

"Why?"

"Because I liked the guy who did *Evil Dead II*. It's schlock and it's superficial and it's frightening and it's scary and it's outrageous and it's clever and it's fun."

Whatever you say, Keanu.

Like many people in this business, Keanu doesn't seem to pay as much attention to certain recurring patterns in the roles he chooses as, say, critics. Asked why he repeatedly has affairs with older women in his films, not to mention the bedroom scene with Tracey Ullman in a recent episode of her show, Reeves just shrugs it off: "I don't know. Maybe it's my youthful, boyish character. Besides, it's only happened three times." Asked about the exotic hairstyles he uses in his films—the demi-Mohawk in *Prince of Pennsylvania*, the asymmetrical razor-cut in *Parenthood*, the shaved look in the upcoming *I Love You to Death*, he says, "It's just hair." Asked about the arms and hands and shoulders and hair and what-not flying all over the place, Reeves says he's not aware that he's doing it. He's doing it.

Unlike previous incarnations of Keanu Reeves, who were prepared to go on record on such controversial issues as bathing and whom he'd like to have sex with, Reeves now goes out of his way not to say anything unpleasant or impolite about anything or anybody. He lives in New York, but that's no reflection on Los Angeles. He likes the directors he's worked with. He respects other people in the field. He would be more than willing to do roles like Charlie Sheen's in *Wall Street*. He buys trucks for members of his family. He loves the theater, but he loves movies, too. He would like to be in a play, he would like to accept roles that would broaden him a bit, he would like to do all sorts of things. Mostly he wants to get the interview over with so he can go home and play his bass guitar. Here are a few Keanuisms:

On Steve Martin: "He seems like a genial fellow."

On Ron Howard: "I enjoyed working with him."

On Toronto: "It's basically just a big shopping plaza now."

On New York: "It blows me away."

On Sean Penn: "He has so much power and intelligence, it's incredible."

On people he'd like to work with: "Sean Penn, Christopher Walken, and Dianne Wiest."

On Henry Thomas, who plays the Danceny role in *Valmont:* "Who's he?"

On whether or not he's going to become a big star: "There was one day last week . . . I don't know."

Oh yes, and other than William Hurt playing a tree being William Hurt playing a tree, which we've already heard about, is there anything else Reeves has to say about his costar in the upcoming *I Love You to Death*?

"He's a real serious, tense guy, you know? So I went up to him and asked him, 'Hey, Bill, what kind of movie do you think we're in?' And he said, 'Well, Keanu, if your name is Marlon and my name is Harlan, I guess we're in a comedy.'"

Like all twenty-four-year-old actors who have spent more time on a skateboard than in the library, Keanu would like to play Rimbaud, the irrepressible French poet who burned out at age nineteen and died in, or not far from, a gutter. But until *The Arthur Rimbaud Story* begins production, the young man will have to be satisfied with scripts like *Bill and Ted's Excellent Adventure II*.

Actually, Reeves says, there is, as yet, no completed script for *Bill and Ted II*, and even if there was, he hasn't yet made up his mind he wants to be in it.

"If we do it, I'm going to be twenty-six, so I don't know. I was twenty-two or twenty-three when I did the first one."

But he does know enough about the preliminary plot to say: "We die and go to Hell. Then there's a parody of *The Seventh Seal* where we have to play Death at chess. But we don't know how to play chess. So we play Battleships instead."

Those who marveled at the infinite subtlety of *Bill and Ted I* will be pleased to know that in the sequel, Death will be portrayed as inhabiting a "stark, sterile suburban house." "It's like condo death," beams Keanu. Rimbaud would have loved it.

When last seen, Keanu Reeves is standing at the corner of Fifty-ninth Street and Fifth Avenue in front of the Plaza Hotel, where Robin Williams winds up at the end of *Moscow on the Hudson*. The actor is looking this way and that, trying to decide whether to go back uptown, or downtown, or across town, or perhaps into the park. His hands are thrust into his pockets, his shoulders are all hunched up, he's doing that thing with the hair again. He looks kind of worked up. Gee, Keanu, why don't you just try relaxing? Everything's going to be fine. Everything's going to be *just* fine.

24 WHINE, WOMEN, AND SONG

In 1980 Woody Allen made an amusing but cynical film called *Stardust Memories* about a famous director who is sick of hearing his fans say, "We enjoy your films, particularly the early, funny ones." Master of understatement that he is, Allen was successful in conveying his middle-aged angst to his admirers. But he was not successful in getting them to stop saying, "We enjoy your films, particularly the early, funny ones." The most that the folks who had been with him since *Take the Money and Run* were willing to do was to award him a cultural Purple Heart for valor in a doomed cause (*Interiors*). But after the dismal failure of that 1978 hooterama, his first foray into "serious" drama, you would have hoped the guy would have gone back to his bread and butter, or, as he says in *What's Up, Tiger Lily?*, to his "various breads and various butters," for good.

But he didn't, and he hasn't. Though he occasionally cooperates with his public by making fine, entertaining, clever movies such as *Zelig* and *The Purple Rose of Cairo*, if you take your eyes off him for five minutes he'll be right back to the suicidal interior decorators and the blind rabbis dancing with brides. Shadows and fog indeed.

The sad fact is, those extraterrestrials in *Stardust Memories* had this guy pegged. "You wanna do mankind a real service? they say. "Tell funnier jokes." You tell him, guys: What mankind needs is Howard Cosell broadcasting a live presidential assassination. What mankind does not need is a woman in a restaurant approaching Gena Rowlands to tell her that her essay "Ethics and Moral Responsibility" changed her life. What mankind needs are burglars being interrupted in mid-heist by a telephone call from "Name That Tune." What mankind does not need is Mariel Hemingway leaving a message on Woody's answering machine telling him that *Grand Illusion* is being shown on public television that evening. What mankind needs are jokes like: "Don't knock masturbation; it's sex with someone I love" and "Those who can't, teach, and those who can't teach, teach gym." What mankind does not need are lines like: "I accept your condemnation" or "Did you read my novel?"*

In recent years, Allen seems to have agreed to a compromise, alleviating the Sturm und Drang of his melodramas like *Hannah and Her Sisters* and *Crimes and Misdemeanors* by livening them up with some high-octane comic material. These hybrids are amusing, but they don't quite pull off the trick, because while the comic material rings true, the dramatic material often seems stiff, rehearsed, self-conscious, faked. Woody Allen declaring that show business is "worse than dog-eat-dog; it's dog doesn't return other dog's phone calls" is hilarious. Michael Caine ruminating about marriage, procreation, or anything is not.

The bitter truth, which has been repeated time and again by critics far wiser and better dressed than I, is that none of Woody

---

Allen's most recent film is the lugubrious, self-important Husbands and Wives, *in which the characters say things like: "Her approbation was very significant to me."*

Approbation?

Allen's later movies is as clever, entertaining, or memorable as
the early films: *Sleeper, Love and Death, Bananas, Take the
Money and Run* because, like Jimi Hendrix, the Ramones, and
even the Beatles, the more Allen learns about his craft, the less
fun he is to be around. But, with the exception of the deadly
Interiors, the claustrophobic *September* (*Interiors II*), the dreary
Another Woman, and the embarrassing *Shadows and Fog,* all of
his films are worth seeing, if only because this is the age of John
Hughes, John Milius, John Candy, Jo(h)n Peters, John Belushi's
brother, and various people named Adrian. Woody Allen, whatever his failings, does not make movies for morons. Most directors do. Of course, most directors are morons.

Woody Allen's career is an inspiration to megalomaniacs
everywhere, since this diminutive, bespectacled bagel philoso-
pher who is not without his own schlemielish personality components, has been able to spend the past two decades making films
in which the spotlight is always on himself and his tiny circle of
narcissistic noshers at the Russian Tea Room and Elaine's. Yet
none of his fans seem to hold it against him. A great writer, a
great comedian, a great comic actor, and a great employer of
great Swedish cameramen, Woody Allen is as good a director as
a person can be without being great—like Bergman or Kurosawa
or Fellini or Renoir or any of those other guys who never got to
work with Diane Keaton.

Because his films are literate, intelligent, visually opulent,
beautifully played, and filled with some of the best jokes ever
("Sex and death. Two things that come once in a lifetime. But at
least after death you're not nauseous."), Woody Allen's die-hard
fans have been willing to gloss over the fact that he keeps making
the same movies, with the same plot lines, the same Gershwin
soundtracks, the same settings, the same actors, the same jokes
about postcoital nausea, and the same references to Kierkegaard
for twenty-five years.

His is a severely constricted universe that stretches from
Greenwich Village to 105th Street on the West Side of Manhattan,

and from Fifty-seventh Street to Ninety-sixth Street on the East Side. (Although *Love and Death* takes place in Russia, and *Sleeper* in the future, they are set in a Russia and in a future where people clearly spend an immense amount of time eating lox.) These are films by a New Yorker for New Yorkers—plus perhaps 323 people in Los Angeles, plus France. Lucky for Woody that he has those eleven million residents of the Greater New York area to sell tickets to. Were Woody Allen making black-and-white movies with all-George Jones soundtracks that paid visual homage to the Astrodome and Gilley's while chronicling the exploits of the most pretentious, self-absorbed people in Houston, Texas, the studio would have probably pulled the plug years ago.

Woody simply cannot let his audiences forget the titans who have influenced him; he has long exhibited a self-conscious need to refer in his films to the work of his betters, often showing snippets of their movies in his own. How do we explain this? One theory is that Woody Allen has never outgrown his formative intellectual experiences at City College and New York University, both of which he attended for one year. That's why one can say, in the best possible sense of the word, that his movies are "sophomoric." The humorous but superficial conversations involving Kierkegaard, Schopenhauer, Nietzsche, McLuhan, etc., that occur again and again throughout Allen's films are not really the way grown-up pretentious people talk in New York, but the way pretentious college kids talk everywhere. (This was particularly true in the fifties and sixties when students caught anywhere in North America without a copy of Herman Hesse's *Siddhartha* or *The Glass Bead Game* were abducted by the Weathermen, hacked to pieces, and buried in swamps.)

There is no evidence that Allen has ever read the philosophers he cites, but even if he has, there is never any attempt to incorporate any of their theories into what are still fundamentally commercial films. (I am *certainly not* suggesting that this would be a good idea.) The references are thrown out as jokes or, more often, as window dressing. This passion for the highfalutin resembles the healthy fascination with esoterica that many college students feel when they are first introduced to the great books and can stop reading Harlan Ellison. But the references have no other importance; they're simply there to create a mood of serious jejeunitude and total heavyosity.

The influence of the writers, artists, and composers a student is exposed to in those first two years of college surfaces again and again in Allen's films: the Emily Dickinson verse-trading in *Crimes and Misdemeanors*, the volume of Edna St. Vincent Millay poised on Mia Farrow's nightstand in *Alice*, the e.e. cummings balderdash in *Hannah*, the two-credit Classical Music Appreciation selections Allen uses in *Crimes*, *Hannah*, and *Love and Death*. The idea of having a character escape from a film (*The Purple Rose of Cairo*) comes directly from Luigi Pirandello's *Six Characters in Search of an Author*, a staple of those Introduction to Western Drama courses you get in your second year of college. The scene where Allen recovers from a suicide attempt by going to see a Marx Brothers movie is a direct lift from the opening of Albert Camus's *The Stranger*, where the protagonist Meursault learns of his mother's death, murders an Arab boy, then goes to see a movie by the French Charlie Chaplin, Fernandel. (Camus's role in Western civilization is largely to serve as a bridge over which confused adolescent boys can pass from the adolescent sass of J. D. Salinger to the mature, full-blooded nihilism of Franz Kafka.) Camus, like Woody, was a master of Posing the Big Questions, as if this were the same as Presenting the Big Answers. He was French, of course.

In many ways, Woody Allen's movies are sort of like term papers, where a student dresses up a flimsy thesis with a bunch of impressive quotations from people with names like Northrop Frye. In *Hannah*, for example, Sam Waterston takes Dianne Wiest and Carrie Fisher on an architectural tour of Manhattan, enabling the director to display his knowledge of gorgeous New York buildings. Thanks, Woody, I took my mom on that tour, too. More seriously, by appropriating a visual image of something that is *already* indisputably beautiful and indisputably great, Allen makes his own project seem weightier and more important. Which it usually isn't.

This use of other people's material as a crutch (all standup comics steal material) runs throughout Allen's work, ranging from the excerpts from famous movies to the photographs of landmark buildings to his incessant use of established Jazz Age classics on his soundtracks. In fact, Allen's whole obsession with Gershwin and Benny Goodman and Artie Shaw and the rest of that crew is a trifle unsettling. Maybe he's a snob or maybe he's too cheap to hire Maurice Jarre, but after seventeen virtually interchangeable soundtracks, the joke is starting to wear thin. Instead of commissioning a brand-new soundtrack that would seek to evoke emotions related to the images on the screen, Allen uses preposterously famous pieces of music that already evoke a mood, that already have their own emotional connotations, and then seeks to hitch a ride on them.

Although this may be more sophisticated than using Bon Jovi's Greatest Hits or the Best of the Temptin' Temptations to establish a mood, I can't see how it is one bit of an improvement over extended music videos such as *Top Gun*. It's cheating. It's borrowing from other people's battle-tested, well-established work to help achieve artistic objectives through the loudspeakers that you're supposed to be achieving through the lens.

And it's incredibly anachronistic. A musician himself and a big-time Louis Armstrong fan, Woody Allen's most profound musical influence is probably the rhumba. (His only experiment with *hip* music was the Lovin' Spoonful in *What's Up, Tiger Lily?* The Lovin' Spoonful were *never* hip.) Allen is clearly one of those people who was born longing for the good old days, hearkening back to the music of an earlier, simpler era (when folks only had the Depression and the Gestapo to worry about). But unlike Martin Scorsese, who fills his films with music that was popular when he was young, Woody Allen fills his movies with music that was popular when his *parents* were young. Moreover, you're not allowed to be in a Woody Allen movie unless you're the sort of person who always goes over to the turntable to put on an Art Tatum record. The rare characters in his films who express any interest in music recorded more recently than Benny Goodman's "Stompin' at the Savoy" are treated as hopeless buffoons: Shelley Duvall as a starstruck Dylan fan in *Annie Hall*, Dianne Wiest as a less-than-believable punk rock enthusiast in *Hannah*. It's worth noting that Wiest eventually recants, undergoing an intellectual conversion from the Duke of Earl to the Duke of Ellington, hooking up with Allen in the jazz section of Tower Records (though she's carrying a copy of *Pagliacci*), while Allen abandons Duvall in bed so he can go kill a giant cockroach at Diane Keaton's apartment. A fitting fate for anyone who would rather listen to Bobby Dylan than Bobby Short. Barbarian harpy.

Don't get me wrong. I find many of Allen's films enormously appealing, and one of the reasons Allen's fans like him so much is that in his own films he gets to fire off all the zingers and snappy comebacks we all wish we could uncork in real life, but never can because we don't have Woody Allen as our scriptwriter and because the people we wish to insult have tattoos. (Besides, we are wearing our Sunday clothes.) Allen, like Groucho before him, gets to mercilessly tee off on his victims, and *they* just have to sit there and take it, like Michael Murphy in *Manhattan*. Like Tom Wolfe, the only other great American satirist of the past quarter-century, Allen is one of the most accomplished hypocrites of our time, earning his living by pillorying the social milieu in which he is clearly most comfortable, eviscerating people who are obviously his dinner companions.

The logical result of this two-facedness is the absurd finale in *Alice*, where the wealthy Mia Farrow abandons her Upper East Side penthouse life to visit Mother Teresa, then chooses to raise her kids in the slums. One anxiously awaits the moment when Moishe's Movers pull up in front of the Allen-Farrow uptown digs to effectuate *their* decampment to the more spiritually uplifting environs of the Lower East Side. One *anxiously* awaits that. One also anxiously awaits the moment when Woody and his lefty uptown buddies abandon their Park Avenue apartments, grab some baseball bats, and go over to Jersey to break up a Neo-Nazi rally instead of writing scathing satirical op-ed pieces in *The New York Times*. One *very* anxiously awaits that.

One of the greatest shocks caused by the release of the interminable *Interiors* in 1978 was the public's realization that Woody Allen, the Ingmar Bergman imitator, could show such compassion for the very same people that Woody Allen, the satirist, had torn to shreds in his earlier films. How could we have known while watching *Sleeper* that when Diane Keaton played an airhead poetess so dumb she had to be told that butterflies do not turn into caterpillars, she was really only rehearsing for her role as a pretentious poetess in *Interiors*? How could we have known when Allen was heaping abuse on self-centered artists in his early films, that in *Interiors* he would introduce us to the dominant theme in most of his subsequent work: that the greatest torment a human being can suffer is not death or blinding or the loss of a child or leprosy or even eviction from one's co-op, but being unable to express oneself artistically.

Characters afflicted with this horrid curse include Sam Waterston, the aspiring novelist of *September*, and Dianne Wiest, who in addition to being a failed actress in *Hannah* is also a failed screenplay writer in the dull movie of the same name. Then there's Woody himself as a failed documentary filmmaker in *Crimes*, as a frustrated TV show writer in *Manhattan*, and as a frustrated standup comic in *Annie Hall*. We also have a failed writer (Diane Keaton) in *Manhattan*, a frustrated singer (Keaton again) in *Annie Hall*, and a failed TV writer (Farrow) in *Alice*. New York *is* in fact a city filled with failed writers, failed dancers, and failed musicians, but most of them have the good grace to die or go to work for Merrill Lynch or something. In Woody's universe, they simply hang around the Museum of Modern Art and whine.

What is one to do in a world where it is so hard to achieve artistic success? Well, you can always try sleeping with your best friend's wife or lover (*Play It Again, Sam, Manhattan, A Midsummer Night's Sex Comedy, September*). If that doesn't work, try sleeping with your wife's sister (*Interiors, Crimes, Hannah*). And if that still doesn't work, you might consider suicide (*Interiors, Crimes, Hannah*). Or, in a pinch, you could always take in a flick. After attempting suicide in *Hannah*, Allen is restored to what passes for sanity in his personality by going to a Marx Brothers movie. Allen, who grew up in the 1940s, belongs to the first generation of Americans to regard films as something other than mere diversions. (This is an idea imported from France, and like most ideas imported from France, it is basically stupid).

Because of this, he has an obsession with films that is unnatural even for a native New Yorker. *What's Up, Tiger Lily?, The Purple Rose of Cairo, Stardust Memories,* and *Crimes and Misdemeanors* are all films about films, while *Zelig* and *Take the Money and Run* are pseudodocumentaries. The most famous scene in *Annie Hall*—the one with Marshall McLuhan—takes place in a movie lobby where Woody and Keaton have gone to see *The Sorrow and the Pity*. Later on, they will attend a double-feature of an unpronounceable Japanese film and an unpronounceable Russian film. When Allen first meets Keaton in *Manhattan*, she so ires him with her putdowns of his cultural icons that he later tells Hemingway that Keaton was just one more Bergman insult away from a pop in the kisser. Woody, like Buford Pusser, is clearly a man who can only be pushed so far.

"You've seen too many movies," Martin Landau remarks in *Crimes and Misdemeanors*. Seen too many movies? Hell; he *makes* too many movies: twenty-two and counting.

The movies about movies, the quotations from movies, the parodies of movies, the obsession of characters inside the movies with movies (usually *The Sorrow and the Pity*) make Woody Allen seem more like an archivist or a rap sampler than a director. What, after all, are his movies *about*? In the great films by

Renoir, Fellini, Kurosawa, Bergman, Ford, Godard, and Satyjit Ray, the characters are concerned with such issues as war, fate, fascism, injustice, poverty, deceit, betrayal, and having one hell of a good time with another human being. They are not obsessed with getting to the Bleecker Street Cinema's 2:35 showing of *Grand Illusion* so they'll still have enough time to screw their neurotic sister-in-law before schlepping uptown to see the 6:45 showing of *Rules of the Game* at the Thalia. One of the major differences between Ingmar Bergman and Woody Allen is that Ingmar Bergman's characters have never seen Kurosawa's films.

In one sense what we've got on our hands here are lite foreign films: pretentious but witty fare leavened by pleasant music and some good jokes. In another sense, we've got the world's highest-class nostalgia act. With its sex-without-genitalia-or-even-underwear and its lack of political conviction, the Woody Allen universe makes Fred and Ginger's look like Hiroshima. Consider Woody Allen's *Manhattan*. Although New York is one of the most ethnically rambunctious cities in the world, there are virtually no blacks or Hispanics in his movies, and those who do appear are maids, doormen, masseurs, convicts, or Bobby Short. There's virtually no violence in Woody Allen movies: The murder in *Crimes and Misdemeanors* is carried off with such taste and civility it looks like Noel Coward broke in and brained Anjelica Huston; and the botched assault on Kristin Griffith in *Interiors* still gets my vote for Least Successful Cinematic Rape/1970–79 Division.

Attempts to deal with more serious matters are often jarring, as in the thoroughly unconvincing scene in *Crimes and Misdemeanors*, when Allen reacts to the news that a man his sister met through the personals has tied her up and defecated on her. It is fair to say that Allen, a kindly, gentle soul, has no real appetite for unpleasantness, which is why comparisons to Bergman are so ludicrously inappropriate. Bergman is all about toads in the bread loaves, splintered glass in the vagina, defiled virgins, whipped schoolchildren, guys in black cloaks who want to play

chess. When push comes to shove, Woody Allen can *never* pull
the trigger, which is why Broadway Danny Rose forgives the two-
timing Tina Vitale; which is why Cecilia in *The Purple Rose of
Cairo* ends up smiling at the movie screen like an idiot; which is
why Hannah doesn't have a falling out with her sisters. The only
thing Woody Allen has in common with Ingmar Bergman is Sven
Nykvist.

Woody Allen's problem is that he is trying to make movies
with a message when all he really has to work with is an attitude.
Woody Allen's idea of serious filmmaking is to *pose* the big
questions, then turn around and admit that he really doesn't have
any answers. He has done this time and again, and he's not
getting any closer to being Tolstoy. A century that has lived
through Adolf Hitler, Josef Stalin, and Pol Pot doesn't really need
any smartass New York filmmaker to tell it that life isn't fair. And
a society with AIDS, crack babies, and institutionalized poverty
could care less about movies focusing on women in furs who want
to meet Mother Teresa.

Woody Allen is a big New York Knicks fan, but the Knicks
suck, so let's finish up with an anecdote about the Chicago
Bulls.* Michael Jordan, captain of the Bulls, is the greatest
basketball player ever to play the game, a man who can literally
do anything with a round ball. Is Michael Jordan satisfied with
being the world's greatest basketball player? Of course not; he
wants to become a golfer. Fine. But when Michael Jordan does
hang up his jock and starts slicing the ball into the water trap,
he shouldn't be surprised or offended when people say, "We
liked you better when you played for the Bulls" or "Go back to
doing what you do best."

Woody Allen is the Michael Jordan of film comedy. When he
makes a funny film (*The Purple Rose of Cairo, Broadway Danny
Rose, Zelig*) nobody does it better. When he makes the stuff with

---

**Since this article was written, the New York Knicks no longer suck. Now the
New York Knicks choke.*

the women gazing out the windows and rearranging the minimalist vases, it's time to fetch the truncheon. And he should stop blaming his fans for reminding him of this. After getting that early fix from *Sleeper, Bananas, Love and Death,* and *Take the Money and Run,* the rest of us are always waiting for the robot clothiers named Ginsberg & Cohen, for the computerized confessionals, for the giant banana peels. We are always waiting for the one-liners about interstellar space cookies, or "weird, futuristic" creatures with "the body of a crab and the head of a social worker." We are always waiting for the Woody Allen who declared that he could never get involved with any religion that advertises in *Popular Mechanics,* always waiting for the "teleological existential atheist" who believes that "there is a motivating intelligence to the universe, with the exception of certain parts of New Jersey." We are always waiting for the cellist in the marching band, for the escaped convict with the soap gun trapped in a thunderstorm, for the man who correctly pointed out that although "sex without love is an empty experience, as empty experiences go it's one of the best." The Woody Allen the world needs is not the man who asks "Why are we here?" and "What is the meaning of life?" but the one who asks, "If Christ was a carpenter, what does he charge for bookshelves?"

And will he take Diners Club?

INDEX

God

   and career of Steve Guttenberg, 158

   and career of Mariel Hemingway, xix

   and career of Christopher Reeve, 65

   and career of Daphne Zuniga, 65

Goodman, John

   as the American Gerard Depardieu, 95

Griffith, Melanie

   ability to turn a man's saliva into gravy, 209, 211

   addresses issue of fist-fucking, 217

   Betsy Wetsy voice of, 156

   Chatty Cathy voice of, 210–11

   frustrated in attempts to study philosophy at the Sorbonne, 209

   inexplicable career of, 217

   large butt of, 210, 211–12

Guttenberg, Steve

   chemotherapeutic looks of in *Don't Tell Her It's Me*, 72

   compared to John Ritter and Lou Diamond Phillips, 65

   difficulty of determining whether he was better in *Police Academy III* than in *Police Academy II*, 152

   as proof that God exists, 158

Harlin, Renny

   astonishing grooming influence of Steppenwolf on, 113

   proximity of house to Hell, 54

   role of Soviet Union in obstruction of career, 117

   spelling mistakes and, 117

   winner of Finland's *Best Industrial Short Film of the Year* award, 115

Harper, Valerie

   and rabies jokes, 9

Hemingway, Mariel

   ability to act badly while asleep of, 13

   role of God in career of, xix

Hitchcock, Alfred

   inability to get people like Grace Kelly to sit on his lap, 195–206

Hopper, Dennis

   as jazz-buff hitman, 71

Jones, James Earl

   as Cher impersonator, 38